Main Resources
TEA
COPRA
HEMP
MINERALS
TIN
RICE
TEAK
QUININE
OIL
RUBBER
SUGAR
PHILIPPINES
CELEBES
NEW GUINEA
AUSTRALIA

SOUTHEAST ASIA IN PERSPECTIVE

THE MACMILLAN COMPANY
NEW YORK • CHICAGO
DALLAS • ATLANTA • SAN FRANCISCO
LONDON • MANILA
BRETT-MACMILLAN LTD.
TORONTO

SOUTHEAST ASIA IN PERSPECTIVE

by

JOHN KERRY KING

THE MACMILLAN COMPANY NEW YORK 1956

Printed in the United States of America

FIRST PRINTING

Library of Congress catalog card number: 56-11449

ACKNOWLEDGMENT

Permission to quote copyright material is acknowledged to authors and publishers as follows: Cambridge University Press, *Colonial Policy and Practice,* by J. S. Furnivall; Cornell University Press, *Nationalism and Revolution in Indonesia,* by George McTurnan Kahin, copyright 1952 by Cornell University, Cornell University Press; Council on Foreign Relations, *The Future of Underdeveloped Countries,* by Eugene Staley (Harper & Brothers), copyright 1954 by Council on Foreign Relations; Harvard University Press, *A Documentary History of Chinese Communism,* by Conrad Brandt, Benjamin Schwartz and John K. Fairbank; Institute of Pacific Relations, *Japan's Role in Southeast Asian Nationalist Movements, 1940 to 1945,* by Willard H. Elsbree (Harvard University Press), copyright 1953 by Institute of Pacific Relations; Institute of Pacific Relations, *The Left Wing in Southeast Asia,* by Virginia Thompson and Richard Adloff (William Sloane Associates), copyright 1950 by Institute of Pacific Relations; The Macmillan Company, *The Memoirs of Cordell Hull,* copyright 1948 by Cordell Hull; W. W. Norton & Company, *The Stakes of Democracy in Southeast Asia,* by H. J. van Mook, copyright 1950 by H. J. van Mook; Princeton Center of International Studies, *The Requirements of Deterrence,* by William W. Kaufmann, copyright 1954 by Center of International Studies, Princeton University; Princeton University Press, *Realities of American Foreign Policy,* by George F. Kennan, copyright 1954 by Princeton University Press; and The Twentieth Century Fund, Inc., *Approaches to Economic Development,* by Norman S. Buchanan and Howard S. Ellis, copyright 1955 by The Twentieth Century Fund, Inc.

The New York *Times* kindly granted permission to reprint the map on page 176 and the International Cooperation Administration the endpaper map.

The author is indebted to William W. Kaufmann's study, *The Requirements of Deterrence* (Princeton, Center of International Studies, November 19, 1954), in developing parts of the analysis of retaliation in Chapter Seven.

J. K. K.

TO EDNA

FOREWORD

by Edwin F. Stanton, Former United States Ambassador to Thailand

The world has witnessed many important political changes since the end of the last war. Two of the most potent influences upon the course of international developments have been the steady spread of communist imperialism and the rising tide of nationalism in revolt against colonial rule. The one is a menace to free institutions and governments; the other is the manifestation of a spirit we recognize and admire.

Many areas of the world have been affected by these two forces, but the story of the struggle of the countries of Southeast Asia to achieve independence and to become masters of their own destinies is a profoundly moving one. Six new nations have been born. Their problems and their future may well determine whether war and chaos or peace and progress are to dominate the immediate future of mankind.

Dr. King, in the pages of this book, describes for us what has happened in that part of the world during the past decade and why the United States is both interested and concerned with these developments. He does so not only with the scholar's sense of the historic importance of these events but also with a keen appreciation of the vital necessity of seeking to understand their needs, aspirations, and feelings in an effort to strengthen our relations with them. This is the heart of his book. His concern over the misunderstandings that have arisen between them and us and the imperative need to reestablish trust, confidence, and goodwill is evident on every page.

Before World War II the United States did not have direct diplomatic relations with the countries of Southeast Asia with the exception of Thailand, and our interests in these colonies of Great Britain, France, and the Netherlands were nominal. With the ousting of the colonial powers by the Japanese, the eventual defeat of the latter by the Allies, and the upsurge of strong nationalist movements clamoring for independence and the end of colonial rule, it was evident that a new era had dawned in South Asia.

The United States desired to see free, independent nations emerge from the long twilight of colonial rule. However, because we were committed to the support of our Allies, who were also our partners in building up the defenses of the West in Europe, we have failed to take an unequivocal position on the burning issue of colonialism. In consequence we have lost much of the goodwill of the peoples of Southeast Asia, who have noted the gulf between public pronouncements of our leading statesmen on this issue and our obvious support of the colonial powers, particularly our support of France in Indochina. Because of the intensity of feeling among the Asian peoples concerning colonialism, which has left a legacy marked by bitterness and suspicion of the West, there is great need for us to make an earnest and intelligent effort to win the goodwill and confidence of these new citizens of the free world.

The pangs and problems connected with the struggles of these countries to establish stable governments and viable economies present enormous inherent difficulties, but they are being dangerously aggravated by the restless, pushing force of communism which seeks to spread its tentacles throughout the area. The United States believes that collective security through an agreement, such as the Manila Pact, is the most effective deterrent to communist ambitions. On the other hand, it is clear that although some Asian leaders are not blind to communist objectives, they are not inclined to join defensive military alliances initiated by the Western powers. For them the new spirit of nationalism is the bulwark upon which they choose to place the greatest reliance. After all, very similar sentiments animated our Founding Fathers and governed our own early foreign relations.

With care, Dr. King describes the policies of the United States with respect to these Asian countries. He doubts whether the communists have been greatly impressed either by the doctrine of massive retaliation or by the military assistance we have been giving to some countries, which although very substantial in the case of Indochina did not prevent the communists from scoring important victories in Vietnam. As to the effect of this policy upon the countries of the area, it is evident that it ranges from acceptance in the case of Thailand to outright rejection by Burma and Indonesia.

What should the United States do? Dr. King cogently urges that we attune our actions and statements much more closely to the political, economic, and psychological currents flowing through Southeast Asia today. Certainly, we must dispel the feeling prevalent in those countries that we think of them as pawns on the international chessboard. Furthermore, while maintaining an adequate level of military preparedness against communist aggression, let us shift the emphasis of our aid to meet the pressing economic and technological needs of each country in the area. Above all, let us seek to understand the new Asian spirit of nationalism, which is basically the same spirit that has made our nation great, and to form firm, equal partnerships with our Asian friends in pursuit of the common good.

INTRODUCTION

Southeast Asia may be defined roughly as the area of continental Asia and the offshore Philippine and Indonesian archipelagoes which lies south of China and east of India. Mountainous for the most part, covered by rain forest and jungle, the area has a tropical climate whose high temperature and humidity, dominated by the monsoon from May to November, allow for no cool season except in the mountains. Elsewhere the weather year round is either hot or hot and wet.

Several mighty rivers carry the torrential monsoon rainfall south and east to the Bay of Bengal, the Gulf of Thailand, and the South China Sea. In continental Southeast Asia, such rivers as the Irrawaddy, Sittang, Salween, Chao Phraya and the Mekong pass through great central basins, forming tremendous deltas which provide the rich soil and annual flooding that is ideal for rice cultivation—the major occupation of the majority of the people. In the Philippines and Indonesia, this area of rice cultivation is extended onto the mountain slopes by banks of terraces thousands of years old.

In addition to rice, Southeast Asia's major products include rubber, tin, oil, tungsten, zinc, iron, coal, sugar, hemp, copra, kapok, quinine, sticlac, teak, forest products, and fish.

Southeast Asia may be said to constitute nine countries, whose area approximates half the size of the United States, with a population roughly equivalent to that of the United States. The countries are Burma, Thailand, Malaya, Laos, Cambodia, North Vietnam, South Vietnam, the Philippines, and Indonesia. Newly independent of Western colonial rule for the most part, only one of these countries, Thailand, never was held under a colonial yoke. Seven of the countries won their independence within the past ten years; the Philippines being granted independence as part of a preconceived plan, the others being forced to fight for it. To Malaya, the only country without sovereign independence, the British have promised full freedom by 1957.

To most Americans, startled by the recent appearance of this galaxy of new Southeast Asian states on the international scene, the conditions in which their foreign policy must operate in the area are as confusing as the problems are knotted and perplexing. Without a history of close contact with the area, such as characterizes American relations with Europe, the peoples and countries of Southeast Asia seem to be an indistinct part of a "mysterious Orient." For their part, the people of Southeast Asia have little real knowledge of the United States or of the role the United States is seeking to play in their world today. The two parts of the globe are separated by time, distance, and experience. It is these new and unfamiliar relationships which partially are responsible for difficulties that the United States has been encountering in developing and executing foreign policy toward the area.

As an area, Southeast Asia has great political, cultural, ethnic, linguistic, racial, religious, and historical diversity. Its people do not think of themselves as Southeast Asians. They identify themselves with their ethnic groups or, more recently, with their nations. If they feel the need of a wider self-identification, they think of themselves as Asians.

Southeast Asia is an "in between" area, caught always in the cross fire of two major influences. It is in between Asia's two great cultural centers, India and China, and so has drawn heavily from both Indian and Chinese culture, religion, art, architecture, social and political institutions. It is in between two great competing political and ideological movements—communist totalitarianism and representative democracy. It is bounded by continental Asia's mass land armies and the West's vast sea power. It has governments which lie roughly in between representative democracy and military-intellectual oligarchy. Its national economies are far from the modern industrial age, yet they are not entirely primitive. The peoples of Southeast Asia are in between centuries. They no longer sleep under the opiates of feudalism and colonialism, but they have not yet fully awakened to the clamor and speed of the twentieth century. Western civilization and institutions pull at the minds of the Southeast Asians, but the heritage of ancient Asian cultures and values fill their hearts. Today, nationalism, the most powerful dynamic force in Southeast Asia, is passing through a transition period whose duration is uncertain and whose outcome remains unpredictable.

The peoples of Southeast Asia are involved in a revolutionary experience which has few parallels in history for diversity, scope, and speed. Momentous events and sweeping changes in the area which mature national societies would have found difficult to accommodate in half a century have been compressed into a tumultuous fifteen-year period.

Since 1940 Southeast Asia has experienced major war, the defeat of the Western colonial powers by an Asian power, a disillusioning occupation by Japan, a great upsurge of nationalism, and the rapid growth of communism. Since the end of the Second World War, a wave of independence has swept South and Southeast Asia, leaving in its wake some 600 million people freed of colonial rule, a host of new sovereign states, and a vast ideological and power vacuum. Indigenous social and cultural institutions, long weakened by the impact of Western civilization, have begun to disintegrate rapidly. Economic and political problems have multiplied in number and increased in complexity. Every state in Southeast Asia, except Thailand, has experienced major communist insurrection or invasion. A new Asian power—communist China—has emerged as an immediate neighbor and, since the war, the issues of the global conflict between communist and noncommunist states have focused sharply in the area.

Perhaps the most important change of all is the demand of the Southeast Asian people, after centuries of marginal existence, for a better life. Although the better life which they envisage includes higher living standards, it is not limited solely to food, clothing, and shelter. The Southeast Asian peoples also demand equality, respect, and prestige among nations and an end to their long period of foreign-imposed spiritual, physical, and intellectual eclipse. The changes which are sweeping Southeast Asia today are the culmination of a long historical process that has not yet reached its climax.

For United States foreign policy, six specially significant features dominate the Southeast Asian scene. They are: (1) the newness of national independence and the growing force of nationalism; (2) the political, economic, and social revolution sweeping the area which carries in its wake all the uncertainties of revolutionary upheaval; (3) the wide gap between Southeast Asia's potential and actual level of economic development; (4) the sharp focus of the cold war on Southeast Asia; (5) the vulnerability of the area to political, economic, and intellectual communist penetration; and (6) the power vacuum created in the area by the retreat of Western colonialism.

As former Secretary of State Dean Acheson once said:

> The peoples of Asia are so incredibly diverse and their problems are so incredibly diverse that how could anyone, even the most utter charlatan, believe that he had a uniform policy which would deal with all of them? On the other hand, there are very important similarities in ideas and in problems among the peoples of Asia and so what we come to, after we understand these diversities and these common attitudes of mind, is the fact that there must be certain similarities of approach, and there must be very great dissimilarities in action.[1]

It is in the spirit of this statement that United States foreign policy in Southeast Asia is treated in this book. Despite Southeast Asia's great internal diversity, a number of basic problems and attitudes concerning economic development, national independence, colonialism, racialism, neutralism, communism, and collective security lend themselves to a general approach. These, translated into concrete actions at specific times and places, however, must contain, as Mr. Acheson points out, "very great dissimilarities." To make valid any general treatment of United States policy in Southeast Asia, such as is attempted in this book, this point must be borne in mind.

United States policy toward Southeast Asia must be viewed within the context of global policy considerations. Southeast Asia is but one area of conflict in a global crisis. Other areas of conflict,

[1] Address to the National Press Club, Washington, D.C., Jan. 12, 1950. *Department of State Bulletin*, Jan. 23, 1950, p. 111.

both actual and potential, exist which call for United States attention and make demands on United States resources. Because United States responsibilities are global and capabilities are limited, United States foreign policy from time to time must shift emphasis to meet challenges and to take advantage of opportunities. Today Southeast Asia as an area of critical vulnerability and special opportunity warrants greater relative concentration of United States policy effort, attention, and help than it is receiving. Today, matters of vital United States concern are the progress of Southeast Asia's revolution, the success or failure of communism's thirty-five-year-old effort to harness and guide the revolutionary and nationalistic forces of Southeast Asia to communist ends, and the future political and economic orientation of Southeast Asia's peoples and governments.

Until the Second World War, United States policy and interest in Southeast Asia, except for the Philippines, was marginal, almost non-existent. Since that time the degree of United States interest in Southeast Asia has increased greatly, as it undoubtedly will continue to increase in importance in the future.

The conditions in which United States policy in Southeast Asia must function have been many decades in the making. As former Ambassador George F. Kennan sees it, "If there is any great lesson we Americans need to learn with regard to the methodology of foreign policy, it is that we must be gardeners and not mechanics in our approach to world affairs. We must come to think of the development of international life as an organic and not a mechanical process." [2] For United States policy in Southeast Asia, a gardener's long-range organic view is particularly apropos. No dramatic change in United States–Southeast Asian relations is likely to be produced by the sudden courting of a national leader, "stepping-up" of United States information activities, or increase in American foreign aid appropriations for a year or two. Only the gradual accumulation of common experience and effort in working together toward mutual goals on a basis of national equality and respect can possibly bring together the two areas. That is tomorrow's test.

Through this book an attempt is made to explore four broad

[2] George F. Kennan, *Realities of American Foreign Policy* (Princeton, Princeton University Press, 1954), p. 93.

questions which are of immediate concern to United States and Southeast Asia relations. First, United States interests in Southeast Asia are introduced in Chapter I. Second, the conditions in Southeast Asia in which United States policy must operate are considered in Chapters II, III, and IV. Third, Chapters V and VI attempt to outline the major contours of United States policy in Southeast Asia. Fourth, the major gaps and problems in the structure of United States policy in Southeast Asia are the tenor of Chapters VII, VIII, and IX. The final chapter is a summation of conclusions and recommendations.

And so, for making this book somehow inevitable, the author takes the opportunity to offer his several grateful acknowledgments: to the United States and Thailand Fulbright program, for valuable background months of residence, research, and lecturing in Bangkok, Thailand, and for making possible the opportunity to visit Laos, Cambodia, Vietnam, Malaya, Indonesia, Burma, India, and Pakistan; to the Council on Foreign Relations, New York City, for the Carnegie Research Fellowship, which afforded time from university chores for further research; to the University of Virginia's Institute for Research in the Social Sciences, for additional months of research and travel throughout Southeast Asia; to the peoples of Southeast Asia for the fact that they did not seem to flinch from the research, travel, or scrutiny of their various fascinating lands. To Ambassador Edwin F. Stanton, both in his knowledgeable capacity as Ambassador to Thailand and in his objective status later on as private citizen, always generous with his time and the valuable object lessons of his wide experience, I wish to express special appreciation for consistent encouragement and many splendid suggestions. Without being superfluous or attempting to deny the obvious connection, I can scarely overlook the credit and admiration due throughout to that willing editor of innumerable pages of manuscript and ideas, Edna Grodman King. Responsibility for the study rests solely with the author.

JOHN KERRY KING

CONTENTS

SOUTHEAST ASIA IN PERSPECTIVE

1. THE NEW IMPORTANCE OF AMERICAN INTERESTS IN SOUTHEAST ASIA

For several breathless days in April 1954, as the eyes of the world watched the merciless drama of Dienbienphu unfold, the United States verged on war in Indochina. For a moment in time, direct American participation in another Asian war was averted; but, immediately afterward, the United States became committed as never before to involvement in Southeast Asian affairs.

By the summer of 1954, following the Indochina Armistice Agreements negotiated at Geneva, the United States had assumed a new and precarious responsibility for the survival of a troubled segment of the area, the weak and disunited South Vietnam.

By September 1954 it had added a solemn pledge through American representatives meeting in Manila to defend a large part of Southeast Asian territory against communist aggression.

By April 1955 the United States could tot up obligations for expenditures totaling some $1,500,000,000 for military, economic, and technical aid in the effort to help the Southeast Asian states maintain their independence and achieve a certain amount of political stability and economic progress.

Ten years before the name of Dienbienphu flashed across the world's headlines, Southeast Asia as an area was practically unknown in the United States, except as the embattled Allied armies continued to slug their way through World War II to release occupied territory from the throttlehold of the Japanese.

Today Southeast Asia looms so large in America's national interests that it fights for position with all other international interests, and secures military and economic commitments of a scope never previously anticipated.

What lies behind this sudden potency of the Southeast Asian area? How has the United States been snared into adding further burdens and responsibilities to an already long list of them? Does the United States have a vital stake in Southeast Asia?

Cold-war strategists of recent years contend that Southeast Asia is the last barricade against communism in all Asia, and that, if communism were to sweep through Southeast Asia, it would blanket the entire continent and tip the balance of world power to the communist bloc.

Military analysts contend that Southeast Asia is vital to United States security in terms of military strategy alone.

Economists contend that Southeast Asia is of utmost importance to the United States because of its vital natural resources and its trade potential.

All these are evidence of the new conditions and threats to American security and interests which have developed in Southeast Asia since the beginning of the Second World War, when the United States interests in the area were slight, and confined, for the most part, to the Philippines, then an American possession.

Present acute American concern for the area emerges from four principal events: (1) the Second World War revealed the strategic importance of Southeast Asia to the United States both in military and in economic terms; (2) the independence achieved by Burma, Indonesia, the Philippines, and the states of Indochina resulted in the formation of new relationships between these states and the United States; (3) through the communist victory in China the relatively weak states of Southeast Asia became exposed to the possibility of communist aggression and domination; (4) the key role assigned to Great Britain and Japan in American security planning enhanced American interests in Southeast Asia because of the economic fact that access to the trade and resources of Southeast Asia is vital to both American allies. Thus, the United States not only has interests *in* Southeast Asia; it also has interests *in relation to* Southeast Asia.

Of all the reasons for American concern over the area, there is little question that the overriding consideration remains the threat to Southeast Asia of communist domination. If there were no threat of communism creeping into Southeast Asia by infiltration and subversion or crashing into the area by Chinese or Viet Minh aggression, American concern undoubtedly would be far less acute than it is. Although communism is the major factor in considering American interests in Southeast Asia, it is not the only one.

American interests in Southeast Asia are ideological, humanitarian, political, economic, commercial, and strategic. When considered individually, it is hard to see where any American interests at stake in Southeast Asia are clearly vital to the minimum conditions necessary for American security today. America will not collapse if Indonesia closes its borders to American trade or if Cambodia falls to the communists or if Burma remains neutralist. However, when the area is considered as a whole, and when American interests are taken in combination as a multiplicity of interests in the perspective of present world conditions which extend from the cold war to an intense global effort by the United States to prevent international communism from engulfing the entire Eurasian land mass, American interests in Southeast Asia become extremely significant, perhaps even decisive.

Today the economic, political, and social relationships among the countries of the world are more interrelated than ever before, and the major issues of life rapidly are becoming global. The prophesy of Sir Halford Mackinder, the famous British exponent of geopolitics, is near fulfillment. Some fifty years ago he wrote:

> Every explosion of social forces instead of becoming dissipated in a surrounding circuit of unknown space and barbaric chaos, will be sharply reechoed from the far side of the globe, and weak elements in the political and economic organism of the world will be shattered in consequence.[1]

Until recently, to the United States most of the countries of South and Southeast Asia were part of a "surrounding circuit of unknown space." That gray area is now filled by a number of new independent national states which, by choice, seek to adapt their philosophies and institutions to the values and institutions of democracy.

Through changing conditions and threats, the United States has maintained its persistent interest in preserving and promoting basic democratic values—in widening the area of democracy and representative government. Although this interest has not been pursued with utmost vigor in Southeast Asia, traditionally it has provided a primary point of reference in the determination of American interests. Emotionally, intellectually, and historically, the United States is committed deeply to the basic values of democracy—national independence, individual liberty and dignity, representative government, the concept of the state as the servant of the people, economic, political, and social opportunity and progress. In the broad sense, American well-being and security are perpetually related to the way in which these values fare in the rest of the world. The basic values of democracy do not exist in isolation. Nor can they prosper in isolation. A threat to democratic values anywhere ultimately becomes a threat to them everywhere.

Both the substance and the form of democratic government have far to go in Southeast Asia where democratic institutions and concepts are an alien importation with few roots in local tradition and culture. The circumstances in which the bid for democracy and representative government is being made in Southeast Asia are difficult ones; the obstacles are many and formidable. If their progress seems slow to Americans, it must be remembered that in the United States and the states of western Europe, democratic institutions developed gradually. Adapting to the new problems and changing conditions with measured pace, the Western countries had time for ideological and political evolution. But the problems of the modern world came abruptly to Southeast Asia, imposing on the countries of the area the task of adapting democratic values and building democratic institutions in the midst of internal social and economic revolution and unprecedented global tension. The governments of Southeast Asia must race against time to achieve some results. Before mounting impatience, disillusionment, economic or political collapse can work their demoralizing way into a pattern of totalitarianism, they must acquire some of the benefits of democratic government, must satisfy some of the aspirations and needs of their people. The experiment culminating in the success or failure of democratic government in Southeast Asia naturally is of deep interest and import to the United States.

As for United States diplomacy, this American interest in widening the area of democracy is a source of major frustration. On the one side, there is the sincere concern for the progress of democracy and representative government everywhere; on the other there are the strict limitations the nature of democracy and of foreign policy imposes in furthering democratic progress. It is in the very nature of democratic government that democracy cannot be forced, exported, loaned, or granted. It can only be aided, encouraged, and demonstrated. In Southeast Asia there is no guarantee that the institutions of representative government will develop or that democracy will succeed merely by relieving some of the pressures on the states through the assumption of partial responsibility for their defense and through making available economic and technical aid. The governments and people of Southeast Asia must carry the major burden of building democracy and, at the same time, of overcoming the protagonists of nondemocratic values in their midst.

Today the most powerful bearers of these nondemocratic, totalitarian values are the communists. Wherever the conflicting values of democracy and communism meet, it is inevitable that they clash; and, because they have already chosen Asia as a major meeting ground, the ominous sounds of warfare are clearly discernible. Whether by words or deeds, the battle for Southeast Asia and adjacent areas is not only on but will undoubtedly continue for some years to come. Already China has fallen to the communists, leaving the Chinese people to the brutal communist ordeal of organized brainwashing and regimented hate. The blow against freedom in China has resounded to the detriment of the free world everywhere, particularly the United States. But this does not lessen the fact that the fate of the rest of Asia is yet to be decided, and it is urgent as never before that Southeast Asia retain a choice for freedom.

Apart from political considerations, the United States has an even simpler interest in Southeast Asia—that is, the United States is interested simply in the people of Southeast Asia. For humanitarian and practical reasons, the prosperity, progress, and happiness of the Southeast Asians are a matter of American concern. It is an intangible element to assess, but it is part of the American national character and history to have an interest in the dignity, security, and progress of other peoples. United States policy has given frequent expression to its idealism and humanitarianism in Wilson's Fourteen Points, the Atlantic Charter, Roosevelt's Four Freedoms, Truman's Point Four, the United Nations Charter, the underlying concepts of the United Nations Relief and Rehabilitation Administration, the World Health Organization, and the United Nations International Children's Emergency Fund.

On the practical side, 165,000,000 unhappy and depressed people in Southeast Asia would pose a threat to the peace and an opportunity for totalitarian gains.

In his address to the National Press Club in Washington, January 12, 1950, Secretary of State Dean Acheson reminded the world that "Americans as individuals are interested in the peoples of Asia. We are not interested in them as pawns or as subjects for exploitation but just as people." Again, he told the Commonwealth Club of San Francisco in March of the same year:

> So far as we are concerned, we know that we are interested in the peoples of Asia as people. We want to help them as people. We do not want to take anything from them for ourselves. We do not want to deny them any opportunity, any freedom, any right. We do not want to use them for any purpose of our own. On the contrary, we want to help them, in any sensible way we can, to achieve their own goals and ambitions in their own way. We want to do this, because we believe that what the peoples of Asia earnestly desire will make for the kind of a free and productive world in which we and they can live out our lives in peace.

America's increased interest in Southeast Asia coincided with several significant American developments—the abandonment of isolation as a basic tenet of American policy, the acceptance of the role of major partner in the free-world coalition, and the assumption of international responsibilities and burdens heavier than those ever before undertaken by a single nation. America's increased sympathy and concern for Southeast Asia coincided with the outward thrust of a greatly strengthened international communist movement, dedicated by its own admission to world domination, into weak and disorganized areas of the world. Under these conditions, the principles of power politics, balance of power, and collective security have been propelled to the front. If the United States has appeared at times to pursue its humanistic and idealistic course with less vigor than expected, generally speaking, the reasons have been the limitations of foreign policy and the requirements of security rather than any conscious abandonment of the principles involved.

In Southeast Asia the American interests in democratic values and in the principles of human progress are buttressed but not necessarily dominated by a number of narrower, more specific, interests of an economic, security, and diplomatic nature, all of them intensified by the threat of international communism.

In geopolitical terms, Southeast Asia occupies a position of global strategic importance roughly comparable to Panama and Suez. Thailand, the states of Indochina, and Malaya jut south and east from continental Asia more than one thousand miles into the South China Sea. Offshore, the Philippine and Indonesian archipelagoes complete a great barrier between the Pacific and Indian oceans. Only through the narrow Straits of Malacca, which are dominated by Singapore, may this barrier be penetrated conveniently. In Southeast Asia, too, the great international air routes converge from the west coast of the United States, from Australia and Europe. In the hands of a hostile power, the peninsula and offshore islands of Southeast Asia in effect would cut the world in two. South Asia and Africa would be isolated from the Pacific; India, New Zealand, and Australia would be threatened immediately. The entire area of Southeast Asia and the western Pacific, including Australia and New Zealand, is an interconnected strategic unit of far-reaching importance.

Another geopolitical interest in Asia is bounded by the recently awakened knowledge of American security needs. This may be illustrated by historic reference to events in the Atlantic covering the periods of the two world wars. Although the American public was never fully aware of the fact at the time, and American leaders were reluctant to admit it, a basic reason for American participation in the First World War was to prevent continental Europe from falling into the hands of a single hostile power. With German submarines sinking merchant vessels within a scant distance of Boston and New York harbors and the resultant loss of American life and property, for the first time there were demonstrated two facts pertinent to United States security: (1) the Atlantic Ocean no longer was a great protective barrier for the United States; (2) the protection offered by the Atlantic Ocean and the legal concept of Freedom of the Seas depended, in fact, on the role of the British Navy. The Second World War repeated this early lesson of power politics which, the second time round, made a deeper impression. It is now generally recognized that the Atlantic is a source of protection only when policed and that the problem of policing the Atlantic would be infinitely greater if continental Europe were dominated by a single hostile power. Thus, America's first line of defense is the continent of Europe rather than the Atlantic. The principle, recognized in British foreign policy for centuries, at last has become a principle of American policy.

The same principle of American security applies in the Pacific. During the Second World War the question of Japanese domination of continental east Asia and the islands of the western and southwestern Pacific was a vital Pacific issue. Through such experiences as Pearl Harbor, the instances of the shelling of west-coast towns by Japanese submarines, the defense of Alaska, Australia, New Zealand, and India, there is ample indication of the threat to American security of an unpoliced Pacific Ocean and domination of continental Asia by a single power. Today, with the Moscow-Peking Axis in established control over a large part of Asia, it is just as consistent for the United States to have a continuing interest in free, strong, and independent states in South and Southeast Asia as for the United States to maintain its interest in the free, strong, and independent states of Western Europe.

The American interest in trade with Southeast Asia must be reckoned in strategic terms rather than in terms of volume or dollar value. From available figures it is estimated that trade between the United States and Southeast Asia runs to approximately $1.5 billion annually or, roughly, 7 per cent of the total American foreign trade. Although the amount constitutes an important segment of American foreign trade, it is hardly on a scale to be considered vital. The general trend of trade with Southeast Asia ap-

ond World War, American private investment in Southeast Asia appears stagnant, if not below prewar levels, because of the general political and economic instability of the area and the more secure and rewarding investment opportunities elsewhere. There is no certainty of a favorable climate for increased private American investment in the future; nor, by the same token, does it appear likely that American investment will soon become a major American interest in the area.

Despite this paucity of private American investment, the United States has made substantial investments in the future of the Southeast Asia countries through the program of government grants and loans, through assistance of an economic, military, and technical nature. A basic purpose was to protect American interests, and to help serve American security interests in Southeast Asia by promoting economic and political progress in the recipient countries and by strengthening their military defenses. By a curious evolution which occurs in such situations, an effect of these investments was to increase the American stake and to expand American interests in the area, because interests serious enough to warrant large-scale foreign aid and assistance for their protection tend to increase in importance in direct ratio to the amount invested for purposes of protection. This self-feeding characteristic of national interests whereby the national interests require protective measures which, in turn, help to increase the extent of the national interests accounts, in part, for the resistance to American aid encountered in several South and Southeast Asian countries. For example, Burma, Indonesia, and India would prefer to see a diminution rather than an increase of the American stake in their security, stability, and economic development.

Again, the United States has a major interest in Southeast Asia resulting from a variety of previous security commitments in Asia. Already concluded are mutual defense treaties with the Philippines, Korea, Formosa, Japan, Australia, and New Zealand. Through the Manila Pact, American security commitments have been extended to include Pakistan, Thailand, Laos, Cambodia, and the southern zone of Vietnam. Not only have these agreements greatly increased American interests in the area, but they also have engaged the national prestige irrevocably. Like economic aid and assistance, collective security arrangements have their self-feeding characteristics.

Many Southeast Asians assert that the United States is interested not in themselves but in their potential as a bulwark against communism. This assertion is neither entirely true nor entirely false. All states, including the states of Southeast Asia, seek to promote their own welfare and security first of all, but it is an oversimplification as well as a harsh rendition of the case to assert that United States policy in Southeast Asia is motivated solely by the selfish national interest. Just as every government seeks to create conditions which ensure the national security, and just as no government knowingly or willingly sacrifices that security, so does the United States guard its security interests in Southeast Asia. There are other subsidiary interests, some complementary and some contradictory, but it goes without saying that the *key* United States interest in Southeast Asia, as it is in other areas of the world, is in United States security and welfare.

In applying such a standard to Southeast Asia, the question of the conditions necessary for United States security arises. How is United States security in Southeast Asia best served? If the power vacuum which exists in Southeast Asia were filled by strong, independent, and friendly Southeast Asian states, if the Southeast Asian states were economically advanced and prosperous, providing internal economic strength and conditions for extensive mutually profitable trade, if the states of the area, in an association with a similarly endowed and stimulated India, possessed sufficient unity, strength, and vitality to serve as a center of dynamic democratic leadership in Asia and so offset the magnetism of communist China's dramatic rise to power, then indeed America's interests would be outstandingly served. But these maximum conditions represent wishful thinking rather than reality in Southeast Asia. At the present time most of the Southeast Asian states are divided and weak, their governmental fumbling with democracy uncertain, their political and economic progress slow. Even if they were to achieve the peak of their potential strength, it is dubious whether, individually or collectively, they could balance the power potential of China.

If the maximum conditions for United States security appear unattainable, what representations may be made for minimum conditions essential to United States security interests in Southeast Asia? The character of the factors involved is a shifting one, but four general conditions may be stressed as basic minimum requirements for meeting United States security interests in the area. These are:

1. Government institutions in Southeast Asia must win popular loyalty, confidence, and active support. The needs are for governments to achieve sufficient strength and unity to maintain internal law and order, to provide leadership which is dynamic and imaginative enough to reduce threats of internal subversion and which, in turn, will help develop government institutions to a point where they will accommodate peaceful and orderly change. Without these minimum conditions, Southeast Asia is bound to remain an area of weakness and confusion, running the constant risk of having its national aims corrupted by communist interference.

2. Economic progress and development in Southeast Asia must be sufficiently rapid to show quick results and sufficiently sound to promise basic improvements in living standards and national economic health. Although short-run visible results are essential to alleviate existent distress and to prevent general demoralization, it is only through long-run economic construction and development that the states of Southeast Asia can have a sound basis for a viable economic system, which will bolster the political system.

3. There must be an easing of the existent tensions between Southeast Asia and the United States resulting from suspicion of American motives, fears of American imperialism and race antagonism. Even in the Philippines and Thailand where relations with the United States are relatively free of tensions, good relations and understanding are inhibited by strains of suspicion, fear, and antagonism.

4. America and Southeast Asia must develop between them a mutually acceptable analysis of the nature and intent of communism. At the national level today, conflict on this question causes significant differences between the United States and Indonesia and, to a lesser extent, between the United States and Burma. Between the United States and India, it is a matter of special im-

portance because of India's influence in Southeast Asia as well as India's own inherent potential. To the people of Southeast Asia generally, the need to gain a broader perspective of the communist threat is equally critical, for, above all, the people should not be won away from their own nationalist aspirations through ignorance or false promises.

Apart from the meaning of the multiplicity of United States interests—ideological, humanitarian, geopolitical, economic, commercial, strategic, security, and accumulative—all signs point in one direction. In the years ahead, Southeast Asia and the surrounding areas are bound to play a role of increasing importance in world affairs, a matter which will be reflected by the continued growth of United States national interests in the area.

2. CONDITIONS FOR POLICY

The conditions in Southeast Asia in which United States foreign policy must function cannot be controlled, but at least they must be understood and taken into account in formulating both objectives and policies because they set the limits and provide the opportunities for policy. In Southeast Asia a number of indigenous conditions prevail—political, economic, social, and psychological in nature—which determine the climate in which United States policy toward the area must operate. Some of the conditions stem from elusive and remote forces difficult to define and assess, but most stand out clearly against the backdrop of recent history.

THE LEGACY OF COLONIALISM

Perhaps no single experience has so deeply influenced the states of Southeast Asia as their years of domination by Western colonial powers. In each of the newly independent states of the area, the political orientation and structure, the political immaturity, the economic organization and disabilities and the disintegration of traditional social structures may be traced, in large part, to the practice or the negligence of the colonial powers or to the impact of Western civilization.

Western colonialism embraced a time span in Southeast Asia which suggests the degree to which it has infected present conditions in the area. The Dutch ruled Indonesia for three hundred years. French interests in Indochina, dating from the seventeenth century, became more widespread when the French occupied Saigon in 1859 and, in the ensuing fifty years, managed to cover all Indochina. In Malaya the British took the first step toward colonial rule in 1786 when Francis Light took possession of Penang Island; the second, in 1819, with the settling of Singapore. By a gradual process of working out from these two strong points, the British rule in time included all the Malayan peninsula. In Burma the British assumed rule by annexing Arakan and Tennasserim to secure the borders of India in 1826, and finally, within sixty years, completed the job by annexing the rest of Burma. Three hundred years of Spanish rule preceded American annexation of the Philippines in 1899. Only Thailand, by agreement between the British and French, and by its own prudent willingness to part with certain border regions, was able to maintain a precarious independence over the past several centuries.

It would be unrealistic to assume that the era of Western colonialism was entirely black or devoid of benefit to the peoples of Southeast Asia. The colonial powers created political entities in Southeast Asia where none had existed, bringing these entities to the threshold, if not the drawing room, of the modern world. The colonial powers introduced Western political and philosophical ideas of individual freedom, equality, and representative government wherever they moved, making a deep impression on many Southeast Asians in an area of activity which cannot help having certain lasting effects. The colonial powers provided the formerly colonial states of Southeast Asia with whatever start they possess toward modernization and industrialization and, in this respect, like it or not, the indelible stamp of its one-time colonial mentor is borne by every formerly colonial state. But, for all their positive elements, the colonial powers had an unfortunate tendency to emphasize their role as masters rather than their opportunity as mentors; and this, inevitably, is a negative force for future relations between the states of the West and of Southeast Asia.

Except for United States policy in the Philippines, none of the colonial powers gave convincing evidence of serious intentions to release their colonial territories voluntarily. When independence came to the states of South and Southeast Asia, it therefore came primarily as a consequence of pressures applied by the nationalist forces in those countries and not by a planned relinquishment of control on the part of the colonial powers. These struggles for independence generated emotions which still cloud the relations between most new Southeast Asian states and the West; needless to say, the communists do everything in their power to keep the sparks of resentment and hatred alive.

Although the colonial policies and practices of Britain, France, the Netherlands, and the United States differed in certain essentials, there is great similarity in many of the broad political, economic, social, and psychological consequences of their colonial rule in Southeast Asia.

In the political sphere, one important consequence of colonialism in Southeast Asia is the establishment of territorial political units lacking national unity. When the Western colonial powers arrived on the scene, they found no organized political units comparable to the present-day states. Southeast Asia was a heterogeneous and disorganized area ruled by innumerable sultans, kings, and nobles. Personal loyalty was feudal in character, limited to the hereditary chieftains and the local community. With the exception of Thailand, present-day states of the area owe their administrative unity and geographic definitions to colonial administrative organization. Generally, the administrative units created by the colonial powers were held together only by military supremacy, by the ability of the colonial power to dominate its various parts, and by the manipulation of local rulers. On the whole, the colonial powers formed their administrative and territorial units without regard for linguistic or ethnic considerations. The size, shape, and nature of their colonial territories were determined by the extent of local resistance and by competition from other colonial powers. Interested in maintaining domination by the most inexpensive means, they found it expedient to play off one indigenous group against another and to suppress the growth of national unity. In addition, European colonial rule must bear a large part of the responsibility for intensifying problems of national unity for the Southeast Asian states by their policy of importing of alien workers, mainly Chinese and Indians, in order to secure abundant supplies of cheap labor.

Although nationalism is the strongest single force in Southeast

Asia today, several Southeast Asian governments are experiencing difficulty in holding together their national states. Separatist movements, demands for local autonomy, and denial of the authority of the central government are aspects of a colonial legacy of territorial and administrative unity which has little real basis in national unity. In Burma, Indonesia, Vietnam, and the Philippines, the newly independent governments have been forced to by-pass acute economic and social problems in the first years of their national existence in order to devote a major part of their energy and resources to establishing law and order and to overcoming sectional animosities.

A second political consequence of colonialism is the rudimentary stage of development of political institutions in the newly independent states of Southeast Asia. At the time they achieved their freedom, not one of the states of Southeast Asia could be considered prepared for orderly self-government by Western standards. But when the urge for independence and the pressures of nationalism reach the boiling point, as they did in Southeast Asia after the Second World War, the question of preparedness for independence as a basis for independence becomes academic. All the colonial powers made some effort to prepare their colonial territories for self-government but, before the training program had advanced beyond the primary grades, independence came.

Because the colonial experience failed to provide full opportunities for the early growth of party and parliamentary institutions, the states of Southeast Asia were left without an institutional or philosophical framework of their own for orderly or responsible government. Patterning their political institutions on the limits of their experience, the national leaders of states recently under British rule seek to use British parliamentary institutions as their model, former French colonials model their political institutions on French standards, and so on. Quite obviously, this situation is fraught with danger of further political dislocation because of the difficulties inherent in adopting unassimilated Western political practices and institutions. There is always the chance of making erroneous application of imperfectly learned lessons. There is further risk in the attempt to apply advanced forms of Western representative government in Asian states in advance of a popular demand for or understanding of them. The development of political institutions is a phenomenon of indigenous evolution and growth rather than revolution, decree, or direct outside influence.

The nature and structure of political parties in Southeast Asia also reflect the lack of political experience under colonial rule. Because the colonial authorities frowned on the development of political organizations and parties, no foundation of experience was constructed for organizing or using political parties as institutions of responsible government. As a result, the political parties which mushroomed over Southeast Asia after independence had been won tended to have little practical relationship to the problems of government or representation. Today, most of these parties are based on personal loyalty to individual political figures, with the party following, in general, having little regard for the political philosophy or program of the party leaders. The party leader enjoys considerable freedom to use his position in any way suggested by expediency or opportunism. This has, in turn, weakened concepts of party discipline, leadership, and responsibility, and shaped the character of Southeast Asian political parties in the direction of factionalism and the growth of multiple splinter parties. Ambitious would-be politicians, able to muster a circle of personal followers, may and often do set themselves up in business as heads of political parties. The net result has been that a number of coalition governments in Southeast Asia lack even the minimum political strength to adopt necessary reform legislation.

A third legacy of colonialism of special political significance in Southeast Asia is the critical shortage of trained and experienced administrators willing and able to assume responsibility, to make decisions and to delegate authority. The colonial powers, trapped by a dilemma, developed very few such officials. Although they wanted to promote the growth of an indigenous educated class to serve in the colonial service, the colonial authorities feared that the people whom they trained and educated might become a threat to the perpetuation of colonial rule. Consequently, while creating a small Western-educated intellectual élite, they restricted the opportunities of that élite. This had a double-barreled effect. Some educated nationals, seeking to apply in their homeland the liberal Western education which they had absorbed, became revolutionaries or independence leaders, just as the colonial authorities had feared. Others, after years of relegation to inferior posts and routine assignments in the colonial service, lost their enthusiasm, initiative, and self-confidence. Therefore, when the time came and the states of Southeast Asia became independent, the new governments were hard put to it even partially to fill essential administrative posts in the ministries and the provinces with officials who had experience in any way commensurate with the responsibilities of their new tasks.

A fourth, and extremely important, political legacy to the new governments of Southeast Asia is the extremely narrow popular base upon which they can build and operate a system of democratic government. Most colonial governments made little effort to provide the educational facilities or the opportunities for experience necessary to develop a politically conscious and articulate electorate. Except in the Philippines, colonial practice discouraged popular interest in politics and government. Thus, when national leaders took over the newly independent governments of Southeast Asia intent on setting up political systems resembling those of the Western democracies, they found the basic ingredient of representative government—an interested, informed, and sensitive electorate—was lacking. Moreover, because colonial government had been imposed from the outside, often without adaptation to local institutions or traditions, to the vast majority of colonial peoples central government came to mean something foreign and restrictive and, therefore, something to be either actively resisted or evaded, as far as possible. This common attitude toward government has not been entirely overcome in the postindependence period.

Following independence, the members of the intellectual élites soon found themselves in positions of government leadership and responsibility rather than in their accustomed role as opposition and resistance leaders. They were forced by circumstances to broaden their political knowledge. As a result of their new contacts with national and international problems, they broadened their horizons and arrived at new levels of political and economic competence. But the mass of Southeast Asian populations, not as prepared to assimilate new experiences or to adapt themselves to modern political and economic life, have developed political awareness more slowly. In fact, so slow has been the change that there is an ever widening gap between the national leaders and the followers which today adds the burden of communication between the two groups to other problems. Because differences in the terms of reference, the levels of knowledge, between the governors and the governed are so great, it has proved difficult for the national leaders of Southeast Asia to rally around them sufficiently resolute popular opinion adequate to support their programs or ideas. Until a reasonably broad popular base is built, it is clear that responsible and orderly representative governments cannot easily be developed through Southeast Asia. Faced with heavy international pressures and internal tensions, the Southeast Asian countries are hardly in a position to construct such a base effortlessly.

In the economic sphere, the conditions resulting from colonial practices created problems for the newly independent states almost as difficult as those of political construction and growth. Upon achieving their independence, the Philippines, Burma, Indonesia, Cambodia, and Vietnam were confronted immediately both with political and with economic disorder, each complementing and intensifying the other.

Throughout the colonial period in Southeast Asia, the traditional concepts of mercantilism prevailed. The basic motives of the colonial powers, profitable trade and commerce, were mitigated only mildly and inconsistently by concern for the welfare of the local populations. Observers differ in their estimates on the indigenous standards of living: whether they remained about the same or actually decreased during the colonial period. Very few maintain that the local populations gained from the exploitation of their land and resources in any degree comparable to the mother country.

One heritage of colonialism was the growth of large numbers of landless, debt-ridden peasants and, in some instances, the concentration of large-scale landownership in the hands of foreign groups. In Burma the British imposed legal concepts and a money economy on a population unprepared to cope with the accompanying problems and temptations. Under the new system, unsuspecting and uncomprehending Burmese peasants mortgaged away ancestral lands, which formerly could not be expropriated under Burmese customary law, to the alien Hindu caste of hereditary money-lenders, the Chettyars. By 1930, through foreclosure, absentee landlords owned more than 50 per cent of the most fertile rice lands in lower Burma. The former peasant proprietors became either tenants paying excessive rent or landless farm laborers. In the apt description of one authority:

> The people were freed from servitude to their hereditary chieftains only to find themselves bound to foreign money-lenders in chains firmly riveted by western law. Economic force, subject to no restraint but law, upset the balance of native economy, sapped the foundations of religious life and institutions, ousted native arts, crafts and industries, and killed the social pastimes and recreations.[1]

In Indochina the French development of large plantations for the cultivation of rubber and rice (the latter especially in the Cochin China delta regions) led to the displacement of native landholders. While unoccupied land often was developed in this way, native owners, if involved, soon became landless agricultural workers. In central Luzon in the Philippines an unhealthy concentration of landownership also developed.

The concentration of colonial investors on profit led to the specialized production of a few export products, such as rice, rubber, tin, copra, and oil. This unbalanced economic development has since proved a severe economic handicap to the newly independent states. Their ability to pay for numerous essential imports depends entirely on their ability to sell profitably one or two export products in the world markets. The risks of overspecialization are latent in the economic position of every Southeast Asian country. Along with the colonial development of plantation economies or mineral export specialization, the economies of most colonies became heavily dependent on the mother country, forcing the new governments to face major problems of trade reorientation.

Another heritage of colonial economic practice is the very low per capita productivity in Southeast Asia. Most colonial investors were content to base production on cheap mass labor, which they imported when it was not available locally, rather than on increased capital equipment.

If the Southeast Asian states were properly to export and manage the raw material resources originally developed by colonial investment, they would have on hand a valuable means to help finance their own economic development and diversification. But here again the states are handicapped by early colonial practice which principally used nationals of the mother country as technicians, engineers, and managers. With few local technicians prepared to take over the plantations, mines, oil fields, refineries, and transportation facilities at the time of independence, any timetable on economic development and growth is bound to be seriously delayed during an interim period of training the needed professional assistance.

The Southeast Asian countries lack not only engineers and managers but also businessmen who can mobilize capital for use in initiating commercial and industrial enterprises and agrarian improvements essential to economic growth. Generally speaking, the role of the businessman throughout Southeast Asia has been left to foreign minority groups, principally to Chinese, Europeans, and Indians. Under colonialism there was developed no indigenous middle-class business group. The indigenous peoples, generally isolated from contact with the world of national and international commerce, had limited opportunities to acquire experience or knowledge in the fields of capital accumulation, marketing, investment, or modern business administration. The result is that industrial and business initiative today rests in the hands of government. No national industrial or entrepreneur class has the capital, the experience, or the psychology essential to the growth of a free-enterprise economy.

One further consequence of colonialism is especially important on this economic side. During the colonial period, free-enterprise capitalism carried on the bulk of economic activity in the colonial territories. The colonial powers introduced foreign investment, foreign managers and bosses, and a foreign economic system. As a result of the association of colonialism with foreign investment and capitalism, a residue of profound suspicion and hostility toward both tinges the minds of many Southeast Asians. The Secretary-General of the Indonesian Ministry of Foreign Affairs has expressed this attitude in the following words:

> In our experience, colonialism is the child of capitalism. In its inevitable wake, colonialism brought us national disunity and poverty of a

degree which has probably never been known in the West. For us, colonialism is not a theoretical evil, for its effects are seen everywhere in our countries. The development, physical and mental, of our people has been stunted by colonialism, and colonialism is the offspring of capitalism. Therefore, for us, socialism is an essential ingredient of nationalism, since we believe that socialism offers our people the quickest escape from the poverties of the colonial heritage.[2]

The countries of Southeast Asia have experienced a number of cultural invasions in the course of their long histories. Before the arrival of the European on the scene, Muslims, Hindus, Buddhists, and Confucians from Arabia, India, and China made their social and cultural impact in successive waves over large parts of Southeast Asia. These outside influences were absorbed, for the most part, without serious disruption of indigenous social patterns. They were peaceful, gradual cultural intrusions from which the indigenous societies borrowed religious concepts, social organization, art, architecture, drama, and literature. Western civilization and the machine age, which accompanied the European colonials, was so different from the earlier alien contacts that it could not help being more disruptive to indigenous political, economic, and social institutions. Not that Southeast Asia absorbed more Western social and cultural characteristics (the contrary is possibly truer), but the new forces, represented by the West, created wider divergencies and heavier pressures and, in the end, had a greater disruptive impact on the traditional social structures of the area.

The legacy of colonialism in the social sphere is not easy to assess because the social disruption and change manifest in colonial Southeast Asia were the result of a combination of the general impact of Western civilization and of colonialism. Western colonialism was the vehicle for the penetration of Western civilization. The changes in indigenous social systems, in large measure, were forced and unbalanced owing to the purposes and methods of the colonial powers. Under Western colonial régimes, all the aspects of Western civilization were not automatically or intentionally brought to Southeast Asia. Either through colonial policy or the sheer weight of the impact of Western civilization, often the colonial powers introduced social changes which were of a superficial or structural nature. The extent of truly basic Western social orientation in Southeast Asia is uncertain. It is clear that urban centers in Southeast Asia felt the impact of the West and its industrial society far more than the rural areas. In many ways some rural communities appear to be little changed from the precolonial period. However, even the most isolated communities of Southeast Asia have felt the opening up of roads, railways, canal systems, and air lines to remote parts of the country, the increased possibilities for trade, the introduction of money economies, the facts of cash crops and Western legal codes.

From the beginning of the present century until the Second World War, the Dutch attempted to preserve the rural cultural and social organization of Indonesia; the British in Burma appeared indifferent to the preservation or protection of the Burmese social structure, although they actually laid the framework for its disruption by introducing Western legal codes and a *laissez faire* economic policy; the French, with their colonial objective of "assimilation," made a studied effort in Indochina, beginning with the indigenous élites and working through the social hierarchy, to replace local socioeconomic systems with a French one. The United States, in the Philippines, by political, social, and educational policies, attempted to shape local societies in the American pattern. Despite the differences in approach, the results in all cases were very much alike. Indigenous social systems were weakened or disrupted, but new systems did not evolve to replace the old. When colonialism ended, there was revealed throughout the area the social disruption inherent in alien rule, intensified by the unique impact of Western civilization and its industrial orientation.

Mr. Furnivall, reporting on traditional social structures in his study of the impact of British and Dutch colonialism, lists five adverse consequences of colonialism, most of them applicable throughout Southeast Asia. These are: (1) the failure of Western self-governing institutions; (2) the growth of debt and agrarian distress; (3) the multiplication of litigation and crime; (4) the rise of disaffection and unrest among the indigenous clergy; and (5) the widespread corruption in the judicial and administrative service.[3]

The High Commissioner for the Philippines in his Annual Report for 1941 summed up the nature and extent of social and economic dislocation in these words:

> . . . neither a sizable independent middle class nor an influential public opinion has developed. The bulk of the newly created income has gone to the government, the landlords, and to the urban areas, and has served but little to ameliorate living conditions among feudal peasantry and tenantry. The relative numbers of these have not been materially reduced. Maldistribution of population, of land, and of wealth in many forms continues. The gap between the mass population and the small governing class has broadened, and social unrest has reached serious proportions.

Mr. Kahin outlines four ways in which the impact of Dutch rule in Indonesia "substantially altered the basic structure of Javanese social organization": (1) Javanese society was changed from moderately authoritarian to strongly authoritarian; (2) the political power of the indigenous nobility over the peasantry was substantially increased; (3) the relative economic and political strength of the peasantry was weakened; (4) the Javanese merchant group and middle class were eliminated.[4]

Southeast Asian societies were noticeably affected by the introduction of large numbers of alien laborers, mainly Chinese and Indian, by the colonial powers. These immigrant laborers, in time, managed to displace the indigenous entrepreneurs and middle-class elements in the national populations. Because these groups were not assimilated—neither the colonial powers nor the indigenous peoples encouraged them to do so—they became a source of social tension. Even in noncolonial Thailand, where a large unassimilated Chinese population controls much of the economic activity of the country, a Chinese minority problem developed. This suggests that the colonial powers are not entirely to blame but, in Malaya and Burma especially and, to a certain extent, in Indonesia, the colonial powers deliberately encouraged alien immigration and showed considerable economic favoritism for the alien groups.

Although overpopulation is a problem today in only a few areas of Southeast Asia, such as Java and central Luzon, the population increase which all Southeast Asia experienced during the colonial period is an additional source of social disruption. The colonial powers introduced minor sanitation and health measures which sharply reduced death rates in the colonies at the same time that birth rates remained the same or increased. As a consequence, in the first half of the present century the populations of the

Philippines, Indonesia, and Thailand more than doubled; the population of Malaya increased more than 400 per cent; and the population of Burma increased nearly 40 per cent.

> One of the worst heritages of Western colonial rule in parts of Asia (quite unintentional, even motivated in part by humanitarian intentions) was a partial modernization which brought enough modern ideas to keep more people alive but not enough to alter social institutions so that not so many would be born. . . . This heritage of partial, unbalanced modernization means that these countries face the problem of transforming their economies and social structures from a starting position where population is already as dense as in highly industrialized regions. Consequently they have little "slack" to absorb the population upsurge that has always accompanied modern economic development.[5]

Colonial rule and Western influences caused an impact on nearly every aspect of Southeast Asia's indigenous social structures. Disruption came to religions and educational systems, family and communal relationships, traditional values, customary law, concepts of property rights, historic political and socioeconomic patterns. Although Western influences disrupted established social orders, they did not replace the social systems or provide suitable alternatives. The new states of Southeast Asia, unable to retreat to their ancient social order or adopt Western social systems, are faced with only one way out—a long task of building new social systems which satisfy their own cultural and social traditions and which at the same time accommodate the desired modernization and industrial development.

So profound an impression has the colonial experience made on the attitudes and psychology of the peoples of Southeast Asia that today these formerly colonial peoples value their independence from foreign rule as undoubtedly their most highly prized possession. The newly independent states give anticolonialism significance in their foreign policies, insisting that the Western powers must never again be allowed to revive colonialism and that colonialism must end everywhere in the world. Evidence that these issues are kept alive is frequent and repetitive.

Because colonialism in Southeast Asia historically was a Western institution, its psychological reaction today is manifested by some form of rejection of the West. The trend is often apparent in

Southeast Asian attitudes on political, economic, and military cooperation, and it is even clearer in matters of culture and philosophy. From the viewpoint of formulating and executing United States policy in the area, four of the many psychological consequences of colonialism may be considered of special importance. They are: (1) suspicion of the West; (2) desire for individual and national prestige; (3) racial tension; (4) the urge to return to traditional social and philosophical concepts.

Except for Thailand and, to some extent, the Philippines, the colonial legacy has left Southeast Asians with a persistent tendency to suspect Western conduct and policy as a continual threat to their national independence. Still fresh in the minds of the people is the bitterness of the recent struggle to end the colonial era and, in the minds of the leaders of the newly independent states, their personal part in the very personal struggle for national independence. Suspicions cannot easily be overcome by verbal assurances from the formerly colonial powers that colonialism is dead. Only the passage of time, the growth of internal strength and confidence, and the most circumspect Western conduct can create conditions in which this psychology of suspicion may diminish.

Like all the "Western" states, the United States falls under the shadow of suspicions common to Southeast Asia. Distinctions among Western nations are scarcely recognized by any but the more sophisticated or informed Southeast Asians, and many of the latter perceive imperialistic ambitions in America's postwar conduct. Nor is the United States cleared of suspicion by the fact that it readily granted independence to the Philippines. A great number of noncommunist Southeast Asians are wary of American motives because the United States retains military bases in the Philippines and Japan. Southeast Asian memories of the colonial role played by British, Dutch, and French military bases in the past dim practical considerations of Philippine and Japanese security in the present. A great number of Southeast Asians, other than the communists, consider American support of the French in Indochina as an indication of American sympathy for colonialism. In Indonesia, others place the responsibility for delayed independence on American Marshall Plan aid to the Netherlands. Regardless of the merits of the case, in the minds of a great many Southeast Asian people the

United States is identified with the West and, therefore, with the formerly colonial powers; increased American interest and activity in the area in the postwar period strengthen the illusion that the United States is a potential "successor" to the European colonial powers, a fear which the communists have not hesitated to use to their advantage.

A second psychological impact of colonialism, the strong and understandable desire among Southeast Asian people for individual and national prestige, was built up during the prolonged period of colonialism. Although the concept of "face" is not exclusively Oriental, there is a special sensitivity attached to it today by the peoples of Southeast Asia because during the colonial era they suffered national frustration and were relegated to a secondary personal status. The urge for equality, respect, and prestige is so significant that it possibly has a place in personal relationships out of proportion to other matters.

This urge, for example, is reflected in the attachment of Southeast Asian leaders to concepts of absolute independence and sovereignty which, though understandable in countries long denied a sovereign voice in world affairs, can also become extreme. To most of these leaders, independence means more than freedom from foreign political and economic control: it also means freedom from unwanted foreign, especially Western, influence. Under present circumstances the Southeast Asian leaders' adherence to the concept of absolute national sovereignty increases the difficulty of smooth relations between East and West. By one of those tricks of history which sometimes occur, the Southeast Asian states won their national sovereignty at the very moment in time when most Western states were abandoning, in favor of collective security, the concept of national sovereignty in its absolute sense as one which failed to meet present international realities. The intellectual and emotional adjustment necessary for close political and security coordination with the Western nations is therefore a very difficult transition for many Southeast Asian leaders to make.

Racial tension is a third psychological remnant of colonialism. The wind of discrimination and exclusion on a racial basis was seeded by the colonial powers and is now being reaped in the sensitivity and feeling among the Asian peoples for one another and by their inclination to exclude predominantly white nations from their affairs where possible. Racial consciousness in Southeast Asia today is due probably to resentment of past experiences under colonial rule rather than to inherent racial complexes and prejudices. Although the latter exist as well, the "Asia for Asians" psychology, the demand for Asian prestige and recognition, are significant aspects of the present emotional climate in most Southeast Asian countries.

Psychologically, colonialism has had a strange reverse impact. By forcing Western concepts into the jaws of Southeast Asia, it has helped regenerate a national psychology which tends to reject these Western concepts. Many Southeast Asians today have a strong psychological urge to return to their ancient cultural traditions, as evidenced by the current Buddhist revival in Burma and Cambodia and the Islamic revival in Indonesia whose bases are not only political but also religious and sociological. Unhappily, the tendency to revert to the traditional, away from the modern, is a psychological paradox for the Southeast Asian people who crave modernization in the economic sense at the same time that they seek this return to traditionalism in their cultural and social activities.

In light of the history and background of colonialism in Southeast Asia, it is surprising to note the extent of the impact made by Western ideas of government and individual freedom. But it cannot be assumed that the impact is permanent or that these Western ideas ultimately will prevail. The Southeast Asian leaders were afforded Western orientation by the colonial experience but the experience will not serve to produce a replica of Western political, economic, or social organization in Southeast Asia in the future. The future Southeast Asian structure is more apt to be a synthesis of Western and indigenous concepts.

The legacy of the colonial experience remains an uneven mixture of opportunity and limitations within which United States policy must operate. United States policy may be conducted in such a way that, in time, it will diminish the limitations and widen the area of cooperation and mutual affiliation of national interests between America and the states of Southeast Asia. But one thing is certain. If American policies are formulated without regard to the fears and aspirations of the Southeast Asian people and governments, and if policies are executed without regard to Southeast Asian sensibilities and justifiable pride, the gulf between the United States and the states of Southeast Asia can be easily widened—to the certain disadvantage of all concerned.

THE SECOND WORLD WAR

The Second World War marks a decisive turning point in the history of Southeast Asia. During the war and immediately afterward, forces which had been steadily gathering momentum in colonial Asia for several decades suddenly were unleashed. Patience with foreign privilege and alien rule snapped. The colonial peoples no longer were content to suppress their aspirations for independence, for a better life, and for individual dignity and national equality. Even with the war won by the Western powers, the nature of the relations between the states of colonial Asia and the Western colonial powers could never be the same as before the war. Britain recognized the fact relatively early; the Netherlands recognized it slowly and reluctantly in the face of international pressure; the French were unable to recognize it until seven years of bloody and costly war failed to restore their colonial status in Indochina.

Engrossed in the war against the Axis, cut off from contact with Japanese-occupied Southeast Asia, the United States and the European colonial powers lost touch with the mood and temper of the area. As a result, they entered the postwar period with policies which were unacceptable to the newly vitalized nationalist movements and which were inadequate for coping with the current conditions in colonial Asia. Britain, France, and the Netherlands expected to resume their colonial activities essentially where they left off before the war. Their first consideration was to reestablish economic production in the colonies without giving serious regard to local demands on political and social matters. It was evident that none of the European colonial powers planned early independence for their Asian colonial territories.

But, as a result of the war, the balance of capabilities between the colonial powers and their Asian territories changed. On the one hand, the nationalist and independence forces in India, Burma,

Indochina, and Indonesia had increased in size and achieved considerable unity. They were organized, armed, and their spirit was high. On the other hand, Britain, France, and the Netherlands were near economic collapse and military exhaustion. As subsequent events demonstrated, they were in no position to reimpose colonial rule in Asia by force, especially in the face of resolute and armed nationalist opposition, without seriously endangering their own postwar recovery.

The many and varied effects of the Second World War form an important part of the background conditions within which United States policy in Southeast Asia must function. Although the widespread physical destruction caused by the war in Southeast Asia is the most obvious effect, it is also temporary in nature. Of the Southeast Asian countries, Burma, the Philippines, and Malaya suffered extensive physical destruction from wartime military operations. Their roads, railways, communications, mines, oil fields, industrial plants, plantations, homes, and cities were heavily damaged, first as a result of scorched earth tactics or bombing and, later, as a result of looting and neglect. During the war, peasants generally were impelled to reduce their crops to subsistence levels because of the impossibility of transporting surplus production to markets and because of the unavailability of consumer goods in exchange. Japanese requisitions and famine took heavy toll of livestock, including the all-important draft animals. When the war was over, some fifteen million acres of the rich rice land of Southeast Asia lay abandoned and overgrown by jungle.

In Burma, where the maximum total war damage was sustained, rice cultivation dropped to less than half prewar levels, oil and mineral output were at a standstill following destruction of most of the productive facilities, timber production fell to less than 30 per cent of prewar activity, and railway rolling stock was more than 90 per cent destroyed. Burma's over-all productive capacity was reduced to one-third of prewar levels. Its damage claims for both private and public property were estimated at approximately $2.6 billion. Independent Burma's first Minister of Finance in a 1948 budget speech succinctly stated the effect of the war on Burma's economy:

Burma before the war was a surplus country in many respects. . . . She had surplus rice, timber, petroleum, kerosene, lead, tin, wolfram, silver, hides, rubber, etc. . . . If war had not come to Burma she, like India, would have emerged as a creditor country, with her mineral resources greatly developed. . . . The Anglo-Japanese wars twice fought over the length and breadth of Burma have wiped out all her sources of income.

Although not as dire, the postwar picture in the Philippines and Malaya was similar. In both instances, however, large-scale outside help was available immediately for economic reconstruction. British government and private investment capital hastened repair of war damage and restoration of production in Malaya. The Malayan rubber trees, untapped and unmolested during the war, provided greater yields in 1948 than they could ever have offered in 1941. In the Philippines, American economic aid and payments of various kinds amounting to more than 1.5 billion American dollars hastened recovery between the years 1945 and 1950.

Although Indonesia and Indochina suffered much less war damage than Burma or the Philippines, mineral and agricultural production dropped considerably in both countries owing to the lack of world markets and the Japanese oppression. Initially, Indochina suffered extensive damage in the postwar period by the looting Nationalist Chinese troops who occupied Laos and northern Vietnam; later, as a consequence of the long and bitter Indochina war. Although Allied bombing raids caused some damage to railways, docks, and power facilities near the end of the war, the destruction in Thailand was slight compared to the other states of Southeast Asia.

The war's physical destruction increased the weakness and the problems of the Southeast Asian states in the postwar period of readjustment. It reduced the states' economic capabilities at a time when every ounce of economic strength counted. Although reconstruction proceeded rapidly in some places, production was slow to follow except in the case of rubber and tea, which were the only important commodities to recover production immediately at the close of the war. This relatively low volume of production of export commodities, owing to the effects of war devastation and civil strife, proved early to be a major limitation to economic improvement in that postwar period when the population continued to grow and, more important, when local economic demands and expectations were increasing.

So handicapped during a critical period of their histories, the Southeast Asian states nonetheless have demonstrated such impressive rates of reconstruction and production recovery when conditions of relative internal peace prevail that hope of greater recovery from war destruction may be indicated. In general, Southeast Asian production was restored to prewar levels by 1950. But exports, so necessary to economic health, have revived unevenly, and still constitute a major economic problem in the area.

The Second World War also drastically disrupted international patterns of trade and payments. Before the war, the economies of the Southeast Asian countries were closely integrated with the colonial powers and geared to established international trade channels. Following the war, the violent stresses of European economy and of established trade channels tossed unprecedented economic problems into the laps of the totally unprepared Southeast Asian states.

Southeast Asia, forming a part of a global network of multilateral trade and payments, before the war managed to have a considerable export surplus with the United States and continental European countries. The area met its deficit with the United Kingdom together with deficits on "invisible account" by merchandise surpluses in other directions as well as by an inflow of long-term capital and occasional short-term borrowing. Except for the international depression of the 1930's when the amount of goods moving through international trade channels was reduced sharply, when many countries adopted restrictive trade policies, and when foreign investments and loans, especially from the United States, were drastically curtailed, the traditional pattern of multilateral trade remained essentially fixed until the Second World War.

In the postwar period, serious Southeast Asian trade deficits replaced the substantial export surpluses of the prewar period. Southeast Asia's trade with the United States, for example, shifted from an over-all export balance to a serious deficit, with a consequent acute dollar shortage. Where the prewar system of multilateral exchange once operated to offset deficits with other countries through the region's surpluses with the United States, the wartime devastation and economic disruption led to sharply reduced production and export of key commodities such as rice, timber, tin, petroleum, and copra. The changed postwar conditions, including principally the increased importance of the United States and the dollar area as a supplier of both raw materials and manufactured products, the low level of United States investment abroad, and the fall in the real value of Europe's "invisible income" seem to indicate that a return to the traditional trade pattern of the prewar period is unlikely.

For the Southeast Asian states, there are a number of real problems resulting from the economic dislocations of the Second World War. Some of the adverse economic effects of the war which were of a temporary and local character, such as physical destruction, low postwar productivity, and emergency import needs, are much improved today and, in time, may be entirely overcome. However, they caused much economic strain in the countries of Southeast Asia at a critical time by depressing the already low standards of living and delaying general economic development and diversification. Other effects, such as the scrambled international trade patterns, war-induced changes in world production patterns and in the demand for key Southeast Asian export items, the dollar shortage, and the relatively low level of foreign investment in Southeast Asia—due to other reasons as well as to the war—are part of a long-term international economic problem. Somehow, the export levels of the Southeast Asian countries must be increased and stable markets found for their products. Actually, global needs for Southeast Asia's primary products probably will increase over a period of time, and a full and efficient exploitation of their basic commodities could provide much of the capital necessary for increased standards of living and economic development. Meanwhile, the Southeast Asian states do not have adequate trade revenues to meet their needs or to satisfy their people's economic aspirations.

United States policy must function in an area which, in general, is depressed economically and runs either trade deficits or surpluses too small to keep abreast of growing requirements for defense, economic development, and popular demands for better living standards. In the context of over-all United States policy, it is also important to keep in mind the fact that Southeast Asia trade is a significant factor in the economic welfare of the United Kingdom, western Europe, and Japan. Since the causes of the economic problems in Southeast Asia which result from the Second World War are global as well as local, their solution must be sought in the realm of multilateral international trade as well as in local development.

The disintegration of the traditional social structures of Southeast Asia, in process throughout the colonial period, was accelerated by the war turmoil and confusion. All the Southeast Asian countries, with the exception of Thailand and Malaya, achieved their recent independence following long periods of social disruption such as are inherent in alien rule. The shattering experience of the war intensified the disruption, removing to all intents and purposes the stabilizing restraint of law and order for its duration, increasing economic hardship, making destruction and bloodshed appear commonplace. In Burma, Malaya, Indonesia, Vietnam, and parts of the Philippines, the traditional social mores and restraints tended to lose force in the struggle for individual survival. For the first time thousands of young men came into possession of firearms and, learning to use them, left home to join underground forces or bandit gangs. Families, uprooted from their farms, fled to the cities seeking protection and many, once there, were forced to live by looting and thievery. No longer did the family and village units afford security and stability. Only Thailand, Cambodia, and Laos, affected to a lesser extent by the war, seemed islands of relative calm.

Still, by some curious contradiction, the war experience and the following nationalist struggles for independence precipitated an urge for social and cultural rejuvenation. A great many people, witnessing the unhinging of traditional behavior patterns in the wartime eruption of amorality, were impressed with the need for preserving and strengthening the traditional social fabric. This gave special impetus to the cultural and religious renaissance which is observable in Burma, Indonesia, and Cambodia.

The requirements of modern statehood and the fact that

social disruption has gone too far for a complete revival of old traditions preclude complete reversion to traditional social institutions and organizations in Southeast Asia. In addition, national aspirations for industrialization and economic diversification are contrary to the ancient social and cultural patterns. But the phenomena of social change and readjustment are among the conditions in which United States policy must operate in Southeast Asia. It would be as easy to revert to an earlier century as to try to stop or ignore Southeast Asia's social revolution. Because United States policy can no more hope decisively to influence the Southeast Asian revolution than to predict its outcome, it would seem that United States policy should have a sufficiently high degree of flexibility and tolerance to function in an atmosphere of social uncertainty and instability, a policy whose concepts can accommodate basic social changes in the area, whether or not the latter invariably are in accord with American concepts.

THE GROWTH OF NATIONALISM AND THE JAPANESE OCCUPATION

The Second World War and the Japanese occupation provided both the stimulus and the opportunity for the rapid growth of nationalism in Southeast Asia. On the eve of the war, the Southeast Asian nationalist movements were weak and poorly organized; the spirit of national consciousness had penetrated no more than 6 or 8 per cent of the population of any Southeast Asian colonial area. By the end of the war, nationalism had become a dynamic force of first magnitude everywhere, except perhaps in Malaya.

The roots of nationalism in Southeast Asia may be traced to the early part of this century and to the Russo-Japanese War. The defeat of a major European power by a small Asian nation in that war opened new avenues of hope in Southeast Asia for independence, self-government, and equality. Equally important, many Southeast Asians began to regard Japan as the most likely source of assistance in their struggle for independence. The First World War gave further stimulus to incipient nationalism, which was kept alive during the opening years of the twentieth century by a small minority of educated Southeast Asians trained in the liberal and nationalist traditions of the West. The idea of self-determination, postulated at the Paris Peace Conference and the League of Nations primarily to help solve nationalist and ethnic group problems in central Europe, spread to the nationalist groups in Southeast Asia. Nevertheless, the nationalist instinct remained weak in Southeast Asia until the Second World War. Its main rationale and substance were a growing dissatisfaction with colonial rule.

The growth of nationalism in Southeast Asia obviously was aided by cultural and ethnic bonds, but anticolonialism was its primary ingredient. It is doubtful that modern nationalism in Southeast Asia would have developed, at least along its present lines, without the historical basis of colonialism and the galvanizing experience of the Second World War. After long periods of slow growth nurtured by a few nationalist leaders, there "was a deep change of the nationalist spirit caused by the experiences of war and occupation. . . . Simultaneously all the accumulated and repressed feelings of nationalism burst loose." [6]

Even now, some ten years after the war, there is minimum awareness of the tremendous impact of the Japanese victory over the Western colonial powers and of their subsequent occupation in Southeast Asia. The Japanese victory broke the grip of Western colonialism in Southeast Asia. It provided other Asian nations with a basis for confidence in their own ability to resist Western military power and political mastery. It contributed much to those postwar conditions which made independence for colonial Southeast Asia inevitable. The apparent ease with which the Japanese carried out their military conquest of Southeast Asia and the barrage of anti-Western propaganda during their occupation of the area diminished the prestige of the colonial powers almost to the point of non-existence.

The Japanese victory seemed to many Southeast Asians a vindication of their long-standing faith that the Japanese would prove the best source of help in achieving independence. In fact, the Japanese occupation was greeted at first as "liberation" and a prelude to independence. Most of the local population welcomed the Japanese with enthusiasm. Except for the Philippines, few raised a hand in support of the colonial powers as harbingers of independence. In Malaya, the Malays generally were apathetic and resistance to the Japanese occupation forces was limited almost entirely to the overseas Chinese. In Indonesia, the coming of the Japanese brought anti-Dutch feeling into the open. Many Indonesians regarded the Japanese occupation as temporary and as a prelude to national freedom. In Burma, many nationalist leaders and common people alike eagerly awaited the arrival of the advancing Japanese troops. In Indochina, nationalist hopes for independence under Japanese sponsorship soon faded only because the agreements concluded between Japan and the Vichy régime in France left the French in nominal control of Indochina. Regardless of the exceptions and the degrees of variance, the Southeast Asian people and their leaders as a whole anticipated independence under Japanese sponsorship and an equal partnership with Japan in the Greater East Asia Co-Prosperity Sphere.

Southeast Asian attitudes at the end of the war are in marked contrast to the early ones, owing in part to Japanese arrogance and cruelty, in part to the economic hardship and suffering under Japanese occupation and, most important of all, owing to the amazing growth of national consciousness among the masses. By 1945, in the hour of crisis, those who had welcomed the Japanese as "liberators" gave them little or no support, and local guerrillas or organized nationalist armies under indigenous leadership harassed the Japanese throughout Southeast Asia. Although the Japanese, as part of their strategy for controlling and administering Southeast Asia, utilized and encouraged many nationalist leaders and supported some nationalist groups, they failed to identify their interests with those of the Southeast Asian nationalist movement. The Japanese, as the returning colonial authorities were to do later, miscalculated the nature and strength of indigenous nationalism.

Japanese occupation policy differed in the different countries of Southeast Asia. In Burma and the Philippines, the Japanese attempted to rule indirectly by establishing in the summer and fall of 1943 nominally independent régimes. In Indochina, by agreement with the Vichy Government, the Japanese permitted continuation of the French colonial administration until March 1945 when, having outlived their usefulness to the Japanese, the colonial administrators were rounded up, disarmed, and interned. Within a month of this change, independent régimes were proclaimed in Vietnam, Cambodia, and Laos. In Indonesia, Japanese rule was direct. Japanese occupation authorities replaced the Dutch colonial officials and did not give Indonesians substantial governmental and administrative responsibility until the closing months of the war. Then, faced with increasing nationalist pressures and the Allied offensive in the Pacific, they began preparations to establish an independent Indonesian régime. Although the Japanese surrendered before arrangements could be completed, the Indonesians declared their own independence within a few days of the Japanese surrender.

In such diverse ways, six Southeast Asian states achieved some measure of independence in the course of the Japanese occupation. But in every case, far from satisfying nationalist demands, independence served to increase them. Whenever they could, the wartime régimes pressed the Japanese authorities for full and complete independence to satisfy national aspirations. The following excerpt, taken from a wartime document which the Burmese Government prepared for the Japanese, illustrates this attitude.

> The Burmese understand independence to be primarily the concrete right and power to administer their own affairs in their own way and with their own authority. Where they see this right with their own eyes they see independence. . . . Burmese national independence must be as real and visible as possible by leaving everything in Burma to the Burmese Government and people.[7]

Thus the Japanese occupation provided stimuli to nationalism in Southeast Asia, first by evicting the colonial powers and encouraging the hopes for independence, later by short-sighted and often brutal occupation policies which alienated the Southeast Asian peoples. In their disillusionment with the degree of independence permitted by the Japanese and in their hardship under Japanese occupation, the Southeast Asian people found greater national consciousness than they ever before had known.

Even though the periods of national independence enjoyed by

African Conference at Bandung in the spring of 1955, and in cultural exchange programs. National consciousness also has been stimulated by exchange visits of prime ministers and other government leaders among the Asian states. The latent force of national pride is manifest in such diverse enthusiasms as the Malayans for their world-champion badminton teams and other Southeast Asians for their teams or individual athletes sent to participate in the Olympic games or in regional contests.

Although the transition is proceeding, it undoubtedly will take many years for nationalism in Southeast Asia to achieve a state of development necessary for stable and responsible political life. Certain dangers are implicit in the interim phase. For example, the full significance of the transition has not yet fully penetrated to some national leaders who still revert to the slogans and appeals of the preliberation period in order to maintain artificial and surface appearances of national unity and patriotism. The broad intellectual and social gap which exists between the national leaders and the ordinary citizens creates the burden of effective communication between the two groups. The groups as yet fail to share a common body of national concepts, symbols, and ideals necessary for understanding. Real or imagined external threats, especially those conceivably connected with the Western colonial powers, still can be used to evoke emotional mass response in the newly sovereign states. To perpetuate and use this convenient political tool is a strong temptation for some national leaders. In the transition stage opportunities exist for political extremists of either the left or right to corrupt the growth of a healthy nationalism. Extreme manifestations of economic nationalism may endanger chances for rational economic development. Over all lurks the added specter of nationalism in Southeast Asia which, failing to develop along lines conducive to viable political and economic systems, can lead to national disintegration or a communist-subverted nationalism and unity imposed by force.

Nationalism may be expected to be a major feature in United States relations with the states of Southeast Asia for some time to come. Undoubtedly, the nationalist drives in several Southeast Asian states may take unpredictable and even extreme forms because of the revolutionary conditions which prevail. The extent to which

United States policy can influence the transition phase is limited both by the nature of nationalism and by the past role of the Western powers which has given the nationalism of formerly colonial nations a generally anti-Western bias.

As long as indigenous bases for nationalism—a unity of national culture, beliefs and a sense of destiny—as opposed to its anti-Western motivations continue to develop in the area, these forces may be considered in the American interest. Such a concept emerges from the premise that, without national unity, the new governments of Southeast Asia would find it difficult to maintain internal order and a rate of political and economic growth satisfactory to their citizens, and also that nationalism in Southeast Asia could present a major shield against external communist pressures or internal communist subversion. As an alternative to communism, the effectiveness of nationalism is significant but it should not be exaggerated. From a United States policy viewpoint, there are still the dangers that as long as nationalism in Southeast Asia retains a large element of anti-Westernism, it can work to the advantage of the communists. Furthermore, it is possible that the communists may capture nationalist emotions and divert them to their own basically antinationalist ends.

Nationalism and the general conditions prevailing in Southeast Asia may lead in time to the development of economic, political, and social institutions of a distinctly national character whose guise will be unlike any preconceived American image or any European colonial model or even, barring forcible seizure of power by the communists, like any communist icon. United States policy in Southeast Asia may succeed or fail to the extent that it may be willing to appreciate and work with the indigenous institutions and forces which are developed. Advancement of American objectives in Southeast Asia—continued freedom and independence, political and economic progress—is possible through this development of mature national consciousness on indigenous bases. Potentially, Southeast Asia's nationalism offers a basis for staunch support of United States objectives and policy. The proviso is that the United States is willing to work with it on a level approaching its terms.

3. NATIONAL OBJECTIVES IN SOUTHEAST ASIA

The internal conditions of the Southeast Asian states constitute one dimension in which United States policy toward the area must operate. A second is the manner in which these internal conditions, when combined with geographic and historic factors, are manifested in the national objectives and policies of the Southeast Asian states. United States objectives and policies must reflect and accommodate, insofar as possible, the national aspirations of the Southeast Asian governments and peoples, if they are to have the desired effect in the area.

In the formulation and execution of United States policy, the expressed objectives of the Southeast Asian governments warrant special consideration for their intrinsic merit and for the imperative and urgent quality given to them by the very newness of independence to many Southeast Asian states. In their initial enthusiasm for freedom from alien rule, it is true that some Southeast Asia leaders expressed overly ambitious aspirations and expectations which they have only recently begun to modify in taking a sobering second look at independent statehood with its responsibilities and limitations. But this is not to deny the validity of national efforts and aspirations. To do so would be to deny the most dynamic and revolutionary occurrence in Southeast Asia in modern history—the remarkable development of nationalism and national consciousness in the Southeast Asian states.

According to one viewpoint extant, no Southeast Asian state has yet developed a true national will; the goals which pass for national objectives in Southeast Asia in reality merely represent the desires or wishful thinking of a handful of national leaders. Based on the fact that complete rapport does not always exist between the national populations and the national leadership élites, this view overlooks the cogency of national opinion which is quite accurately represented by the national leadership, and which does exist on a number of basic national issues.

Despite differences in interpretation and emphasis among the independent states of the area and in spite of the differing kinds of policies resulting from their objectives, the peoples of Southeast Asia essentially are united behind their governments in a number of general national objectives, which flow naturally from their colonial backgrounds, recent independent struggles, growing self-consciousness, and economic ambitions. For example, they are determined to maintain their independence against all recognized threats. They are especially anxious to perfect their independence by minimizing outside cultural influences and their economic dependence on outside powers. They are determined to achieve the form and substance of international status, prestige, and equality. They want to formulate and to pursue their own domestic and foreign policies in their own way. They aspire to rapid industrialization and economic development both as a means of raising living standards and as a symbol of international prestige and status. Above all, they want to complete the transition from a dependent colonial society and economy to an independent national society and economy.

Prime Minister Nehru, addressing the first Asian Conference at New Delhi in 1947, in a broad sense summed up the basic aspirations of all Asian peoples. He said:

> For too long we of Asia have been petitioners in Western courts and chancellories. That story must now belong to the past. We propose to stand on our own feet and cooperate with all others who are prepared to cooperate with us. We do not intend to be the playthings of others. . . . The countries of Asia can no longer be used as pawns by others; they are bound to have their own policies in world affairs. . . .

In addition to these general objectives, the various states of Southeast Asia, owing to their specific geographic situation, historical experience, and national needs, have certain individual objectives and policies. It is to take into account these differing contours of major individual objectives and policies that United States foreign policy must be shaded.

Thanks to the manner in which the Philippines gained independence and the reasonably good relations which have prevailed between the Philippines and the United States, the Filipinos began their independence without rancor or resentment. At the present time their most immediate national aim is to maintain close relations with the United States on a basis of political equality and, as their economic strength grows, to decrease their economic dependence. The Philippines, as an insular republic of more than 7,000 islands and a heterogeneous population of 20,000,000 people, faces her goals with tremendous problems of internal organization, administration, and unity. Like most Southeast Asian leaders, the postindependence leaders of the Philippines have preferred to concentrate their efforts on domestic issues and such internal threats to stable government as land-distribution problems, corruption and inefficiency in government, low living standards, underemployment, and communist subversion. Unlike some Southeast Asian states, however, the Philippines have adopted an active anticommunist foreign policy, collective security, and outside aid and investment as the basis for maintaining independence and hastening the transition from a colonial to a national economy.

In a general sense, the focal points of Philippine foreign policy are: (1) the establishment and strengthening of an Asian collective security system with primary dependence on the United States for defense protection; (2) the establishment of closer political, economic and cultural ties with its noncommunist Asian neighbors; (3) the satisfactory settlement of reparations claims against Japan and subsequent expansion of commercial relations with that country; and (4) the insistence that Formosa be kept out of communist hands. Filipinos have good reason to remember Formosa as the place from which the Japanese launched their attack in 1941, and they are anxious to prevent any recurrence by doing their part to see that Formosa is kept out of hostile or potentially hostile hands.

Except for Vietnam, Indonesia faces greater internal problems of economic development, political control, and national unity than any other Southeast Asian country. And, more than any other country in the area, Indonesia prefers to be left alone to cope with these problems in her own way. Far from attained are the revolutionary aspirations of the Indonesian nationalist leaders expressed in the slogan, "One nation, one people, one language." So slow, in fact, has been Indonesia's general economic development as to be scarcely perceptible at all. Beneath the surface of her problems lies another festering sore. Resentment and suspicion of colonial and formerly colonial powers, and non-Asians generally, color all of Indonesia's domestic and foreign policies.

Indonesia's state philosophy is given utterance in the constitution as Five Postulates designed to lend continuous guidance to the Indonesian government and people. The postulates are: belief in Divine Omnipotence, humanism, nationalism, democracy, and social justice. These objectives have a high moral tone whose intent on the part of most Indonesians, official and others, is unquestionably sincere but whose pursuit, in a world torn by international tensions, conflict, and power politics, often tends to give Indonesian foreign policy an air of unreality. Similarly, the resounding generalities expressed in the United Nations Charter have a strong attraction for the Indonesians who feel—and rightly so—that if these were observed the world would be a better place in which to live. Indonesia itself places a great deal of reliance and emphasis on the United Nations as providing the proper philosophical and institutional framework for international relations, especially those relations concerning non-Asian powers.

Apart from this concept, Indonesia is a staunch advocate of Asian solidarity and of an "Asia for the Asians." For a country which has made scant marginal progress toward the solution of extremely difficult and urgent internal problems, Indonesia has played a surprisingly active role in Asian and, more recently, Asian-African affairs. Indonesia has initiated or participated in many bilateral and multilateral Asian meetings and conferences in the past years, climaxing these lesser publicized events by playing host at the more widely heralded Asian-African Conference at Bandung. As has become increasingly evident in the past few years, Indonesia is highly attracted by India's international orientation, and the two nations generally are in close rapport concerning relations with the communist and anticommunist blocs.

Although confronted by similar, if not the same, considerations of a geographic, political, economic, and social nature as the Philippines, Indonesia has elected to pursue quite a different foreign policy in the international struggle between the communist and the democratic ways of life. The key to the policy is neutrality but, in Indonesian terms, it is an "independent" or "nonalignment" policy. This attitude toward the cold war contains several facets. Foremost is the overwhelming desire for peace which, in the Indonesian belief, is served neither by individual nor by collective preparations for defense. Then, there is the traditional isolationist reasoning, implicit in the words of Vice President Mohammad Hatta:

> This island archipelago is in a very different kind of position from that in which the Netherlands and Belgium found themselves at the beginning of World War II. It does not share a common boundary with any of the possible belligerents. . . . Further, Indonesia does not have common frontiers with Soviet Russia or China. A direct threat from that direction to Indonesian independence neither exists nor is possible. Only the domestic Communist movement is a political factor in Indonesia, but in this regard Indonesia's position is no different from that of the other democratic countries. Consequently, there is no pressing need for her to make a choice between the two big blocs. Her independent policy keeps her from enmity with either party, preserves her from the damage to her own interests that would follow from taking sides, and permits her to be friends with all nations on the basis of mutual respect.[1]

And there is Indonesia's self-deluding analysis of the intent and nature of the international communist movement. Indonesia views the cold war as another traditional power conflict, this one between the Soviet Union and the United States, intensified and rendered even more illogical by atomic weapons. The only vital Indonesian concern in the conflict, in the Indonesian view, is the hope for peace. Obviously, even the causes and issues of the cold war stand in a different relationship for the Indonesians than they do in the United States. According to Vice President Hatta, "The opposition between the two [the American and the Soviet blocs], due to different economic systems, has been heightened by a conflict of ideologies in every particular," [2] which would seem to suggest that Indonesians consider communism as basically a "different economic system" and the choice between communism and noncommunism as a choice in internal economic organization. In this sense, Indonesia's inclination toward socialism provides a natural ideological attraction for the communist side.

A perennial Indonesian foreign policy objective is to wrest West Irian (Netherlands New Guinea), the rump of the old Netherlands East Indies, from the Dutch. This demand for added territory for the Republic of Indonesia probably is due in part to a flat and unqualified opposition to Western colonialism, in part to the latent fear that, as long as the Dutch retain a toehold in Asia, there is danger to Indonesian independence. However, the emotional forces involved in Indonesian demands for West Irian are sufficiently strong that, at times, it appears as if the issue were raised to rally the nation and divert the people from dissatisfaction with internal political and economic progress since independence.

Prime Minister Ali's first government in Indonesia, 1953–1955, tended to lean toward the communist position both on the internal and on the international fronts. This was probably due more to politics than to national sentiment, for the government relied on the communist minority in Parliament to remain in power. The Indonesians, valuing their independence and freedom of decision above all, are likely to be most sympathetic in terms of foreign policy to those states which seem to represent the least threat to their freedom, peace, and independence. It must be admitted, the Soviet Union and communist China have been reasonably successful in creating such an illusion.

Thailand, in contrast to the insular Philippine and Indonesian republics, is critically located by virtue of her geographical position for any menacing communist activity in Southeast Asia. With communist China pressing close on the north, with the vulnerable states of Laos, Cambodia, and South Vietnam sharing her eastern borders, and with an uncommitted Burma to the west, Thailand understandably feels exposed and threatened. She is even more security-conscious as a result of the Viet Minh thrust into Laos and Cambodia early in 1953, the establishment of a "Thai Autonomous

People's Government" in south China, announced by the Chinese communists in January 1953, and the fifth-column potential of 3,000,000 overseas Chinese within her borders. Faced with this situation, Thailand proposes to thwart the communist menace and any possibility of conquest through aggression or subversion. As a result, Thailand, the first nation to ratify the Manila Pact, is a staunch advocate of Asian collective security and also is a willing recipient of American military aid and economic assistance. Without a colonial history to nourish excess fear and suspicion, and with acceptance of her independence and equality as a matter of fact, Thailand does not recoil from close association with the United States and European nations, but is willing to pursue her general objectives in concert with other nations, both Asian and non-Asian.

Like the Philippines, Burma, and Indonesia, Thailand's foreign policy places heavy emphasis on the United Nations. When the communist Viet Minh invasion of Laos and Cambodia brought their forces to within a few miles of Thai borders, it was to the United Nations that Thailand turned. Generally, Thailand's foreign policy, both within and without the United Nations, parallels United States policy.

Aside from a historic fear of Chinese encroachments, Thailand's traditional antagonist has been Burma. Before the advent of British colonialism in Burma, the two neighbors engaged in a number of wars which culminated in 1767 with the sacking and burning of Ayuthya, the ancient Thai capital. Recently, in the interest of security and mutual benefit, both countries have endeavored to replace their traditionally cool relations with warmer and closer associations, but the suspicion of centuries is arduous to overcome and takes more than a short few years to erase.

After the issue of security, Thailand's major concern is rice, the basis of her economic strength and prosperity. Rice-surplus Thailand and rice-deficit Japan have enjoyed a long history of close economic and political relations, even including the period of the Second World War when Thailand acquiesced to Japanese occupation. There is, consequently, no legacy of ill-will such as plagues Indonesian, Burmese, and Philippine relations with Japan. America's recent entry into the Asian market as a major rice and wheat exporter to food-deficit areas of Asia, especially to Japan, contains some potentially dangerous implications for Thailand's economic position and for smooth relations between Thailand and the United States.

Recently, Thailand has acknowledged some long-range traditional interests involving Laos and Cambodia, large parts of which once belonged to the ancient Siamese Kingdom. Although France forcibly separated Thailand from sizable pieces of territory in both these areas at the beginning of the twentieth century, the Thais never really accepted the loss as permanent. Aided by the Japanese, Thailand temporarily regained some of this territory during the Second World War, only to lose it again in 1945 upon the Allied victory. Prudently, Thailand has suppressed her aspirations to control again these "lost territories" but, with the present independence of Laos and Cambodia and the threat of communist aggression or infiltration from the north and east, Thailand is showing renewed interest in reviving a closer relationship with her neighbors, Laos and Cambodia. As a possible trial balloon, a Thai spokesman suggested at one period in 1954 that the three states might unite. The following year, Thailand officially urged the kingdoms of Laos and Cambodia to join Thailand in an anticommunist bloc, emphasizing the fraternity of religion and race among the three Buddhist countries and the mutual economic, political, and cultural advantages of closer relationships. Recently, the Thai have agreed to give advanced military training to the Royal Lao Army.

To both Laos and Cambodia, the idea of an affiliation with Thailand offers considerable appeal not only because of the affinity of cultural, religious, ethnic, and economic bonds but, more important, because of the impulse toward a bulwark against the more numerous and aggressive Vietnamese to the east, whose domination the Cambodians and Laotians have long feared. This distrust and fear of the Vietnamese has been similarly instrumental in building Cambodian and Laotian dislike of communism, because the communists within their borders are predominantly Vietnamese.

The constitutional monarchies of Cambodia and Laos enjoy popular support and loyalty. As yet, however, neither government has clearly defined its foreign or domestic programs. Laos, a primitive, underpopulated, jungle and mountain country, is held together loosely by tradition, inertia, and the institution of the King of Luang Prabang. Its small cadre of officials and administrators would like to unite the country and to move along the road of economic and social progress, but first they must cling to independence, to keep from being swallowed by the avaricious Vietnamese or Chinese communists. In this objective, undoubtedly, they are followed by most Laotians who are in touch with the important events taking place around them. To maintain independence, Laos is dependent on outside help, and today this means the United States and Thailand primarily.

Although more advanced and in closer contact with the outside world, Cambodia shares many of the Laotian problems and aspirations. The Cambodian government has expressed dissatisfaction with the pacts governing the economic relations with Vietnam and is especially eager to break the grip which Saigon has on the Cambodian economy as a result of the fact that Saigon serves as Cambodia's major outlet to the sea. Since becoming independent, the Cambodian government has begun to modernize her own river port of Phnom Penh and to reorient her trade toward Thailand. Cambodia has a vigorous and imaginative but highly unpredictable leader in former King Norodom who abdicated the throne in 1955 in favor of his father in order to develop a grass-roots political organization and to create greater national unity behind the constitutional monarchy. At the Bandung Asian-African Conference, Prince Norodom declared that his country desired to pursue a neutral policy, like India and Burma. This statement notwithstanding, Cambodia signed a Mutual Defense Assistance agreement with the United States in May 1955 under which the country has been receiving military and economic aid. Then in the next twelve months Cambodia signed a treaty of friendship and an aid agreement with communist China and began pursuing a vociferous neutralist policy marked by frequent anti-American outbursts. Although the Cambodians, like the Laotians, are eager to be rid of French colonial influence, neither shares the extreme bitterness which Vietnamese harbor toward the French.

The specific objectives held by the Republic of Vietnam remain somewhat obscure. Survival is probably the basic objective as it is the basic problem. It is safe to assume that most Vietnamese are united in the desire to rid the country of the French and of all vestiges of French domination. The Vietnamese people certainly want to achieve some sort of peace, stability and, presumably, economic progress, aspirations shared by the government of Premier Ngo Dinh Diem. Beyond these simply stated hopes, the unity of opinion between people and government appears to be tenuous. Again, the immediate objectives of the Vietnam government are easy to chart but, under prevailing conditions, extremely difficult to realize. They are: (1) to consolidate internal political control and (2) to build sufficient internal unity and strength to survive in the face of both internal communist and noncommunist opposition. The Diem government has professed its desire to move as rapidly toward democratic and representative government as possible, has held nation-wide elections for a constituent assembly, and prepared a constitution, but it is caught in the dilemma of being regarded unrepresentative, when fearing to risk such political order as exists by widening representation. The existence of southern Vietnam is almost wholly dependent on United States support and assistance.

Immediately after gaining independence, the Burmese government, starting in 1948, was forced to wage an extremely difficult war against both separatist elements and communist-led insurrectionists to establish its authority. Despite an unpromising beginning, Burma won the war by 1950 and, since then, has made remarkable strides toward economic and political rejuvenation and national unity.

Apart from the maintenance of law and order, Burma's major domestic policy emphasis since independence has been the socioeconomic reorganization of the country—the Burmanizing of the national economy and society. Focal point of this objective is the Pyidawtha (Welfare) Program of Burma, a series of economic, political, and social development plans announced in August 1952 following several years of careful study and thought. To achieve the program's aspirations, Burma's leaders envision a democratic socialist system which, according to Prime Minister U Nu, "will combine full political rights, economic security and a high standard of living with spiritual uplift and morality." In the view of the Burmese leaders, democratic socialism in Burma must be fully harmonized with the religious beliefs, cultural background and heritage of the Burmese peoples. As a goal, they hope to achieve a national society, a national economy, and a democratic political organization which will be a synthesis of Western democracy and Marxist socialism but, above all, which will be essentially Burmese.

Burma as a country is rich. It has surplus agricultural production, abundant natural resources for economic diversification and industrialization, and no population problem. Burma's internal objectives appear to be to use these factors fully to build a happy and prosperous state. Although the Burmese expect a full measure of international prestige and status, they seem to have little inclination for self-aggrandizement or for becoming a "power to be reckoned with" on the international scene.

The principal part of Burma's foreign policy rests on four major pegs: (1) active participation in the United Nations; (2) relations with India; (3) relations with China; and (4) nonalignment in the cold war. In the United Nations, Burma is part of the shifting voting bloc of African-Asian nations. Like the other Southeast Asian member states, Burma attaches great importance to the United Nations in international diplomacy and to her own role in its deliberations.

Although Burma's relations with India have always been close, they have not invariably been smooth. This is due partly to British colonial administration which, until 1937, considered Burma as part of India, partly to Burma's traditional fear of geopolitical domination by India. Then too, while the other countries of Southeast Asia have been trapped with an "overseas Chinese" problem, Burma has faced an "overseas Indian" problem. Since independence, however, the two countries have worked to establish close and harmonious relations. Both Burma and India have complementary economic interests and share an aspiration to remain outside the cold war. From time to time, Asian reports suggest that Burma has picked India to balance the threat of China and that India has accepted the role of protector, but there has been no conclusive evidence of this at any time. Squeezed between the two Asian giants, India and China, Burma's geographical position clearly points up the vital Burmese interest in maintaining friendly relations with both sides. Of the two countries, Burma's national interests and aspirations would seem to draw her closer to India than to China.

As for China, Burma shares a long, and often disputed, border with that country. Fear of invasion and of intervention from communist China is a recurring theme in Burma's foreign policy. Burma's major foreign policy problem since independence has been the presence in the border regions of remnants of the Chinese Nationalist armies which took refuge there in 1950 following Chiang Kai-shek's defeat and withdrawal from the China mainland. Preoccupied with problems of internal law and order, the Burmese government for the first year failed to concern itself with these Nationalist troops which quickly became reenforced by additional refugees crossing the border from Yunnan in south China, established liaison with Nationalist headquarters on Formosa, and began to receive arms and ammunition of American manufacture by clandestine air drop. Not only did the troops raid and plunder Burmese villages, but they also began to extend their areas of control. Their very presence on Burmese territory spelled a challenge to Burma's sovereignty which was further augmented by their stay on the Yunnan border and by their occasional raids into south China, excellent fodder for an invasion pretext by the Chinese communist government. Burma appealed first to the United States, later to the United Nations to intercede. Finally, a Committee of Good Offices, in which the United States and Thailand played important roles, managed to arrange in 1953 and 1954 for the evacuation of some of the Nationalist troops and to obtain official disavowal of the remainder by Chiang Kai-shek. This helped to alleviate Burma's position but, so long as any renegade remnants of the Nationalist forces remain on Burmese territory, the problem cannot be entirely dissipated.

The KMT troops issue seriously clouded relations between the United States and Burma at a highly critical time. Whatever the truth of the matter, many Burmese were convinced of American implication in it, and almost all were certain that the United States could cause the troops to leave Burma simply by putting pressure on the Chinese Nationalist government in Formosa.

The core of Burma's foreign policy, especially since 1950–1951, has been neutrality and nonalignment in the cold war. Unlike

Indonesia, Burma does not base her policy of nonalignment on isolationist reasoning. On the contrary, because of her geographically exposed position, Burma's policy is reasoned on the premise that her security is best served by nonprovocation, cooperation, and friendship with the members both of the communist and of the noncommunist blocs. Burma was the first state to recognize the communist régime in Peking and has made every reasonable effort since then to maintain "correct" relations with it. More recently, Burma has signed mutual nonaggression pacts with communist China on the basis of the so-called Five Principles [3] which theoretically govern Chinese-Indian relations and an extensive trade and aid agreement with the Soviet Union. This does not mean that Burma's policy is procommunist. Burma's leaders appear to have fewer illusions about the communists than do the leaders either of India or of Indonesia. But it does mean that Burma, as a small nation adjacent to China, is anxious to avoid giving China any pretext for overt interference or invasion, and that Burma, whose economy depends on rice exports, must find markets for rice surpluses.

SOUTHEAST ASIA AS A THEATER OF OPERATIONS IN THE COLD WAR

While the Southeast Asian states are striving for solutions to their own pressing internal problems and are trying to assert their newly won independence on the international scene, a number of world powers have moved their foreign policies into focus on the area. One result of the colonial powers' postwar retreat from Southeast Asia has been the creation of a power vacuum which it has not been possible for the weak and unstable countries of the area to fill. As independence has transformed the Southeast Asian states into participants in international politics, so have their relative weaknesses caused them to become especially vulnerable objects in the game of international politics. This is played in fierce competition in Southeast Asia by communist China, the Soviet Union, Japan, India, France, Great Britain and the Commonwealth, whose foreign policies all pursue specific national interests and objectives. The major aspects of these latter interests are also a part of the conditions in which United States policy in Southeast Asia must function.

Although French behavior in Indochina since 1945 has been devious and complicated, French policy motivation has been simple: to retain the maximum degree of domination, control, influence, and interest in Indochina. Three elementary considerations go far toward explaining French policy: (1) The French had no intention of relinquishing control of Indochina. Although they made some political concessions in the face of nationalist pressures, the fact was that the concessions were not necessarily intended to be permanent. (2) The French colonials, resident in Indochina, held interests and views which were local and short-range. Supported by strong colonial economic interest groups in Paris, they played a prominent role in determining French policy for Indochina. (3) The French government's reluctance to lose Indochina was conditioned by concern over the future of the French Union as a whole. Fear of the loss of Indochina was intensified by fear of the effect of the loss in other parts of the French Union, especially in North Africa, and on France's international prestige in general.

Through successive political and military reverses, the French were forced, step by grudging step, to pare down their objectives in Indochina, to be willing to settle for less. In the face of increasingly heavy political handicaps and the growing strength of the Viet Minh forces, the French managed to enlist American aid and support in pursuing their objectives. This effort to implicate the United States in the Indochina war, yet at the same time to maintain a French buffer between the Vietnamese and the Americans, was made easier by the communist complexion of the Viet Minh and by the outbreak of the Korean War.

Following the Geneva Agreements of July 1954 which ended hostilities in Laos, Cambodia, and Vietnam and which provided for the settlement of political problems on the basis of free general elections in July 1956, the French were left with the problem of salvaging as much as possible of their crumbled colonial privilege in the form of economic and cultural concessions. To this end, the French continued a dual policy line. They sent an envoy northward into the Viet Minh camp to attempt to work out a pattern for co-existence with the communists, which was culminated by a Franco-Viet Minh agreement in December 1954, giving certain assurances and encouragement to French business interests to remain in the communist zone of northern Vietnam. Meanwhile, in the southern zone, the French High Commissioner attempted to cooperate with the United States in bolstering the government of Premier Ngo Dinh Diem in the face of unreliable support from Paris and some obstructionist tactics by middle-echelon French officials and resident colonials.

In terms of the objective of retaining the maximum degree of economic and cultural interest in the area, the French position is palpably difficult. So far as any real influence is concerned, the northern zone, presently controlled by the communists, is lost to the French; the future of the southern zone is questionable. Still, the French hope to reach a modus vivendi with the Ho Chi Minh régime in order to continue as much profitable economic and commercial activity in the north as possible. In the south, they are pledged by the Geneva Agreements to honor the 1956 elections even though the South Vietnam government is opposed to the elections. If for no other reason, the fact that it must depend entirely on the United States for economic and military aid and, probably, on United States policy for any chance of independent survival makes the Diem government pro-American. In this vise, the French can hardly give wholehearted cooperation to a government in South Vietnam pledged to throw them out at the first opportunity, nor can they too blatantly oppose a government which enjoys United States approval and support. The French dilemma has a cubic aspect. If the communists eventually win all Vietnam, as many French anticipate, the French want to maneuver themselves into as firm a position as possible for negotiating the retention of their economic and cultural activities with the new régime. By 1956 French influence in South Vietnam had become weak. Practically all French troops had left and many French business interests were liquidating their holdings as fast as possible. Meanwhile, in Laos and Cambodia, where anti-French sentiment is not so intense, French economic and cultural activity has increased considerably, which would seem to suggest an effort to compensate in those states for the diminished status and influence of the French in Vietnam.

Before the Second World War, British influence in South and Southeast Asia exceeded that of any other power. British land power, based on the Indian Army, and British naval power, based at Singapore and supported by a chain of supporting naval bases, dominated the Indian Ocean and the South Pacific. Since the independence of India, Pakistan, Ceylon, and Burma, only the remnants of the British Empire in Asia remain. However, those remnants—Malaya, British territories in Borneo, Singapore, and Hong Kong—are important in view of the basic motivation of traditional British policy, trade, and commerce. In the postwar period, owing to her rubber and tin exports, Malaya has been the major dollar earner for the United Kingdom. Also important from the earnings standpoint is the entrepôt trade of Singapore and Hong Kong, although the trade embargo against communist China severely curtailed Hong Kong's economic margin.

Undoubtedly the key element to present British policy in Southeast Asia is the Commonwealth of Nations which, in the postwar period, has succeeded the concept of the British Empire. The British, with a good deal of justification, regard the Commonwealth concept as one of their major contributions to the realm of political theory and practice. Prime Minister Attlee, in an address on May 15, 1950, defined the Commonwealth relationship in these terms:

> The Commonwealth . . . is the only instance of the transformation of an Empire built up by a powerful State in which that State has, through deliberate policy, divested itself of its power and transferred sovereignty to units of that Empire which were formerly subordinate. . . . The point is that the conception of the Commonwealth today is entirely different from that of other Empires. It is based on the idea of equal partnership, not domination.

A significant part of the Commonwealth rims the South Pacific and Indian oceans, its pivot lying at Singapore. In the multiracial modern Commonwealth, Asian members predominate in numbers, and their influence is increasing, factors which impel the British to attach great importance to India and Pakistan. Today it is beside the point to determine whether independence was granted to India, Pakistan, Ceylon, and Burma through a remarkably astute sense of political timing or through a simple accident of history which brought Mr. Attlee's less Empire-minded Labor government to power at a critical moment. The point is that such were the timing and conditions of independence, that these key Asian states, except Burma, chose to affiliate themselves with the Commonwealth, and British prestige through all Asia is now heavily dependent on their continuance as Commonwealth members. In addition to its value in political terms, the Commonwealth is important to Britain as the foundation stone of the sterling-bloc economic structure.

The existence of the Commonwealth means that Britain must pursue a form of coalition diplomacy in Asia. This is not intended to suggest that India, for example, has a veto on British policy. Take such a case in point as the Manila Pact to which Pakistan and Great Britain are parties, while India, a bitter foe of collective security, is not. But it does mean that, in the event of substantial opposition within the Commonwealth, Great Britain is somewhat constrained in her actions and that, in practice, London pays deference to wishes of New Delhi in matters of Southeast Asian policy.

The British have scarcely been enthusiastic about independence movements in Southeast Asia, although they have been fully aware of the need for accommodating such movements in the face of communist success in using the nationalist issues to serve communist ends. Although the British were unwilling to match United States attitudes toward Indochina and Indonesia, they regarded as unrealistic French and Dutch resistance to the nationalist forces in those countries. In Malaya, where internal security has been a major problem since the start of the communist guerrilla uprising in 1948, the British have carried on a difficult military campaign at the same time as they have been quickly propelling the country toward self-government. Early in 1956 the British promised Malaya dominion status by August 31, 1957.

In line with their commercial orientation, the British have tended to emphasize economic measures in the effort to stem communism, to seek some modus vivendi with communist China permitting normal trade relations, and to work for economic improvement in the Asian area. In the realm of economic development, an important aspect of British policy is support of the Colombo Plan, a Commonwealth scheme, introduced in 1950, which is roughly analogous in purpose and method to the American Point Four program. At the same time, Britain views with some skepticism the increasing commercial competition offered by the growing volume of American trade with Southeast Asia and the revival of Japanese industry.

Within the Commonwealth, Australia and New Zealand emerged from the Second World War with an acute awareness of their vulnerability to attack and their isolation. This has been further emphasized by the rise and spread of communism in Asia, coupled with the withdrawal of British power in the postwar years. Logically, both countries have grown eager to develop closer and more friendly relations with the barrier of Southeast Asian states which stand between them and a renewal of an attack from the north by either China or Japan. Tending to look for protection to the United States, both Australia and New Zealand have welcomed the organization of collective security arrangements as manifested by the ANZUS and SEATO pacts.

India, by virtue of cultural, economic, geographic, and historical factors, is destined to maintain a strong interest and exert a major role in Southeast Asian affairs. Although Indian spokesmen continually disavow any ambitions for the leadership of Asia or even a leadership role in Southeast Asia, they also are clear on the fact that, in considering problems relating to the area, India cannot be ignored. If a competition were to develop between the leaders of India and communist China for the leadership of Asia, its nature and extent would be far from clear. In fact, on the basis of the Indian leaders' seeming preoccupation with the United States as a major antagonist in Southeast Asia, based on the premise that American imperialism is attempting to replace the British, French, and Dutch brands, it would appear as if there were possible seeds for agreement between the two Asian giants.

India's cultural and historical influence is manifest throughout

Southeast Asia. Through Burma, Thailand, Laos, Cambodia, Malaya, and Indonesia ample evidence exists of the strong impact of both the ancient and present Hindu civilization. From the geographical and strategic standpoint, Southeast Asia is of prime importance to India. On the north, India enjoys some protection from the Himalayan mountain barrier which separates her from Tibet and China. But, to the east, no such formidable barrier exists to protect her from any vital change in the status of the Southeast Asian states. In the economic sphere, it is evident that India aspires to a more prominent role in Southeast Asian trade, one she has tried not to jeopardize through allowing the sizable overseas Indian communities which exist in Burma, Malaya, and Ceylon, and in whose welfare she has a deep concern, to become sources of friction to her Southeast Asia neighbors.

But India's greatest interest in Southeast Asia undoubtedly may be formulated best in political terms. India's soul-search for peace leads obliquely to a neutral, or "independent," foreign policy, to co-existence with the communist bloc, to anticolonialism and anti-Western imperialism. In September 1946, nearly one year before India became independent, Pandit Jawaharlal Nehru, whose judgments and opinions have the stature of Indian foreign policy, laid down the basic principles of Indian foreign policy in the following press statement:

> In the sphere of foreign affairs India will follow an independent policy, keeping away from the power politics of groups aligned one against another. She will uphold the principles of freedom for dependent peoples and will oppose racial discrimination wherever it may occur. She will work with other peace-loving nations for international cooperation and goodwill without exploitation of one nation by another.
>
> It is necessary that with the attainment of her full international status, India should establish contact with all the great nations of the world and that her relations with neighboring countries in Asia should become still closer. . . .
>
> Towards the United Nations Organization India's attitude is that of whole-hearted cooperation and unreserved adherence, in both spirit and letter, to the Charter governing it. To that end, India will participate fully in its varied activities and endeavor to play that role in its Councils to which her geographic position, population and contribution toward peace-

ful progress entitle her. In particular, the Indian delegate will make it clear that India stands for the independence of all colonial and dependent people and their full right to self-determination.[4]

Neither a great military nor economic power, India ranks far behind communist China in terms of preparedness and mobilization. Her real strength lies in diplomacy. Owing partly to her unique position in the Commonwealth, and partly to her role as a leading spokesman for billions of people in the newly developing nations of Asia and Africa, India rates a voice in the councils of the powers which far outweighs her economic or military stature. Neither state nor statesman can disregard the voice of India so long as it speaks for and reflects the moods of these multitudes.

Time and again Nehru and his associates have enunciated India's dynamic but independent policy: that India is free to decide each international issue as she sees it, on its own merits. This is a policy representing not passive neutralism but a vigorous participation in world affairs which denies prior commitment to any world group. By eschewing commitment to the principles of communism or anticommunism, Indian policy acquires an elasticity, leverage, and influence it might otherwise be forced to curtail. An important aspect of India's independent policy is nonalignment and resistance to the concept of collective security which, in the Indian view, increases world tensions and magnifies the danger of war. Rather than seek peace through collective security or through a balance of power, India seeks peace through expansion of the uncommitted group of nations, a process which Nehru describes as "widening the area of peace," and through co-existence with the communist and anticommunist nations. To this end, India has opposed the Manila Pact as bringing the cold war to Asia. The differing analysis of the nature and intentions of international communism, implicit in these aspects of Indian policy, is the key to Indian-American disagreement. Nehru and his associates refuse to admit that danger from a "power vacuum" exists in South and Southeast Asia unless the Western nations attempt to fill it. India appears to seek to balance power in Asia with spiritualism, morality, and good will.

India's active role in high-level international diplomacy sometimes has given rise to the false impression that she possesses marginal objectives and policies at home and in neighboring areas.

Far from the case, Indian policy actually includes some impressive primary domestic and regional issues. Internally, India has launched a vigorous and farsighted program of economic development designed to raise the levels of agricultural and industrial production. In the spring of 1951, for example, India inaugurated the first Five-Year Plan providing the nucleus for India's full economic policy, foreign and domestic. Success of the plan relies largely on the maintenance of international peace, and this again provides an incentive for India's foreign policy of co-existence. To accomplish the tremendous and urgent task of economic modernization and development, India has adopted democratic methods which, through a gradual process, are planned to combine private and public enterprise. And, though seeking co-existence with the communist powers as a foreign policy, India has been chary of the movement within her borders, pursuing a vigorous anticommunist policy internally.

Of a regional nature, the dispute over Kashmir is India's outstanding foreign policy issue, muddying further the previously turbid relations between India and Pakistan. It goes without saying that India considers Pakistan a greater external threat than China or the Soviet Union. The Mutual Security Assistance agreement signed by the United States and Pakistan in May 1954 caused great alarm in India and still clouds Indian-American relations. Following the agreement Nehru claimed, somewhat unrealistically, that the balance of power in Asia was changed, that the cold war had been brought to India's doorstep, and that chances of Indian security were materially lessened.

India's objectives and policy, phrased in positive terms in relation to Southeast Asia, specifically appear to be centered on: (1) enlarging the "area of peace"; (2) promoting Asian solidarity, which includes co-existence with China on the basis of the Five Principles and closer relations among the Southeast Asian states; (3) curtailment of non-Asian influence in the area; and (4) economic development and social progress. Indian policy thus conflicts to a certain extent with Philippine and Thai policy, but is in fair harmony with Indonesian policy and, to a considerable extent, Burmese policy. On Indochina, India supports the Geneva Agreements, in the reaching of which she played an instrumental part and is willing, apparently, to accept an area of special Chinese influence in Vietnam. While firm in her general stand for an end to colonialism, India has evinced little impatience in the specific case of Malaya. Undoubtedly influenced somewhat in this attitude by the British, India also is cognizant of the threats to her implicit in the instability and conflict which could develop on her doorstep if Malaya were set free before achieving a reasonable degree of national unity.

Like Great Britain in the Atlantic, Japan, the industrialized island nation of the Pacific, must live by the theme "Export or die." Despite intensive cultivation of land resources, Japan depends on imports for one-fifth of all food needs and many of the raw materials necessary to support her industries. As a result of this cycle, Japan's desire to dominate the resources and trade of her neighbors provided important Japanese motivation in the Second World War. Stripped of her prewar overseas territories, minus the captive economies of Manchuria, Formosa, and Korea, and the prewar trade with mainland China, plus a vastly increased population, Japan's needs are far more acute today than they were before the war. In former Premier Yoshida's words, Japan today "must double her foreign trade," and looks to Southeast Asia as a promising area for trade expansion.

Japan needs Southeast Asia's food and raw materials; Southeast Asia needs capital equipment and industrial goods which Japan can provide. The trade relationship appears a simple and natural one, but some important limitations and obstacles occur to modify it. For one, Japan's occupation record during the war left a legacy of distrust and hatred in Southeast Asia which has not yet been fully expunged. Such countries as Burma, Thailand, the Philippines, and Indonesia have demanded war reparations from Japan as compensation for the occupation and looting which they experienced during the war. As an initial step in preparation for trade expansion in Southeast Asia, it has been Japanese policy to negotiate these reparations agreements, as a result of which Thailand and Burma have concluded agreements, and negotiations are in process for agreements with Indonesia and the Philippines. For another stumbling block to trade, however, Southeast Asia does not have the capacity to absorb the great number of Japanese imports needed to balance the Japanese trade deficit. This is due largely to the generally depressed economies of Southeast Asia and to the low purchasing power of the Southeast Asians. Japan casts her eyes upon the economic assistance programs of the United States and the Colombo Plan nations which, by increasing Southeast Asian purchasing power, in turn should enhance the demand for Japanese-produced capital goods. In addition, though, Japan would like to serve as economic bridge between Southeast Asia and the West, placing herself in the dual roles of industrial adviser to the Southeast Asian countries and of go-between for the United States in helping the countries of the region to secure their economic construction. Yoshida, advocating a Marshall Plan for Asia in 1954, visualized a vast free-world investment program in which Japan contributed technical skills and industrial equipment to the underdeveloped Asian nations.

As a third difficulty, Japanese trade in the Southeast Asian market is curtailed by competition with Great Britain, India, and the United States. Japan would like to be compensated for this competition somehow; and, because of her current need to import heavily from the United States, her preference for compensation at the moment lies in a more liberal American tariff policy. Considering the mood of the American Congress and the effectiveness of pressures from economic interest groups in the United States, this is undoubtedly wishful thinking, since little likelihood exists for major reorientation of American tariffs, except possibly in terms which could be more disadvantageous to Japan than they are at the present time.

In view of these obstacles, Japan, while continuing to work with a certain degree of success for increased trade in Southeast Asia, finds pressure increasing for expanded trade with communist China. The Japanese election of February 1955 brought Prime Minister Hatoyama to office largely on his promise of seeking new understanding with the communist rulers in Moscow and Peking. This development obviously is agreeable to the communists, who dangle the bait of China trade before Japanese eyes as a major political bargaining lure. Although most informed Japanese realize that they cannot hope to revive the trade they once had with continental China, the lure of the China trade remains strong. If wishes are goals, Japan's aspirations still are to revise and increase both Chinese and Southeast Asian trade. Whether or not prospects of trade with China ever materialize, the issue provides Japan with a useful bargaining point in her negotiations with the United States for increased aid and lower tariffs. Again, the fact remains that, if the time ever came when more of Southeast Asia were absorbed into the communist bloc, then the pressure for Japan to come to closer terms with Moscow and Peking could become compelling.

In contrast to the large areas of conflict, or at least disagreement, in national objectives and policies as they concern Southeast Asia among a number of the noncommunist powers, there seems to be a united front in the objectives and policies by the communist bloc, represented in Asia by the Soviet Union, communist China, northern Vietnam and North Korea, at least insofar as international communism is concerned. Within the international communist alignment, however, several important national aspirations may be separately identified. Of remote and peripheral influence only are the purely nationalist aspirations of the Soviet Union—or of Russia, to make the contrast more clear—as opposed to the broader objectives of international communism. On the other hand, China's national interests, because of that country's geographic proximity to Southeast Asia, and because of historical, economic, and cultural factors, are of prime importance.

Historically, China, whose southward expansionist tendencies are as ancient as her culture, has looked toward continental Southeast Asia as a logical extension of her territorial sphere of interest. In the past, China had suzerainty at one time or another over parts of northern Burma and of Vietnam. This shifting relationship became resolved temporarily when the French and British consolidated those territories under colonial control. Just as they felt toward Tibet, the Chinese never regarded their losses in South Asia as final. And, in such areas as the Tonkin and Hanoi delta regions of northern Vietnam, they had considerable cultural and economic influence. Although the Vietnamese often have resisted Chinese political encroachments in the past, there are strong affiliations between Vietnam and China. Obviously, China is also concerned over the area for reasons of strategy and security. This is demonstrable merely by recalling the fact that the initial French encroachments were made into Vietnam to secure an entry route to west and central China, thus exposing China to penetration on her southern flank. China's reluctance to withdraw her troops from Laos and northern Vietnam following the allied agreement that she occupy those areas from the surrendering Japanese at the end of the Second World War, her resistance to the return of French control in Indochina, and her political activity among the Vietnamese nationalist and independence organizations reflect her traditional attitude toward the area.

From the time of the British occupation of Upper Burma in 1885, China's national interests also meant almost unceasing negotiations over the Chinese-Burmese border. Agitating for the northern Burma area, the Chinese Nationalist government claimed it as part of a state which had paid tribute to China from the seventh century Tang Dynasty onward. Again, Chinese troops were in occupation, this time over Burmese territories to which they laid claim, and they were evacuated only with difficulty in 1946. A considerable extent of the Burmese-Chinese border area still remains undefined, and has been restive since the 1950 arrival of a sizable body of Chinese Nationalist troops, in flight from the Chinese communist armies. Although the communist China government has not pressed China's traditional claim to the border territory, it has not yet seen fit to renounce it either. Unofficial reports of several visiting delegations to communist China mention the sight of wall maps in Peking government offices which display large slices of the border regions of Burma, Laos, and Vietnam, as well as of Nepal and Bhutan, as an integral part of greater China.

The large overseas Chinese population in Southeast Asian countries naturally accounts for another purely nationalist interest of China in the area. Traditionally, Chinese governments adhere to the concept of dual citizenship for overseas Chinese. This, in effect, calls on the Chinese abroad to maintain their loyalty to China. Even before the issue of communism reared up, the question of the loyalties and legal status of overseas Chinese was a matter of contention throughout Southeast Asia. And the overseas Chinese provided a source of foreign exchange, cultural expansion, and political leverage for Chinese governments; today, under communist organization and methods, they offer an unbounded potential for a fifth column.

Significant to China's national interest in Southeast Asia are points which may be formulated in economic and geopolitical terms. In contrast to the states of Southeast Asia, China is large, militarily powerful, dynamic, aggressive, and overpopulated. Faced for years with the Malthusian dilemma of too many people for the amount of food available, China appears bound to have an absolute food crisis sometime in the near future. With the thinly populated and relatively disorganized countries which lie south of her borders producing large agricultural surpluses, the potential for solving the imbalance is fraught with peril. Without regard to the issue of communism, China, countenanced in economic and geopolitical terms, constitutes a real and continuing threat to Southeast Asia.

The same historical trend has moved the Vietnamese to encroach on their neighbors, the Cambodians and Laotians. With the emergence of the states of Vietnam either as separate states or as a single state under a communist or a noncommunist government, Vietnam's traditional national interest in expanding in a westerly direction undoubtedly will continue, fortified as it now is by the existence of large Vietnamese colonies as far away as Thailand. The Vietnamese, especially those in the northern zone, face a smaller version of China's dilemma, a problem of population pressure on limited food resource which may be expected to result in a similarly strong national urge to press outward against less heavily populated border areas.

The characterization of Southeast Asia as a theater of operations in the cold war is of necessity a recurring theme in any present summation of the area's affairs. Up to this point, however, only the groundwork has been laid to reveal the conditions in which United States policy must function, primarily in terms of indigenous Southeast Asian forces and of the essentially national objectives and policies of those states which are especially interested in the area. Above this base stand the issues of the cold war—the potential shadings and rationale of that war—which transcend regional considerations and purely national objectives. Here in the cold war is the competition between two ways of life, two sets of values, two economic systems, two ideologies; a struggle penetrating every level: economic, political, social, psychological, diplomatic, military. Part of the struggle, too, is identifiable as power politics. On the one side is the monolithic communist bloc; on the other, a coalition composed mostly of democratic states operating on the principles of collective diplomacy and collective security. This adds the third dimension to the subject of United States policy toward Southeast Asia: here the United States interest in Southeast Asia is identified along with the threat of international communism, a primary threat to United States interests. With the lines of conflict between communist and anticommunist states and between the peoples of the world becoming more tightly drawn, Southeast Asia exists in actual fact as a theater of operations in the cold war. Like it or not, isolationists by preference or not, the Southeast Asian states must face the fact that their fate directly interests and concerns two contending factions—the international communist bloc and the international democratic coalition.

4. COMMUNISM IN SOUTHEAST ASIA

Communism is not merely an ideology in Southeast Asia any more than it is anywhere on the face of the globe. It is organized imperialism allied with an explosive idea. It is a well organized apparatus and an international conspiracy as well as an ideology.

COMMUNIST APPEALS IN SOUTHEAST ASIA

The appeal of communism is a complex and subtle phenomenon. It varies among individuals and among national, ethnic, and social groups. Not many Southeast Asians view or understand communism in its total sense, but many are attracted by aspects of it. In the promises and slogans of communism, they see reflections of their own aspirations, hates, and fears. Some are attracted to communism as a political ideology. Others find it a formula for utopia. Still others see communism as an opportunity to achieve power and influence, as a means of getting better pay and working conditions, as an outlet for frustration, a means of getting land, or a new social order to replace their own disrupted social traditions. Many are attracted to communism simply because they believe it represents the wave of the future, "the winning side."

The communists deny they can create a revolution unless people and conditions are ripe for it. Therefore, an important aspect of communist tactics is to intensify and direct those forces within a society which can serve the ends of revolution. Communist slogans, propaganda, policies, and appeals usually are built on existing grievances or aspirations. In this sense communist tactics may be compared to a type of political jujitsu which employs the victim's own momentum and force to bring about his downfall. In an over-all sense, of course, communist appeals in Southeast Asia are neither greater nor more compelling than they are anywhere else. But, as elsewhere, the communists have moved in on certain historical circumstances which they find especially malleable, and upon these circumstances they base their major efforts.

In Southeast Asia, as elsewhere, the distinction must be made between the attractions of communism for the educated and semi-educated leadership élite and the attractions of communism for the bulk of the population, composed chiefly of a politically inarticulate, inexperienced, and often apathetic peasantry. The group division holds special significance in Southeast Asia because of the traditional hierarchical type of social and political structure which has meant a wide intellectual and social gap between peoples—the governors and the governed—and a tendency in the postcolonial period for that gap to grow wider. Thus, communism's special attraction for one group often has quite a different meaning or no meaning at all for the other.

On the leadership group the communists use every opportunity to play upon its leadership proclivities as well as on its innate suspicions of Western motives, its fears of revived colonialism. Not an independent isolated force in Southeast Asia, this resentment of colonialism is associated, practically consolidated in fact, with nationalism, anti-Westernism, and antiimperialism, drives which form an emotional complex that is the easy prey for communist appeal. The Southeast Asian suspicion of the West is not entirely due to the fear of a revival of colonialism or some new form of Western imperialism; it is also nurtured by racial tensions and inhibitions which mar relations between non-Asian and Asian states.

From the start of their Southeast Asian activities in the early 1920's, the communists have taken special care to associate themselves with the anticolonialism issue. Despite the fact that local communist parties often have been forced to shift policies to serve the Soviet's European security and policy needs, they have consistently used the nationalism, anticolonialism, and antiimperialism themes in their agitation. This has naturally helped to merge the symbols of communism and nationalism, expressed in anti-Western colonialism, in many minds and places into an indistinct blur. When independence tended to lessen the effect of the anticolonialism appeal, the communists shifted ground to take on anti-Western imperialism, portrayed as the natural successor to Western colonialism.

Today the newly independent Southeast Asian states have integrated anti-Western colonialism into their foreign policies, taking as their special cause the end of colonialism everywhere. Here again the communists attempt to make common cause by identifying themselves with Southeast Asian objectives. The Soviet Union and communist China appear on the international scene with the doves of peace in their fists, to all intents and purposes and certainly to the deluded gaze of the more gullible Southeast Asian leaders, the champions of independence for colonial peoples everywhere. The Peking radio, for example, which broadcasts regularly to Southeast Asia, on January 13, 1955, points up its attitude in reverse fashion:

> The American aggressive clique and its followers are adopting a disparaging attitude toward the Asian-African Conference because they oppose the promotion of mutual understanding between the Asian and African peoples and are against international cooperation and also because the United States is trying hard to maintain and strengthen its colonial rule over many Asian and African areas. . . . The much-publicized "economic aid" to Asian countries reportedly to be examined at Bangkok is only a device to mask U.S. aggressive designs. It is obvious that any "economic aid" plan for Asia is determined by U.S. considerations for grabbing strategic raw materials. The United States is trying to control Asian nations both politically and economically through so-called "aid" and turn them into America's satellites. However, these American tricks have long lost their effect on some of the Asian countries.

For the very reason that the complex by-products of colonialism constitute the major obstacles to closer United States and Southeast Asian relations, the communists use these slanted reminders to telling effect in the attempt to win over the Southeast Asian states or, at least, to prevent consolidation of any strong anticommunist front.

In the economic sphere, above all, Southeast Asian peoples and leaders would like to see their countries transformed into modern industrial states without incurring any obligation to the West, not even an economic toehold for possible future economic exploitation. They visualize a quick transition to the industrial epic which is associated in their minds with high living standards, international power and prestige. The communists respond to this dream with claims of creating modern industrial societies quickly, without risk, capital, or obligation. In Southeast Asia, this is the way that the economic progress of the Soviet Union and communist China is widely advertised. When the human cost of communist-type progress cannot remain concealed, it is revealed as a necessary factor in protecting the state against enemies and agents of foreign powers. Communist peace drives, the characterization of Western economic or technical help as disguised imperialism, disruption of noncommunist economies by strikes and sabotage—these and others are all variations played on the same theme.

The economic appeal of communist dogma has other manifestations in Southeast Asia. One of these is the identification of capitalism with imperialism. During the colonial era capitalism provided the economic framework within which Europeans and such alien minorities as the Chinese and Indians prospered while the economic status of the indigenous peoples remained low. As a reaction, Southeast Asian leaders tend to view capitalism as an exploitive alien economic system. Consequently, their inclination is to some form of socialism.

With the dislocation of traditional social structures in Southeast Asia, the communists have been provided with another fertile area of activity. Colonial practice and the impact of the West in general have contributed greatly to the breakdown of traditional social and philosophical patterns. Although many of their traditional values and authorities have been effected or displaced, so far no new ones have arisen to take their place. The resulting uncertainty is more conducive to political and economic extremism than to the growth of democracy. Here again, communism makes its brash promises—promises of a new social order to go with the new political and economic orders, a social order where class distinctions are abolished and everyone is equal under the leadership of the communist party.

In the midst of the prevailing marginal social conditions in

Southeast Asia, many uprooted individuals are searching for some new social unity, a new order or meaning to existence. The educated leadership élite, members of whom find themselves in a combined social and philosophical vacuum, keenly feel the disturbing social and philosophical impact of the West. Their Western orientation has penetrated too deeply to be cast aside, yet they cannot return to their old philosophical and social heritage. In such circumstances communism exercises a peculiar attractiveness. Unable to revert to traditional values and authorities, unable to find conclusive answers in Western philosophy to the new questions besetting them, some of these Asian intellectuals are drawn to communism and to the philosophy of Marxism by the intellectual and philosophical security which they seemingly afford. Between communism and the communists, complete and absolute solutions are postulated for every political, economic, or social problem. With the lack of philosophical bases for resistance to communism in Southeast Asia, with no obvious economic or political stake in anticommunism, for the gropers, for the uncertain, communism seems to provide the answer.

Another, perhaps a more subtle, attraction to communism emerges from the phenomenon of the disintegrating societies of Southeast Asia. The fact that their traditional societies cannot survive the changeover period intact is recognized by most Southeast Asian people with an awareness of the outside world. At the same time, they are reluctant to accept the degree of Westernization which must accompany industrialization, preferring to preserve their social and cultural traditions. They want the economic benefits that the Western World has achieved while, at the same time, they resist and resent many of the changes necessary for industrialization. To some, the way of communism answers a twofold purpose. It offers a system for industrialization and it represents an effective protest against their former colonial masters who, they feel, were responsible for the retarded economic development, the social disruption, and the lack of international prestige and power of their countries.

Among the educated élites of Southeast Asia, communism's appeal is enhanced by the desire to be part of an important international movement, a movement which prompts Washington, London, and Paris to concern and worry. The communist movement seems to afford opportunities which too often are lacking in the service of the national governments, such as chances for self-realization and for promotion on the basis of merit and performance. Among the literate classes of Southeast Asia, resentment against corruption in government is growing; and here again the communists carefully nurture the idea through propaganda and their own behavior that they are enemies of corruption and champions of those who lack proper defense against corrupt officials.

In Malaya and Thailand, the communist situation is unique. From the beginning in these countries communism has been geared almost entirely to the large overseas Chinese groups, which in Southeast Asia are by no means all communist or sympathetic to communism but rather fall in each country into small groups—one communist, one anticommunist, plus the large majority uncommitted to either group. In Southeast Asia most overseas Chinese would prefer to ignore the issue of communism and concentrate wholly on their economic activities. In 1927 they split along the lines of the Kuomintang-Communist split in China, and ever since both factions have been represented in Southeast Asia. However, it is self-evident that, communist or not, many overseas Chinese have been strongly influenced in recent years by the increased international prestige and power of communist China. They have not assimilated to any marked degree into the cultures where they have chosen to reside, especially since the beginning of the Chinese revolution and the upsurge of Chinese nationalism which accompanied it. In Southeast Asia the overseas Chinese often have been marked as victims of discriminatory legislation and antagonism, more economic than racial and, as a result, have looked to China, whatever that country's political complexion, for diplomatic support and protection.

The development of communism among the Chinese living in Thailand and Malaya, as well as elsewhere in Southeast Asia, has proved a mixed blessing for the communists. While the communists among the overseas Chinese have provided a valuable fifth column for communism, the antagonism and distrust evoked by the Chinese among the indigenous peoples of Southeast Asia have tended to minimize the appeal of communism to the non-

Chinese majority groups. In Thailand and Malaya especially, communism is regarded as essentially a Chinese phenomenon, and that seems to be sufficient reason for the indigenous populations to oppose it.

If these colonial, economic, and social forces at work illuminate the character of communist appeal for the important leadership groups in Southeast Asia, then what of the nature of the communist appeal to the masses of illiterate peasants and laborers? The conditions already described scarcely apply equally to all groups. Then why do the masses follow communism? In large part, the simple answer is that the masses of Southeast Asia do *not* follow communism. Some follow leaders who follow communism. And these carbon copies of the rank-and-file communist followers for the most part possess only the dimmest understanding of communism. Mainly, they are attracted to personalities, to leaders who seem to express interest in their welfare, and to those who promise to fulfill their wants. Among workers and peasants, communist promises of honest government, farms for landless peasants, better living and working conditions for laborers, and the elimination of social classes have been especially effective. Mao Tse-tung in his early writings gave away the communist method of seeking mass support in Asia. Understand the peasant, learn what he wants and what he fears, and then formulate communist slogans accordingly, Mao instructed his cadres.

THE EARLY YEARS

Communist activity in Southeast Asia is not a new or recent phenomenon. For at least twenty-five years communist agents have carried on active propaganda and organizational work in the area. During the early years their activities were scattered and limited to the efforts of a handful of individuals; but, as in China before the success of the Chinese communists, there was a long period of communist planning, experience, and preparation.

No regular pattern is suggested by the development and growth of the various communist parties in Southeast Asia. Instead, there is a wide diversity of the timing, composition, and degree of success of the national communist parties of the area. For example, communist activities began in Indonesia as early as 1914 when four Dutch Social Democrats began organizing various dissident and nationalist groups into a revolutionary Social Democratic Association which, in turn, provided the nucleus for the Indonesian Communist Party (PKI) formed in 1920. Shortly thereafter the PKI was admitted as a national section of the Comintern, the Soviet apparatus which had been organized only the year before in Moscow to support, coordinate, and guide the activities of communist parties throughout the world. In contrast, the Communist Party of Burma (CPB) was formed as late as 1943. Before that date communism in Burma had been largely academic.

The Indochinese Communist Party (ICP) was organized in 1930 and was admitted to the Comintern a year later. It was preceded by an Association of Revolutionary Annamite Youth formed by Ho Chi Minh in 1925. For five years prior to its reorganization as the ICP, party members fanned out from their base of operations in South China to indoctrinate and organize communist cells throughout Indochina. From 1926 to 1930 Ho Chi Minh, one of the key figures of the international communist apparatus in the Far East, traveled about Southeast Asia recruiting and training men for local communist leadership. When he was arrested in 1931, the communists were deprived of the services of a most effective agent in Southeast Asia for two years.

Although individual agents and isolated cells existed earlier, the national communist movement began in the Philippines in 1930 with a mass meeting in Manila to celebrate the thirteenth anniversary of the Russian October Revolution. The Communist Party of the Philippines (CPP) was founded in November 1930, but it floundered almost immediately after, when, following a second mass meeting in May 1931, extremist statements and activities caused the arrest and conviction of most of the leaders and cadres.

The early organization and development of the Malayan and Thai communist parties run parallel. In both countries agitation and propaganda began early in the 1920's, and the communist movements are essentially Chinese in ethnic composition and orientation. Although the Malayan Communist Party (MCP) was not founded until 1931, communists were active in labor organization and agitation for ten years prior to that date. In Thailand communism was outlawed and effectively contained from 1933 until late 1946, which prevented the party from operating openly to any significant extent during that interval. As a result, the actual party organization date and the question of unified party membership of Chinese, Vietnamese, and Siamese adherents are subject to question. Both in Malaya and in Thailand, the communist organizations failed to achieve a national character. Either for that reason or because they were relatively weak, neither organization was admitted to the Comintern as a separate national section. Because of their close ties with China, however, the Malayan and Thai organizations are considered by some observers to be branches of the Chinese Communist Party.

The embryonic struggles of the communist parties in Southeast Asia reveal certain elements at work in the pattern. For instance, the early years of communist activity suggest that the communists have had a considerable amount of difficulty in finding strong, capable, unified, and imaginative top party leadership. Party cadres frequently have been split by personal rivalries or disagreements over questions of doctrine, tactics, and timing.

In cases such as Indonesia, the Philippines, and Indochina, the local parties appeared at times to be so carried away by an overestimation of their own strength that they launched poorly timed adventures which damaged the national movement and even managed to embarrass the international movement. The implication is that party unity and discipline were not as highly developed as the Comintern could have wished. In Indonesia, for example, the early success of the communists in organizing a large following led them to an imprudent use of the strike weapon. As a result of labor disturbances and violent demonstrations in the mid-1920's, the Dutch colonial government outlawed the party and arrested or exiled many of its leaders. This failed to deter other communist leaders who were still free to attempt armed uprisings in the following years. The Dutch not only suppressed the communist revolts easily but also countered with such sweeping measures that they severely curtailed the effectiveness of the PKI for more than a decade. At the Comintern's Sixth Congress in 1928, this ill considered revolution evoked a reprimand. In Indochina the ICP overextended its activities with a series of violent strikes, peasant demonstrations, and local armed uprisings in 1930 and 1931 which forced the French colonial administration to take severe countermeasures.

Obviously, communism cannot be considered a unified movement advancing in all countries of Southeast Asia at an equal rate. From the communist point of view, an equal rate of progress would be impossible in any case because "objective conditions" for revolution differ from one country to the next. Nor is party progress necessarily measured by relative success as encountered in such a country as Vietnam, or relative failure as appears in Thailand. Rather, the variations would suggest the existence of revolutionary movements in Southeast Asia at different stages of development. And it is in this sense that United States policy may profitably regard them.

The extent and nature of the direction given to the activities of the various communist parties in Southeast Asia by the international communist movement is uncertain. However, the apparatus which international communism has constructed in the area, and the manner in which the various Southeast Asian parties have attempted to follow the strategy guidance, or "line," of the Moscow Comintern, suggest an effort on both sides to integrate communist activities in Southeast Asia into the monolithic international movement.

International communism has long had an extensive apparatus in Southeast Asia for guiding and supporting local communist activities. In 1926 the Chinese Communist Party organized a South Seas Committee, later renamed the South Seas Communist Party, to organize and direct communist activity in Southeast Asia. The parties in Thailand and Malaya were especially close to this organization. A Pan-Pacific Trade Union also was organized in China in 1926 to pay special attention to the indoctrination and organization of the Southeast Asian proletariat. To provide a centralized clearing house for communist directives and intelligence, a Pan-Pacific Trade Union Secretariat was established. As the center of authority in the area, a Far Eastern Bureau, which may be regarded as a Far Eastern office of the Moscow Comintern, was set up in Shanghai. For a time the Far Eastern Bureau appeared to maintain branch offices in Singapore, Bangkok and, also, in effect, another wherever Ho Chi Minh, one of its key officers, happened to be.

The agents of international communism were especially active in Southeast Asia during the years from 1926 to 1930. They set up lines of communication, consolidated isolated communist activity, and brought the national communist parties into contact with the Far Eastern Bureau. They inaugurated extensive indoctrination and recruiting drives and distributed communist literature widely. It was in these years that they made a vital start toward coordinating communism in Southeast Asia.

ZIGGING AND ZAGGING WITH MOSCOW

A number of circumstances tended to foster the misleading impression that the local communist movements were national in character or, at most, had only tenuous ties with the international movement. For one, the prewar communist movements in Southeast Asia were assigned a relatively low priority on the international communist program. For another, because communications between Moscow and the outlying regions of Southeast Asia were relatively poor, the Southeast Asian leaders fairly inexperienced and undisciplined, communist activities generally failed to appear as well synchronized there as in other parts of the world. At times the Southeast Asian parties were hard pressed to comply with Comintern guidance without risking self-destruction or the serious loss of following and prestige at home. Their considerations of timing, tactics, and facilities seemed to create the illusion that they were somehow national in orientation and objectives rather than international. Broadly speaking, however, they conformed remarkably well to the main lines of Comintern strategy and functioned to the best of their ability as an arm of Soviet policy in the pattern suggested by the Seventh Comintern Congress (1935) in the following resolution:

> The Comintern shall devise every means and make every effort to strengthen the Soviet Union; it shall fight any enemy of Russia. In time of peace or in time of war, the Comintern shall strengthen Soviet Russia and shall elevate its national power.

An example of this occurred when the communist parties in Southeast Asia felt impelled to shift their strategy to conform to the pattern the Comintern laid down at the time the Soviet Union, seeking a united front in Europe against the threat of Nazi strength, concluded a mutual assistance pact with France. In Southeast Asia local communists, posing as nationalists and patriots, endeavored to cooperate with socialist and independence groups in opposing fascism. Their propaganda deemphasized independence, and concentrated instead on better working conditions and improved economic status. Later, when Stalin found it expedient to enter into an alliance with Hitler, the communist parties of Southeast Asia again made the necessary shift in strategy. They obstructed the allied war effort by strikes, demonstrations, and sabotage until the colonial powers were forced to counter with severe repressive measures which drove them underground. Communist anticolonial agitation took on a new urgency recalling the 1928 Sixth Comintern Congress resolution:

Since the colonies and semi-colonies are the mainstays of Imperialistic countries exploiting the masses in those regions, any movement towards the emancipation of the latter will be a severe blow to the former. Furthermore, revolutions in the Imperialistic countries are requisite for the ultimate emancipation of the inhabitants of the colonies and semi-colonies. Consequently close connection must be maintained between these two movements.

When the Germans finally attacked the Soviet Union in June 1941, causing the Soviet Union to be identified, temporarily at least, with the Allies, the communist parties reverted to the popular-front strategy in Southeast Asia, cooperating not only with nationalist groups but also with the colonial powers in order to contribute their part to the Soviet Union's struggle for survival. This time, they curtailed strikes and demonstrations and, until the countries of Southeast Asia fell before the Japanese invasion forces, worked for the defeat of fascism, the new common enemy. As the Japanese forces occupied one Southeast Asian country after another, the communists retreated to their well established underground positions to prepare for their role in the anti-Japanese resistance movements.

In Indochina, Ho Chi Minh's conduct of communist affairs

was somewhat exceptional during this period. After the fall of France in Europe, under an agreement negotiated by the Vichy government with the Japanese, the French colonial administration remained intact in Indochina, but the Japanese were given the right to station and move troops about the area. Choosing the early days of the Japanese occupation for their purpose, the communists decided on a full-scale revolt to oust the French completely. Before the plot could get under way, the French military learned of it and nipped it thoroughly while the Japanese stood by, aloof to the entire matter. From then until the Japanese surrender, the Indochina communists fought an intermittent war against both Japanese and French, a war whose overtones are reminiscent of Mao Tse-tung's double war against Japan and the Nationalist Government in China.

The communists in Southeast Asia, bolstered by their underground experience which had provided an organizational framework for the development and domination of anti-Japanese resistance movements, were presented a great opportunity by the Second World War. Pursuing their united front tactics, they used the time to inveigle themselves in many instances into positions of leadership in the nationalist movements then growing and sweeping Southeast Asia. At the moment of greatest import, however, they found themselves cut off almost entirely from Moscow's guidance and support. With the Soviet Union fully occupied over the European war effort, Japan in control of all Southeast Asia, and the international apparatus of communism seriously disrupted, the local communist parties had to operate on their own initiative.

Although allied with the Western Allies to stave off Germany, the Soviet Union hoped to improve its international power position and extend its influence by international collaboration and bargaining. In Southeast Asia the communists, frequently aided by Allied arms and support, fought against the Japanese. They cooperated with other anti-Japanese and nationalist groups to form coalition governments, and within these they sought to consolidate their control and extend their influence.

In Burma, for example, communists served as leading figures in the nationalist coalition, the Anti-Fascist People's Freedom League (AFPFL). In Indochina they took the lead in 1941 in organizing the Vietnam Independence League (Viet Minh) which included some fifteen patriotic and nationalist groups. In Malaya they formed a multiracial united front in 1942 as the Malayan People's Anti-Japanese Union and the Malayan People's Anti-Japanese Army. In the Philippines, in 1942, the communists organized the People's Anti-Japanese Army as a wide popular front, including both Filipinos and members of the parallel Chinese communist organization. Another underground under Magsaysay also operated but was separate from the communist-led group. In Indonesia the communist party led a coalition resistance army which held many shades of nationalist and political convictions.

In Southeast Asia the communists did not neglect their political aspirations during the war. From their positions of prestige and leadership, they sought to convert to communism the anti-Japanese guerrillas and the peasants of the countryside. In some areas of Indonesia, Malaya, Burma, and Vietnam, following the pattern of Mao Tse-tung in North China, they organized local soviets and installed communist-type governments. And, as Mao had done, they laid extensive plans for seizing control of postwar governments.

The communist parties of Southeast Asia emerged from the Second World War stronger, more popular, and with greater prestige and following than they had ever before enjoyed. Unlike nationalism, communism in Southeast Asia failed to arise as a great national movement but did emerge as a strong and highly organized force in an excellent position to seize control of the authentic nationalist movements and to dominate the newly established governments.

Echoing the outlines of Soviet policy within the United Nations alliance, the communist parties of Southeast Asia sought to negotiate with the colonial powers at the end of the war. They sought recognition of the wartime "front" organizations. They indicated a willingness to bargain on the issue of immediate national independence in exchange for recognition of their political leadership and status in the nationalist coalitions.

In Burma, Indonesia, and Indochina, the returning British, Dutch, and French officials were forced to negotiate with these organized and functioning popular-front governments which had wide popular support. In Malaya the return of the British was accomplished with minimum resistance and difficulty even though the communists were in firm control of most of the countryside. Whether this was in line with the policy of international communism or a consequence of a communist policy vacuum, or a simple recognition of Britain's superior power and Malaya's weakened condition, is uncertain. In any case, the Malayan communists initially gave the impression of willingness to cooperate with the British.

Although the long-range strategic views of international communism toward colonial Asia undoubtedly remained firm, from the end of the war until 1947, international communist policy apparently had not yet been formulated. Communist liaison in the Far East had to be reestablished, and international communist policy had to be reappraised in view of the Soviet Union's changed position in Europe and the new conditions in Asia. Internally, the Soviet Union faced serious problems of reconstruction. On the international scene, the Soviet Union gave priority to the consolidation of communist influence in eastern Europe. During this period, the Kremlin provided little direct support to the Southeast Asians or to the Chinese communists.

In Southeast Asia the communists continued to participate in the wartime popular-front alliances. They hoped, apparently, to negotiate with the colonial powers a basis for early national independence under coalition governments in which they could exercise decisive influence. But, for the popular-front coalitions, the path of negotiation and compromise was not easy. Dissension over methods, timing, and objectives developed quickly, and personal rivalries among the leaders of the various factions added to the confusion. While the centrifugal forces strained and threatened to break the bonds which had held together the wartime coalitions, the communists kept intact their guerrilla organizations and most of their military equipment. They were a continual threat both to the colonial administrations and to the genuine nationalist groups negotiating for national independence.

Among individual communists, however, party unity at times gave way to strife resulting from personal rivalries among party leaders and disagreements over strategy, tactics, and timing. Some of the dissension in party ranks during this period was due also to the efforts of the Stalinist communists to reestablish party discipline and control in Southeast Asia. Numerous second-echelon communist leaders had emerged from the jungles at the war's end heading guerrilla bands which they had organized, trained and led, and, proud of their wartime exploits, no doubt looked forward to continued independence of decision. The result was that some communist leaders, affected by the upsurge of nationalism among the Southeast Asian people during the Second World War, became as much a problem to the communist movements as they were to the colonial powers, since communism cannot possibly tolerate leaders who place nationalist objectives above communist international objectives. The period following the war was a trying period for Southeast Asian communists, with frequent party purges, expulsions, and the establishment of rival communist factions.

Probably Moscow's planners may be blamed for a great deal of the uncertainty of Southeast Asia in communist strategy at this time. Their knowledge of conditions in Asia was far from complete and, in general, they pursued a "Europe first" policy. By the summer of 1947, the uncertainty had led to an open split over communist policy for colonial Asia within the Pacific Institute of the Academy of Sciences in Moscow. Some of the institute members advocated a militant revolutionary strategy; others backed a moderate popular-front strategy. The Kremlin reached its major policy decision by the fall of 1947.

In recognition of the stiffening opposition of the Western Allies to Soviet expansion into eastern and central Europe, the Soviet Union openly terminated any pretense of cooperation with the Western Allies. At a meeting of major communist leaders from the Soviet Union and the eastern European satellites, held in Belgrade in September 1947, the Comintern, which had been formally dissolved in 1943 as a concession to the Allies, was reactivated as the Communist Information Bureau or Cominform. The new official line was laid down by the Soviet delegate, A. Zhdanov, in a long speech which characterized the international situation as an alignment of the world into two hostile political forces—one dominated by the United States, the other peacefully led by the "anti-imperialist and democratic" Soviet Union. The great task of the communist parties, enunciated in the speech, was to unite "the democratic, anti-fascist, peace-loving elements to resist the new plans of war and aggression."[1] Both Vietnam and Indonesia, according to Zhdanov, already were among those countries "that have broken with imperialism and have firmly set foot on the path of democratic development." Zhdanov spoke the following lines on communism in Asia:

> World War II aggravated the crisis of the colonial system, as expressed in the rise of a powerful movement for national liberation in the colonies and dependencies. This has placed the rear of the capitalist system in jeopardy. The peoples of the colonies no longer wish to live in the old way. The ruling classes of the metropolitan countries can no longer govern the colonies on the old lines. Attempts to crush the national liberation movement by military force now increasingly encounter armed resistance on the part of the colonial peoples and lead to protracted colonial wars.

Thus, in line with the Soviet Union's reversion to a militant anti-Allied policy, the communist parties of colonial Asia were reminded of their duty to aid the international cause by a new offensive in the colonies, "the rear of the capitalist system."

Zhdanov sounded the clarion call for reestablishing discipline and coordination in the international communist movement:

> In the course of the four years that have elapsed since the dissolution of the Comintern, the Communist parties have grown considerably in strength and influence in nearly all of the countries of Europe and Asia.
>
> Some comrades understood the dissolution of the Comintern to imply the elimination of all ties, of all contact, between the fraternal Communist parties. But experience has shown that such mutual isolation of the Communist parties is wrong, harmful, and, in point of fact, unnatural. The Communist movement develops within national frameworks, but there are tasks and interests common to the parties of the various countries. . . .
>
> The need for mutual consultation and voluntary coordination of action between individual parties has become particularly urgent at the present juncture when continued isolation may lead to a slackening of mutual understanding, and at times, even to serious blunders.

Three months after the Cominform meeting, E. Zhukov, Director of the Pacific Institute of the Academy of Sciences in Moscow, outlined the new course of action for communist policy in colonial Asia in even greater detail in an article in *Bolshevik,* an official

Soviet publication. The communists were to bid for power in colonial Asia by a militant forward surge on all fronts, by severing cooperation with more moderate nationalist groups, and by armed revolt, according to this article and several others which appeared shortly afterward in Cominform and Soviet publications.

POSTWAR INSURRECTIONS

The new line was openly disseminated at a major international communist conference held in Calcutta in February 1948 and, within six months, armed communist insurrections began in Malaya, Burma, and Indonesia. There is evidence that Moscow initiated orders for the armed revolts and passed them on to the Southeast Asian communist parties at the Calcutta Conference. Burmese government officials claimed to have captured documents brought into Burma by local communist leaders after the Calcutta meeting which called upon the Burmese Communist Party to move into armed revolt and which laid out in considerable detail tactical plans for the insurrection.[2] The new line was brought to Indonesia by two young communist leaders who attended the Calcutta Conference. The second-echelon leaders, as the "bearers of the true gospel and as ideological experts," in league with other second-echelon leaders were prepared to challenge the top party leadership, and they did, in fact, force party adoption of the policies set down at Calcutta.[3] The available evidence that the communist insurrection in Malaya was an outgrowth of instructions received at Calcutta is less specific. However, an MCP delegate attended the meeting and returned with a full report of instructions. Perhaps more significance may be attached to the fact that a top Australian communist leader spent two weeks in Singapore conferring with MCP leaders en route home from the Calcutta meeting.[4]

Whether the Southeast Asian insurrections were begun entirely as a response to Moscow's wishes or were begun in response to local conditions is uncertain. Probably both factors influenced the local party leaders in their decision. But there can be little doubt of Moscow's implication in the Southeast Asian insurrections. The Cominform called for armed uprisings in colonial Asia, the instructions for revolt were disseminated at the Moscow-inspired

Calcutta Conference, and the progress of the armed struggles was applauded and encouraged by the organs of international communism. It is highly dubious that the sequence of events was entirely coincidental. Moscow's motives in this matter were varied, but one stands out as reasonably clear. In the immediate postwar years the Kremlin expected a general economic collapse in the West which would provide the communists in Western Europe an opportunity to seize power. By armed insurrections in colonial Asia, the "rear of the capitalist system," Moscow hoped to offset the effects of the Marshall Plan aid to Europe already begun and to hasten economic collapse in Britain, France, and the Netherlands. It is possible that Moscow never expected the insurrections to result in local communist success but was willing to expend those parties for European political purposes.

The wisdom of the communist decision to resort to armed insurrection in Malaya, Burma, and Indonesia is open to question. While the insurrections did hamper economic recovery in Western Europe, they did not prevent it. Thus Moscow was frustrated in one primary objective. From the point of view of the communist movements in Southeast Asia, the revolts were probably a serious mistake. In all three cases, as well as in the case of the Huk uprising in the Philippines, the communist parties failed to apply successfully Lenin's classic doctrine of "revolution from within." Except in the case of Malaya, the revolts were put down by the determined efforts of the nationalist governments without outside help. As a consequence of this effort to seize control by force, as a consequence of the embarrassment of the genuine nationalist movements, and of the extortionist and terrorist methods, the communist parties everywhere suffered a loss of prestige, popular support, and good will which was serious although it was not necessarily permanent. In addition, they lost many of their important top leaders.

The communist insurrection in Indonesia began, in its overt phase, in mid-September 1948 when a group of local PKI military officers, without prior knowledge or consent of the top PKI leadership [5] moved on the Madiun area of central west Java in an effort to forestall plans of the Republican government to disarm and demobilize them. Because of the Madiun uprising, the top PKI leadership was forced to enter into the revolutionary phase on a nation-wide basis before it was fully prepared to implement the new Cominform line. With most of its loyal troops lined up against the Dutch forces, the government, on its side, was severely handicapped. The Republic leaders were fearful that any diversion of their strength from the Dutch front would result in a Dutch attack or that the Dutch would use the Madiun uprising as an excuse to intervene.

The communists expected large-scale public support in their revolutionary effort but were disappointed. "In the first place, the Communists were attacking leaders who had become the very symbol of the Republic and of Indonesian independence. Sukarno, in particular, had for an undoubted majority of the Indonesian rank and file come to symbolize the Republic. For them an attack on Sukarno was an attack on their Republic." [6] The communists overestimated the extent to which organized labor, the peasants, and the armed forces of the Republic would rally to their cause. With a few local exceptions, these groups were either apathetic to the communist uprising or, much to the surprise of the PKI leaders, opposed to it.

Within two months the Indonesian communist insurrection was crushed and a great many of its top leaders were either killed or captured. Those who escaped the Republican forces went into hiding, their political organization disrupted and their reputation temporarily destroyed.

The fact that Burma could not be held by force within the Empire was recognized by Britain by the end of 1946. As a consequence, Prime Minister Attlee invited a Burmese delegation to London in December of that year to discuss self-government. A year of negotiations followed during which the communists and other leftist groups in Burma made things extremely difficult for the more moderate Burmese nationalists. Nevertheless, the Nu-Attlee Treaty, concluded on October 17, 1947, pledged Britain to grant full independence to Burma. A very unstable and precarious Burma became independent on January 4, 1948, one month before the Calcutta Conference. In March, the communists began their armed insurrection. Premier Nu continued his efforts to negotiate leftist unity in Burma but failed. In August, large parts of the national army mutinied and, by the following March, the authority of the Burmese government was restricted for all practical purposes to the city of Rangoon. In the countryside, Stalinist White Flag Communists, Red Flag Communists, PVO "White Band" groups, Karens, and miscellaneous bands of roving bandits alternately aligned themselves with and fought one another in constantly shifting combinations. Whatever the combination, however, all were unified on one score: opposition to the Burmese government. The government forces did not begin to score their first important military successes until the spring of 1950, but from then on the situation slowly and steadily improved. Communist disunity and terrorism contributed to this ultimate communist failure, although the most potent weapon in the hands of the Burmese government was the fact of national independence. Without the issue of colonialism, the Burmese communists were unable to rally wide popular support.

In Malaya, from the end of the war until the communist revolt began in early 1948, the MCP failed to retain its wartime strength and prestige. It could neither hide its obvious affiliation with international communism nor expand its membership beyond the ethnic bonds which its Chinese leadership and composition imposed. Although the MCP made considerable progress in organizing and dominating the labor movement in Malaya, their steadily increasing militant tactics built up tension between the MCP and the British and Malayan Federation authorities. In April 1948, when a series of communist-inspired labor demands were refused, a wave of violence was touched off in which recalcitrant employers were murdered and strikers who attempted to return to work contrary to communist orders were terrorized. When the Federation authorities took extensive measures to control the violence, the more important communist leaders fled to jungle hideouts and instituted a reign of terror which included arson, murder, ambush, and looting on rubber plantations, in tin mines, on highways and on railways, in unprotected Malay communities and in Chinese squatter settlements.

Apparently, by armed insurrection, the MCP hoped to drive the British out of the country and to coerce into cooperation or to neutralize by terror the Chinese population of Malaya. With the British gone and the noncommunist Chinese population under control, they knew that the Malay population could offer no serious opposition. Very few Chinese were willing to take up arms against the communist guerrillas, but many contributed to the anticommunist cause by economic and political cooperation. The great majority of the Chinese remained neutral insofar as they could. Although the communists were able to cause considerable hardship and suffering throughout the country, they were unable to push the British out or effectively to curtail the rubber and tin production upon which prosperity in Malaya depends and upon which Britain depends for a large part of her dollar earnings.

The British took extreme and far-reaching countermeasures against the communist guerrillas through the long period of the "emergency." MCP documents captured in 1951 indicated that a change of communist tactics from armed revolt to political penetration and subversion was in the offing. The communists continued their campaign from the jungle, however, on a basis of "selective" terrorism, extortion, and intimidation. Meanwhile, they stepped up their underground infiltration and propaganda activities in the schools, labor unions, and towns. Again, in 1954 and 1955, captured MCP documents indicated a further shift of emphasis to political subversion which is tantamount to a retreat to a lower stage of the revolution, though not a defeat. The MCP was not vanquished or eliminated, although it failed to realize its objectives. The communists continue to hold a potent threat over the Federation of Malaya, for at any time they may order a resumption of unrestricted guerrilla warfare. Meanwhile, they continue their long-range activities designed to soften the will of the anticommunists and to neutralize popular resistance through subversion techniques.

In the Philippines, the armed rebellion followed a somewhat different pattern. After the grant of Philippine independence, the issue of colonialism lost its significance; therefore the Huks based their rebellion on agrarian reform and antifeudalism. In 1945 and 1946 the Huks maintained a popular-front alliance and, participating in the 1946 elections, won several seats in the Philippine Congress. However, their representatives were not seated, and shortly afterward they organized an Army of National Liberation in active opposition to the Philippine government. In 1948 a truce was reached, and Luis Taruc, a Huk leader, finally was seated in the Philippine House of Representatives. Still, the question of demobilizing and disarming the Huk forces precipitated further disagreement which led to the resumption of open warfare. By 1950 Taruc was the commander of a large People's Liberation Army which attempted to follow the tactical pattern of Mao Tse-tung in China. Huk resistance eventually was reduced after a long and costly campaign of attrition, mixed with some land reform in central Luzon.

Only in Vietnam, where the Vietnamese effort had little tactical relationship to the Cominform strategy and where the communists from 1946 on steadily led a nationalist coalition against the French, did armed struggle succeed. Even in Vietnam, however, the objective was only partially achieved, because the Geneva Agreements resulted in a division of the country. In all of Southeast Asia, Thailand was the only country to escape the postwar experience of a major communist insurrection.

On the basis of the outcome of the postwar communist armed insurrection in Southeast Asia, it is possible to make a number of general observations drawn from specific object lessons. First, and perhaps this is most strikingly demonstrated, it is clear that the communists profit greatly from close affiliation with a nationalist or independence cause. The object lessons here are both negative and positive: In Indonesia and Burma, where the communist uprisings failed, they were directed against the local nationalist governments; in Malaya and the Philippines the nationalist issue was either blurred or played no part. In Vietnam the communists managed to rally and maintain wide support for their revolutionary effort. Here the communist armed struggle was closely affiliated with the struggle for national independence. Probably the communists would have won both Burma and Indonesia within a few years of the end of the Second World War if the British and the Dutch had remained in control. Ho Chi Minh's success in Indochina was due more to French refusal to grant independence than to any other reason. If the Southeast Asian peoples are faced with the choice of either an indigenous government, communist or otherwise, or an alien government, they will choose the indigenous government.

Second, the importance of party unification and coordination is indicated by communist experience in Indonesia and Burma. If the communists in Burma had not split into rival factions, their chances of success would have been much better. If the communist uprising in Indonesia had been coordinated, it is probable that the government of the Republic would have had a very difficult time.

Third, the power and influence of the communists in open revolt cannot always be gauged by the extent of communist infiltration into government, the armed forces, and the police. In both Indonesia and Burma, the government services were infiltrated by communists and communist sympathizers, but in both instances the response of these agents disappointed the communist leadership. In open revolt, the "fellow traveler" group proved to be a dubious ally. Although communist infiltration was a serious problem for the anticommunists, it also proved to be a mixed blessing for the communists by leading them to overestimate their strength.

Fourth, proletarian support of the communists throughout the area proved to be unreliable. Much to the surprise of the communists, the working-class groups did not rally to the support of the armed revolutions to the extent the communists anticipated, except in local instances where reliable communists were on the spot and unusually influential.

Fifth, communist methods of terrorism, coercion, and extortion resulted in widespread anticommunist reactions. Even for practical operational purposes, the communists found that the point of diminishing returns of terror was low if the people had some alternate source of protection to which they could turn.

THE MOSCOW-PEKING AXIS

The communist victory in China at the end of 1949 created a new situation for international communist relations. The Chinese communists, employing their own strategies and tactics, came to power primarily by their own efforts in a success which came as a considerable surprise to the Soviet leaders. In power, the Chinese communists have attached great importance to developing policies of their own in Asia and to achieving a "co-equal" status with

Moscow in the world of international communism. These factors, considered with China's size, population, location, and potential power, indicate a relationship between the Soviet Union and communist China quite different from the Soviet satellite status of the peoples' democracies of East Europe. While there is no reason to assume that Peking is a completely free agent in international communism, there is equally little reason to assume that Peking is or can be completely dominated by Moscow. An axis relationship appears to have developed between the two major communist states.

Whatever the precise nature of the Moscow-Peking Axis, the balance of communist influence and operational responsibility in Southeast Asia seems to be undergoing an interesting and potentially very important change. As far as the strategic and tactical guidance of the Southeast Asian communist movements are concerned, the relative influence of Peking has increased greatly. Peking has become the focal point for communist conferences, rallies, good-will missions, social and cultural exchanges, and economic negotiations in Asia. Invitations by the score have gone out to communist groups and front organizations to visit Peking and to view the wonders which have been created by the Chinese communist leaders. The Peking régime has launched a major cultural offense and has increased propaganda activities greatly throughout Southeast Asia.

With communism firmly established on mainland China, it was to be expected that Peking's communist activities would be greatly expanded in surrounding countries. However, the real significance is that these activities have a heavy Chinese and Asian slant rather than a Soviet or communist international orientation.

In the realm of general communist strategy, Peking's increased prestige and influence in Southeast Asia is also discernible. Briefly, according to the Peking or Maoist revolutionary strategies, the peasantry plays the leading role, the armed struggle being conceived as a long-term effort in which the countryside is captured and organized first and the urban centers last. In the Moscow or Stalinist strategies, it is the proletariat which plays the leading role, and the first objective is to seize the urban centers before control is expanded gradually to the countryside. In Southeast Asia the Peking strategies have increased markedly in popularity despite

Soviet doubts on their suitability as a revolutionary model for other Asian countries.

Indonesia provides an interesting exception to the prestige and general pattern of adopting the Peking strategies in Southeast Asia. During 1952, along with other Southeast Asian parties, the PKI applauded the Peking line. Then, the next year, in a struggle for PKI leadership, three young and ardent communists, Aidit, Njoto, and Lukman, the first two of whom, significantly enough, had spent the greater part of 1952 in Moscow, emerged as top PKI leaders. In the party purges which they conducted, the issue of the Peking versus the Moscow strategies was a live one. One or another of three heresies was favored by the purged elements. These were tactical moderation, reliance upon parliamentary development, and emphasis upon organization of the peasantry along Chinese communist lines and at the expense of emphasis on the urban proletariat. The PKI leaders, however, checked pro-Peking leanings and, in effect, declared the party's undivided loyalty to Moscow. Although the PKI called for a concerted drive to convert and organize the peasantry, the fact clearly indicated that this was not an adaptation of the Maoist strategy for revolution. At the PKI's fifth national congress in 1954, Aidit took the opportunity to ridicule the Indonesian communists who advocated the Peking strategy and to warn his party that Indonesia's proletariat class in the cities must remain the vanguard of the communist movement. Possibly, the Indonesian communist leaders hope to pursue both strategies simultaneously, but for the time being they seem to be emphasizing their work among the urban proletariat.

Does Peking's increased influence over the communist parties of Southeast Asia mean a real shift in the balance of communist influence? Or is Moscow still the center of authority and Peking merely a convenient channel for more effective manipulation of the Southeast Asian communist movements? The influences and motivations at work within the Moscow-Peking Axis are little known or understood. Certainly, the rise of Peking's role in relation to Asian communism has not involved Moscow in any withdrawal of a claim to major authority. A division of territorial interest and influence may well advance the common objectives of both Moscow and Peking. However, as far as the changed balance of communist influence in Asia does exist, it would seem to represent Soviet acquiescence to the realities of the Asian situation rather than to any independent tactical decision to use China as the Soviet tool in Asia. It is also safe to assume that the Soviet Union no longer is an absolute and independent authority on communist strategy in Asia nor the sole source of communist inspiration in the area.

As to Peking's increasing responsibility and influence in Asia, there appear to be at least three possible consequences: First, communist strategy and tactics in Southeast Asia in the future are apt to be better adopted to local conditions than has been the case in the past. Although it cannot be foreseen with certainty, the Chinese communists may be willing to permit or even to encourage local communist initiative in devising and adapting strategy and tactics. The Chinese communists came to power by using tactics adapted from Lenin and Stalin and, although the fact remains that attitudes when seeking power are very different from attitudes when power has been achieved, the Chinese leaders, who are in a better position to understand and appreciate conditions in Southeast Asian countries than were the Soviet leaders, may encourage more local autonomy and improvisation of tactics than the Soviet leaders.

Second, communist strategy in Southeast Asia in the future may become coordinated with Chinese objectives and political conditions in the Pacific. This is in marked contrast to the situation when Moscow determined communist strategy in Asia on the basis of Soviet objectives in Europe and political conditions in the Atlantic area. There can be no doubt that Peking's leaders desire to develop and pursue an Asia policy of their own. These factors, as they come into play, may tend to accelerate the rate of increase in Chinese influence and authority over the Asian communist movements.

Third, communist activities in Asia may become more reckless, aggressive, and militaristic, reflecting the mood of Peking. Although it is brash to state that the men in Peking are more impatient or imprudent than those in Moscow, it is conceivable that the Peking forces are more aggressive at this point and that Moscow generally has exercised a restraining influence.

No matter how subtle or incomplete communism's shift of operational and directional influence in Southeast Asia, its potential significance is great. Not only must the change be regarded closely in developing United States policy toward communist China and the international communist conspiracy but it also must be watched for any clues on the future nature of communist strategy and tactics in Southeast Asia.

One likely possibility for future communist strategy and tactics in Southeast Asia is a broader and more vigorous application of the so-called Maoist, or Peking, strategies. This refers to a revolutionary movement based on a major alliance of the proletariat, the peasantry, the intelligentsia, and the national bourgeoisie. When pursuing this strategy, the communists remain firmly and clearly in control of the four-front alliance without the subterfuge of submerging leadership in popular-front organizations. As developed by Mao Tse-tung and successfully applied in China, the preparatory four-class-appeal period is followed by a prolonged armed struggle waged from the countryside.

Following the defeat of the Chinese Communist Party in 1927, Mao Tse-tung apparently decided that two important considerations militated against a communist revolution in China based on the proletariat and the urban centers as provided in the traditional doctrines of Lenin and Stalin. First, the urban-centered proletariat was too small a part of the total population of the country; and secondly, the Chinese urban centers were dependent for survival on the food provided by the countryside. Mao realized that the power of the national government was strongest in the cities and became progressively weaker in the more remote rural provinces. In contrast to the proletariat in the cities, the peasants were self-supporting. Thus a peasant revolt presumably could survive without the proletariat, but a proletariat revolution could not survive long without peasant support.

Putting these observations to practical use, Mao Tse-tung developed a program which concentrated on the peasantry as a main pillar of the revolution and the countryside as a self-sustaining fortress from which the armed struggle could be waged. However, the Chinese communists did not envisage an agrarian revolution merely because of the important revolutionary role assigned to the peasants. To Mao Tse-tung, the peasants were merely the primary means and the countryside the locale for the armed struggle which would lead to power. This is indicated by his postrevolution policy of concentrating on the proletariat and on developing heavy industry to the relative neglect and, indeed, at the expense of the peasants and agriculture.

To this end, the communists employ broad popular-front tactics to gain the widest possible support in order to weaken national resistance during the prolonged armed struggle. Trusted communists from all classes go into the provinces to indoctrinate and organize the peasants, laying the groundwork for establishment of a self-sustaining "liberated area" from which the communists may carry on their armed struggle. Mao's strategy requires a determined long-range program to create a regular armed force composed primarily of peasants who are capable of sustained warfare, of self-support in the countryside, and of recruiting fellow peasants in neighboring provinces. According to plan, the defensible limits of the "liberated areas" are expanded as rapidly as possible until the national armed forces and the government, that are concentrated in the cities, ultimately collapse from the combination of economic strangulation, of internal dissension which the proletariat, intelligentsia, and the national bourgeoisie foment, and of pressure applied by the communist peasant armies.

In the United States, as well as in Southeast Asia, a dangerous tendency exists to focus attention on capital cities and to view the communist threat in terms of the strength and stability of national régimes as evidenced by the strength and loyalty of the national security forces and the unity, or lack of it, of the national leadership élites. The tendency also is to worry about communist influence in labor unions and communist infiltration in city school systems and government bureaus. Although these admittedly are serious threats which could lead to communist seizure of power, the fate of the Southeast Asian states in the long run is likely to be determined by the millions of rural dwellers in the thousands of small villages where conditions provide special opportunities for the communists. With the attention of most national governments riveted on the urban centers, the neglected rural areas become an even greater prey to the communist menace.

Of the people of Southeast Asia, approximately 85 per cent are peasants living in small towns, often remote and isolated. Historically, they have been considered the bottom rung of the social, economic, and political structure, and in the precolonial periods were completely neglected. Today they are as neglected generally by the postcolonial national governments. Their traditional role has been to pay taxes, to provide soldiers for the army, and to abide by government regulations. In return for this major contribution to national welfare and prosperity, they have enjoyed few benefits and little or no voice in government decisions affecting them. Too often they have been the defenseless victims of administrative corruption. Physically and intellectually, most of the rural population of Southeast Asia is isolated from the main streams of international, national, and even provincial affairs and, limited as to sources of information, is generally illiterate and uninformed. In more remote areas the authority and prestige of the central government is often weak.

Such circumstances make the villages an especially soft target for communist penetration, indoctrination and, ultimately, organization and control. In both China and Vietnam, communist village tactics were used on the peasants to telling effect. Communist agents, living and working with the peasants, showed interest in peasant welfare, respected peasant opinion, consulted and arrived at decisions jointly with the peasants, and proved themselves anxious to serve peasant needs and desires. Operating on this level in Southeast Asia, the communists have shown imagination, tenacity, and special talent. They have moved easily at first, accepting the occasional peasant rebuff of their ideas, secure in the knowledge of eventual domination. By this technique they have uncovered leadership talent among the peasants and trained pliable youths as effective village cadres. They have been able to convince a great many noncommunist idealists and intellectuals of communism's interest in serving the people. As the web of communist organization and control is spinning, but before it is strung taut, their tolerance and patience seem to be without end. Here is the pattern which the Viet Minh has employed so successfully in Indochina; here is the pattern unquestionably being introduced by communist agents today throughout the villages of Southeast Asia.

In contrast, the nationalist régimes are so preoccupied with parliamentary and political maneuverings, with the attempt to hold their governments together, to balance budgets, to stabilize economies, to industrialize, and to become impressive on the international stage that they give little time to the peasants and villages upon which their strength ultimately must rest. When the national leaders finally do make spasmodic efforts to win the peasants' loyalty and support, too often they are condescending and, as a result, ineffective. This attitude moves on down the line to the nationalistic youths and civil servants who aspire to government assignments in the capital cities, regarding their higher education as a release from the possibility of uncomfortable and hard work in the provinces and villages. Once in government service, even the more idealistic ones who are fired by the desire to work for national progress too often become disillusioned or are lured away from the nationalist cause by the communists.

The communist threats to Southeast Asia rest on opportunities for overt international aggression, for subversion of national institutions, and for civil war or insurrection. As already indicated, many circumstances favor communist success in the area, and the character of communism is such as to leave little doubt that the communists are organized and prepared to take full advantage of every opportunity which arises to favor them. Add to that the fact that the nationalist governments are weakly organized, uncertain of their objectives and methods, and engulfed by the problems of daily administration, and that they are either unable or unwilling to meet fully the communist challenge to their authority, and the question may well be applied: Why is not all Southeast Asia in the hands of the communists today? Several explanations may be given: (1) The communists recently lost a major source of strength in Southeast Asia—the issue of colonialism. Today they compete *not* with alien, colonial governments for strength and support, but with independent national governments. (2) Just as it hampers the efforts of the national governments, the general lassitude and inertia of the Southeast Asian masses retards communist effectiveness. (3) The "Chineseness" of communism, especially in Malaya and Thailand, has limited and continues to limit communist progress. (4) Throughout Southeast Asia, a basic resistance to dictatorship, coupled with an instinct for democracy, individual dignity, and liberty, is growing. (5) Communist extremist methods of the past have returned to plague their protagonists.

But there is one further explanation most unpleasing of all for the noncommunist world to face. This is the fact that, except for Vietnam, the communists have yet to make their major overt bid for power in Southeast Asia. As they have been for some twenty-five years, the communists are still very much at work, seeking to create the right "objective conditions" for revolution, confident of their hour of final victory.

5. THE SHAPE OF POLICY—V-J DAY TO KOREA

AMERICA'S POSTWAR ASSUMPTIONS AND HOW THEY COLLAPSED

The United States entered the postwar period with Far Eastern policies based on four major assumptions. These were: (1) continued cooperation and unity among the major wartime allies within the framework of the United Nations would maintain the peace; (2) the colonial powers and their Asian possessions would work out arrangements for self-government and independence in a peaceful and orderly manner; (3) a unified and friendly China would become the leading Asian power and the focal point of United States interest and policy in Asia; (4) Japan would never again be permitted to become a major Pacific power. The story of the collapse, or the invalidation, of these four assumptions between V-J Day and the communist victory in China is the background for the new and increased significance of Southeast Asia on United States policy ever since 1950.

At the end of the Second World War, United States policy toward Southeast Asia, viewed in global perspective, may be described as a policy of limited interest and noninvolvement. Aside from the matter of Philippine independence and two other notable exceptions to be mentioned later, the United States gave Southeast Asia relatively low-priority attention. In concerning itself with the Far East as a whole, the major points of concentration of the United States Government were on three specific tasks. First was the job of meeting the many unique and difficult problems related to the occupation of Japan and Korea. Second, in accordance with earlier American pledges, it was necessary to complete arrangements for the creation of an independent Republic of the Philippines. Third, China was to be helped to achieve in fact the big-power status which she had been accorded in theory during the war.

Events leading to the collapse of America's first major policy assumption toward Asia in the postwar period, predicated on peace through friendly allied cooperation, go a long way toward serving as an explanation for American neglect of the significant developments taking place during this period in colonial South and Southeast Asia. Although big-power cooperation collapsed in Asia almost immediately after the war, the decisive breaks occurred in Europe under circumstances which focused primary attention on European issues. On the international scene, two European developments overshadowed everything else for the American people and government. They were the crisis resulting from the economic devastation and disintegration of the European continent with its attendant political confusion and the rapid deterioration of allied relations with the Soviet Union, later known as the "East-West split" which precipitated the cold war.

Confronted by the combination of a near prostrate Western Europe and a hostile Soviet Union armed with vast capabilities, the United States could not risk the consequences of inaction. American security required the creation of some measure of stability and balance in Western Europe where the entire continent seemed ready to drop by default into the arms of communism. By 1947 even the most optimistic Americans realized that peace in the postwar world could not be maintained on the assumption of big-power cooperation inside or even outside the framework of the United Nations. Negotiation and cooperation with the Soviet Union clearly required strength, not merely faith and hope. The collapse of this first assumption of American postwar policy forced the United States to face the realities and responsibilities of leadership in a divided and dangerous world. The American response, carried out within the strategic framework of the "containment" idea, was a series of unprecedented foreign policy programs designed to help reconstruct the economies of Western Europe, to help create conditions for political stability, and to help build military strength adequate for defense of the area. The progress of the programs through the overwhelming efforts of the United States and the countries of Western Europe already is recorded American and European history. Of this covering European operation, three phases—the Truman Doctrine, the Marshall Plan, and the North Atlantic Treaty Organization—represented major innovations in United States foreign policy. Behind each of these decisive moves lay logical reasons which contained significant, if at the time only partially realized, implications for subsequent United States foreign policy in Southeast Asia.

The second assumption, that the colonial powers and the Asian nationalists would work out suitable and peaceful arrangements for self-government and independence, was pulverized in the rubble and flames of the Indonesian and Vietnamese independence struggles. Like the colonial powers, the United States misjudged the postwar strength of the colonial Asian independence movements, especially in Indonesia and Indochina. In general, the United States tended to consider the settlement of independence problems as matters outside the scope of American jurisdiction, which they were, and outside the sphere of immediate American interest, which they were not. At the end of the war, expectation rose high throughout colonial Asia that the United States would express the American heritage and tradition of championing independence and self-determination by a vigorously anticolonial policy. When the hope was not fulfilled, colonial Asia was washed in a wave of disappointment and disillusionment, the effects of which are still apparent in American relations with India, Burma, and Indonesia. Although United States action on Philippine independence was hailed throughout the area, the act in itself, at least in the view of other Asian nationalists, did not fulfill American responsibility on the colonialism issue.

Later, when independence did come to India, Pakistan, Burma, Ceylon, and Indonesia, the United States apparently either miscalculated or ignored the global implications. Clearly significant to the balance of international politics was the vacuum created in South and Southeast Asia by the conjunction of independence with the accompanying withdrawal or drastic reduction of European power. Instead of seeking to influence the course of events throughout by a consistent and active anticolonial policy followed by partnership with the newly emerging Asian states, the United States chose to limit its policy to neutrality, noninvolvement, and occasional general pronouncements favoring self-government and independence. In general, America's anticolonial convictions took active shape only in the diplomatic recognition of the new states as soon as their legal relationship with the colonial powers permitted.

Several factors contributed to this American policy of limited interest and noninvolvement in Southeast Asia. For instance, American concentration on the military aspects of the Second World War seemed to preclude in Asia, as it did in Europe, full consideration of the political and economic issues which were certain to follow victory. Again, American attachment to the idea of China as the focal point of American interest in Asia was so strong as to turn into a weakness after the war. Later, American concern with the postwar crisis in Western Europe inevitably drew attention and interest from Asia. From the outward evidence, the tone of United States postwar policy in Southeast Asia was set by the establishment of the Southeast Asian Command under Lord Mountbatten and the enlargement of the Command's area of responsibility during the Potsdam Conference in the closing months of the war. At that time the Southeast Asia Command was held responsible for the coordination of operations and occupation of all Southeast Asia, except the Philippines and the northern parts of Burma and Indochina which were assigned to the China theater. Responsibility for operations in the Philippines, Japan, and Korea and for their occupation was given to the American forces and, as often happens, these demarcations of military responsibility during the war were perpetuated afterward in postwar interests and policies.

In the advocacy of self-government and independence for the colonial areas of Asia, numerous American officials spoke bravely and wrote bluntly during the war. However, few stirring pronouncements were made in the final stages of the war and in the immediate postwar period. No energetic anticolonial policy followed the earlier expressions of purpose and conviction on the subject. Although the United States sought to avoid any part in the forcible reimposition of colonial rule in Asia, United States policy during the independence struggles was to remain neutral and to stay friendly with both sides—the Asian nationalists and the colonial powers. The general result was that the United States seemed to antagonize both sides.

Again, the United States faced an acute dilemma. How was it possible to champion actively the independence aspirations of India, Burma, Indonesia, and Indochina, and maintain close relations with Britain, France, and the Netherlands at the same time, especially when the European colonial powers considered relations with their colonial territories as matters of specially delicate political, economic, and psychological balance? American officials were confronted by this Asia-Europe dilemma even before the end of the Second World War, as is indicated in Cordell Hull's *Memoirs:*

> . . . we recognized that any change in India's constitutional status could be brought about only if Great Britain were in agreement, and we realized full well that, with Britain fighting for her life, we should take no step and utter no words that would impede her struggle. . . .
>
> At the same time there was a danger that doing nothing would have unfavorable repercussions both on the general war effort and on ourselves. After Pearl Harbor we felt that failure to solve the Indian problem would hamper military operations in the Far East and might later constitute a threat to peace when the war was over. And we also felt that our own position among the Asiatic peoples would be adversely affected by a belief on their part that we were helping Great Britain maintain her imperial policy in the Orient.
>
> With these two viewpoints in mind, we had to keep our discussions with Britain on the subject of Indian independence on as informal a basis as possible. In publicly stating our conviction that subject peoples should be assisted toward self-government and eventual independence, we kept our statements general, without making specific reference to India. But in private conversations the President talked very bluntly about India with Prime Minister Churchill just as I was talking with British Ambassador Halifax.[1]

The challenge of Soviet communist expansion in Europe and the need to strengthen and unify the states of Western Europe to meet that challenge made the dilemma immeasurably more difficult in the postwar period. American officials dealing with the problems held far from unanimous opinions on them, those most cognizant with Asian affairs in general advocating a decisive American stand on Indian, Burmese, and Indonesian independence and an interim trusteeship for Indochina, others knowledgeable primarily on European matters advocating a *status quo* and hands-off policy toward European colonial areas in Asia to avoid irritating or offending the implicated European governments. The Asia-Europe dilemma never was resolved, although now it is clear that the European-oriented voices in the State Department prevailed at a critical time when the United States subordinated its traditional attitude toward colonialism in Asia to the apparent needs for allied unity and strength in Europe.

One notable exception to the general American policy pattern of limited interest and noninvolvement in Southeast Asia is provided by the Indonesian case. Following the Japanese surrender and the Indonesian Republic's proclamation of independence, six weeks elapsed before the first allied troops from Lord Mountbatten's Southeast Asia Command landed in Indonesia. Shortly afterward, with the arrival of the first Dutch military units and civil affairs teams in October 1945, hostilities between the Dutch and Republic forces began. In an effort to break the stalemate, the British, with American support, persuaded the Dutch to negotiate with the Indonesian nationalists for a definition of terms as a basis for solution of the self-government and independence issues. After a year of difficult negotiation and intermittent warfare, the Indonesians and Dutch initialed the Linggadjati Agreement, on November 15, 1946, just two weeks before the withdrawal of British and Indian occupation forces from Indonesia. When the agreement was signed four months later, the United States extended a limited *de facto* recognition of uncertain legal status to the Indonesian Republic. It was obvious that Indonesians and Dutch were far from satisfied and that further armed conflict was certain. The United States, viewing the precarious situation, sent an *aide-mémoire* in June 1947 to urge moderation and cooperation on both sides with the added offer of discussing financial aid for Indonesian rehabilitation upon the establishment of an interim federal government and the assurance of mutual cooperation between the two countries.

When this *aide* not only was ignored but was followed by a

major Dutch military offensive, termed a "police action," the following month, the United States strongly condemned the Dutch act and made strenuous though unsuccessful efforts to induce a cessation of hostilities. On July 31, 1947, the Indonesian Case was placed before the United Nations Security Council by Australia and India, and from that time until its conclusion in the fall of 1949 was conducted in the spotlight of international publicity. Here, with the prestige of the United Nations involved and the issues of global politics engaged, the United States was forced to develop its position accordingly.

Through the course of the Indonesian Case, the United States maintained that the two parties to the dispute would have to initiate any settlement of the long-range issues between them. However, the United States offered its good offices in July 1947 to help reach a settlement outside the United Nations but with United Nations approval. The proposal was rejected by the Indonesians, who preferred United Nations arbitration as being less subject to global political pressures. After considerable searching for an acceptable formula, the United Nations Good Offices Committee was formed, consisting of Belgium as Netherlands representative, Australia as Indonesian representative, and the United States, jointly selected by both parties, as the third "impartial" member. This committee assignment steadily increased the extent of United States involvement in the case. The mutual distrust and hostility of the Indonesians and the Dutch, reflected in the positions of their Belgian and Australian representatives on the Good Offices Committee, meant that the American member, for the most part, held the initiative. When, on January 17, 1948, the Renville Agreement finally was concluded, it was greeted with premature optimism like its predecessor, the Linggadjati Agreement. Although the Renville provisions for troop withdrawals were carried out with relative success, the major issues between the two parties remained unresolved, and negotiations for implementation of the agreement dragged on for nearly a year, punctuated by armed clashes. Finally, negotiations broke down completely and the Netherlands again resorted to full-scale armed force on December 17, 1948.

The American response to the second Dutch "police action" was immediate. The American representative on the Security Council called the body into emergency session to begin full discussion of the Dutch action. The United States position, the strongest yet taken, held the Netherlands directly responsible for the renewal of hostilities without justification. The United States introduced a resolution calling for a cease fire and a Dutch withdrawal to the military lines provided in the Renville Agreement. The administrator of the Economic Cooperation Administration announced that Marshall Plan assistance intended for Dutch use in Indonesia would be suspended.

The vigorous reaction not only of the United States but of all the members of the Security Council apparently came as a surprise to the Dutch and undoubtedly weighed in their subsequent shift of policy which made possible the final settlement of Indonesian independence at the Round Table Conference at The Hague in the fall of 1949. By this time, too, the Dutch finally had perceived the military realities which existed in Indonesia. Although managing to control Indonesia's major cities and lines of communication, they had failed completely in extending their authority to the countryside where the Republic forces waged vigorous and effective guerrilla warfare against them.

Throughout the Indonesian Case United States policy was motivated by the hope of a peaceful negotiated settlement which would preserve as much stability in Indonesia as possible. However, the circumstances precluded such an orderly change. Dutch and Indonesian emotions were too deeply involved; both sides were fearful of compromising their objectives; and mutual distrust was acute. United States policy here coincided with its postwar position of neutrality in the independence struggles and of refusal in aiding the reestablishment of colonial rule in Asia. But the position of neutrality forced the United States into its deepest involvements in the case. In this position, the Indonesians and Dutch both felt, probably correctly, that wholehearted American support could determine the swing of victory. From the Indonesian viewpoint, by equivocating before the second Dutch "police action" and by continuing economic aid to the Netherlands, United States policy prolonged the struggle and made their victory more difficult. From the Dutch viewpoint, United States policy helped lose them a highly prized possession. The loss of Indonesia, in their estimate, resulted from the combination of three important factors: the denial of the use of Allied ships to transport Dutch military units to Indonesia immediately after V-J Day; American denial of support; and foreign interference in what they considered an internal affair. No matter how the American role in the Indonesian Case is assessed, it marks a major exception to the postwar pattern of United States non-involvement in Southeast Asia.

The third major assumption of United States postwar policy in the Far East based on a unified and friendly China as the leading Asian power and focal point of United States interest and policy in Asia collapsed with the communist conquest of the Chinese mainland at the end of 1949. In the next year it became only too apparent that a strong, unified China was destined to become a leading Asian power, but that it would be led by a violently anti-American communist government closely associated with the Soviet Union.

This reversal of American expectations invalidated the most important calculations of United States postwar policy in Asia. More than that, it touched off a serious internal controversy during a highly critical period in the United States. The "loss of China" produced charges and countercharges, cries of treason, and public maligning of even the highest officials, and presented a caricature of America to the world which delighted and encouraged the communist elements while undermining and alarming the nations of the free world which looked to the United States for world leadership.

The facts remain clear despite the wealth of words on the capabilities possessed by the Chiang Kai-shek régime and the influence, short of large-scale military intervention, which the United States might have exercised on China at a certain period of time. The communists decisively defeated the Kuomintang in the villages and cities of China as well as on the battlefields. Their victory was a major disaster for United States policy, and it marked an abrupt turning point in the character of United States policy toward Southeast Asia.

With China under the rule of a hostile communist régime, the United States had to reappraise its conception of requirements for security in the Pacific. Immediately Japan's role assumed new and different proportions, thus invalidating the fourth and last major assumption of United States postwar policy in the Far East; namely, that Japan never again would be permitted to become a major Pacific power. Now in the forefront of American policy planning emerged the idea of a Pacific defense perimeter based on an independent, economically viable and militarily strong Japan. To this end, John Foster Dulles, then special adviser to the Department of State, opened negotiations in the fall of 1950 for a Japanese peace treaty as a first step in transforming Japan from a defeated enemy into a positive contributor to collective security in the Pacific.

Thus, United States policy in the Far East by the beginning of 1950 rested uncomfortably on four major assumptions, all of them invalidated by events. First, a global cold war which dominated every aspect of international relations had replaced the hope for maintaining world peace through big-power unity. Second, two Southeast Asian countries already were in the throes of postwar adjustments with their ruling colonial powers which had been anything but peaceful and orderly. Indonesian independence in the early days of 1950 was an infant of a few weeks, its remembrance of the prenatal struggle as vivid and bitter as that of the mother country which spawned it. Indochina had just entered the fourth year of the war between France and the Viet Minh, which was draining France not only of strength but also of her already limited supply of international prestige. Third, China, under communist domination, had become a major United States antagonist and a close ally of the inimical Soviet Union, revealing in an urgent light the new strength and prestige of the communist régime and the weak and exposed position of the rest of Asia. Fourth, the concept of an independent, strong, and economically revived Japan suddenly seemed to be a vital keystone to American security in the Pacific.

REAPPRAISAL

The sequence of events clearly called for some drastic overhauling of United States policy. An immediate and important change came with the substitution of Southeast Asia and Japan to the position earlier reserved for China in American policy planning. Southeast Asia and Japan now became major focal points for United States diplomacy and interest in the Far East. As a result of the new and abrupt shift of American policy emphasis to Southeast Asia which represented a retreat to previously unprepared positions, the Southeast Asian countries were caught off balance psychologically. As the United States began to implement its policy adjustment with a sudden onslaught of activity in the area, most of the Southeast Asian countries became wary. They were hesitant over the idea of intimate economic, diplomatic, and security relations with the United States; they were suspicious about the new American concept of Japan's dominant role in the Pacific. Only the Philippines and Thailand were reasonably well seasoned by prior experience to withstand the shock of American courtship.

In the Philippines, a fifty-year backlog of close relations with the United States had not been entirely without difficulty, but the grant of Philippine independence had dispelled most suspicion of American motives in that country. Although Filipino dissatisfaction accompanied some of the economic terms and conditions of independence, most Filipino leaders and people recognized and accepted their ties with the United States. They entered their period of independence convinced that the future security and economic development of the Islands depended on good relations with the United States. Nevertheless, there was strong Filipino resistance to America's new plans for Japan. By 1950 general conditions in the Philippines were discouraging. In many instances per capita production and average living standards were lower than prewar, and further economic disintegration seemed to be the trend. The communist Huk rebellion was at its height in central Luzon, spreading a trail of terrorism, looting, and murder and helping to make 1950 the Philippines' darkest postindependence year.

At the beginning of 1950 Thailand's attitude and general economic position was a relatively bright spot in the Southeast Asian gloom. Although there had been confusion and uncertainty in the immediate postwar period, owing to internal political maneuvering, widespread corruption in government and skyrocketing costs of living, Thailand's general situation had improved by 1950. Large export surpluses of rice helped to bring a relatively high level of prosperity to the country, and this did more to minimize popular discontent and unrest in the country than the character of the postwar governments.

In the realm of diplomacy, American-Thai relations were close and friendly for two principal reasons. First, the Thai were eager to mend their wartime political fences. Having capitulated to the Japanese demands early in the Second World War with only token resistance, and having collaborated with the Japanese during the war and taken advantage of the wartime situation to seize four Indochinese border provinces and four northern Malayan states, the Thai governments were now anxious to regain the confidence of the Allies, especially Britain and the United States. Second, the way for the cordial relations existing between the United States and Thailand by 1950 had been paved by some astute American diplomatic spadework. This American diplomatic effort in Thailand was another of the three major exceptions to the general pattern of limited interest and noninvolvement which characterized United States policy in Southeast Asia prior to 1950. The other exceptions were the grant of Philippine independence and the American role in the Indonesian Case.

In the matter of Thailand's wartime strategy, the United States took the position that Thailand's capitulation to the Japanese was not representative of the will of the Siamese people and that the declaration of war which the Thai made on Britain and on the United States shortly after opening the Siamese borders to Japanese troops on January 25, 1942, could be disregarded. The Thai Minister in Washington, who had refused to deliver the official declaration of war to the American government, immediately after Pearl Harbor initiated a "Free Thai" movement which by the end of the war was highly organized and possessed elaborate plans for an uprising against the Japanese in Thailand. Throughout the war, both the United States and British governments cooperated closely with the Free Thai, and the United States especially tended to regard this group, rather than the wartime government in Thailand, as representative of the will of the Siamese people. Although the war ended before the Free Thai were able to put its plans into actions, the facts of its existence and growth, its outspoken pro-Allied orientation, and the personal prestige of its leaders did much to shape American policy toward postwar Thailand. As a result, the United

States regarded Thailand as a liberated rather than an enemy country at the end of the war, and began to lay the groundwork for close diplomatic ties soon afterward.

There was sharp contrast, however, between America's general approach to postwar Thailand and Great Britain's. The British had sustained extensive damage to their economic interests as well as losses of their people in Thailand. Thousands of British citizens had been interred in the country, many laboring and dying on the infamous "railway of death" with which the Japanese attempted to build an overland link from Bangkok to Rangoon. In addition, the British had reason to recollect the Japanese attacks on Malaya, Singapore, and Burma, which had been facilitated by Thailand's conduct. Although the British were not motivated by revenge, they expected full retribution for their losses and were inclined to be harsher than the United States in their treatment of Thailand.

The series of "demands" which the British presented to the Thai government at the end of the war were embodied in the Anglo-Thai Treaty of January 1, 1946, after considerable negotiation and paring. The requirement that the Thai provide 1.5 million tons of free rice as partial reparations payments to the British provided a major storm center in the treaty. Faced with starvation conditions in Malaya and India, the British were eager to enforce this provision. The Thai, depending almost entirely on rice exports for economic stability and recovery, felt that the British demands were much too high. In practice, the rice provision had the effect of diverting the major portion of Thailand's rice surplus into highly lucrative rice smuggling and black-marketing channels in which many Thai government officials were involved. The debilitating effects of the illegal rice trade, not only on Anglo-Thai relations but also on the general moral and economic situation in Thailand, led the United States to intercede with the British in an effort to obtain more lenient terms for the Thai. By this and subsequent acts designed to strengthen Thailand's economic position and to advance Thailand's interests at the level of international diplomacy, the United States established bonds with Thailand which provided a base for the development of even more intimate relations beginning in 1950.

In practical terms, American policy reaction to the new and

dangerous conditions in the Far East had begun some time before the collapse of nationalist resistance on the mainland of China. For example, President Truman, in his inaugural address of January 20, 1949, had advanced the Point Four idea of technical aid and assistance as one technique for influencing social and economic conditions in the underdeveloped areas of the world, including Southeast Asia. By the summer of 1949, the Executive Branch had presented two bills to Congress to implement the Point Four idea, although these were received with less than congressional enthusiasm.[2]

Another step in the adjustment process was taken with the appointment on July 30, 1949, of Raymond B. Fosdick, former president of the Rockefeller Foundation, and Dr. Everett Case, president of Colgate University, as nongovernmental consultants to the Department of State to work with Ambassador-at-Large Philip C. Jessup in a searching review of United States policy in the Far East. The advisory group was charged with conducting continuous evaluation of the conditions and policy problems in the area, with developing long-range plans for Asia as a region, and with lending counsel in the day-to-day decisions arising from the spread of communism in China and adjacent Asian areas. The task was to seek an understanding of the conditions which led to the impasse in China and to devise ways to prevent these conditions from being repeated in the countries of Southeast Asia.

Although the Case-Fosdick policy recommendations never were published, Mr. Fosdick reported his views of the problem and its requisite American response in a widely discussed *New York Times Magazine* article. He wrote:

> As far as American relations with Asia are concerned, one, and only one, door is open to the future: we must identify ourselves with the just and humane purposes of this revolution and make them our own. . . . Our task is clearly defined, although the techniques to be employed are not yet wholly in hand. That task is to make sure, as far as we can, that the aspirations of the people of Asia for freedom and justice and more abundant living have a fair chance. . . . We have the skills and technology, the cultural values and ideals, to make us the friend and counselor of revolutionary Asia. . . . What confronts us is a war not with armaments but with ideas. It is a war to determine which of two systems is really dedicated to the people's

welfare. . . . Those who talk of arms and a display of power as the principal counters in the game misunderstand what the game is about. Arms undoubtedly have their place, but we are up against a set of ideas, and ideas cannot be stopped with bombs or battleships. The only way to beat an idea is with a better idea, and that better idea has got to be an idea that works.[3]

Mr. Fosdick also urged the establishment of a strong Point Four program as vital to America's Far Eastern policy and as the most effective weapon possible to halt the spread of communism.

Although it is not possible to determine the influence which the Case-Fosdick mission had on subsequent American foreign policy, it is clear that the general spirit and philosophy of the Fosdick article coincided with the prevailing convictions of an increasing number of American citizens and government officials. Under constant review by the Department of State since the end of the war, the Southeast Asian situation was felt by many representatives charged with responsibility toward the area either on the spot or in Washington to have been neglected during the postwar period to the detriment of American interests and, ultimately, American security. These officials, convinced that a sympathetic, active support and encouragement of the economic, social, and political awakening of Southeast Asia could best serve United States interests, had pressed for more active and forward-looking American policies toward the area. They sought an approach which would emphasize economic development, technical assistance, health, education, information, and welfare activities, and which would play down military solutions to problems of political unrest, economic instability, and communist organizational and propaganda gains. It was not until the China situation had bogged down to a hopeless morass and the European situation had given some signs of improvement that these views were accorded a more sympathetic hearing.

FACT-FINDING AND FENCE-MENDING IN 1950

For the United States the first six months of 1950 were an anxious period of fact-finding, reappraisal, and fence-mending in Southeast Asia. Such a rapid succession of official missions, major policy speeches, congressional debates, and stepped-up American diplomatic activity was directed toward the area that the suspicious reactions of the governments and people of Southeast Asia are not surprising.[4]

Secretary of State Acheson, in a major policy address before the National Press Club in Washington, on January 12, 1950, laid down American policy essentials towards Asia in direct and forthright terms. He made six key points directly applicable to Southeast Asia. These were:

1. Although the factors influencing United States policy toward the area are extremely diverse, two are common to the experience of nearly all Asian people. First is the "revulsion against the acceptance of misery and poverty as the normal condition of life," and second is the "revulsion against foreign domination. . . ."
2. The basic interests of Americans and of the peoples of Southeast Asia are parallel.
3. American policy is not motivated simply by the desire to stop the spread of communism but by a deeper reason; namely, that communism "is really the spearhead of Russian imperialism which would, if it could, take from these people what they have won and what we want them to keep and develop, which is their own national independence, their own development of their own resources for their own good. . . ."
4. The American defense perimeter runs from the Aleutians to Japan, the Ryukyus and the Philippines. "So far as the military security of the other areas in the Pacific is concerned, it must be clear that no person can guarantee these areas against military attack. . . . Should such an attack occur . . . the initial reliance must be on the people attacked to resist it and then upon the commitments of the entire civilized world under the Charter of the United Nations."
5. "It is a mistake . . . in considering Pacific and Far Eastern problems to become obsessed with military considerations. Important as they are, there are other problems that press, and these other problems are not capable of solution through military means. These other problems arise out of the susceptibility of many areas . . . to subversion and penetration."

6. The United States stands ready to help in any way it can, but the extent of effective American assistance is limited. "American assistance can be effective when it is the missing component in a situation which might otherwise be solved. The United States cannot furnish all these components to solve the question. It cannot furnish determination, it cannot furnish the will, and it cannot furnish the loyalty of a people to its government."

As a reaction to a series of provocations climaxed by the seizure of United States consular property, the American Government recalled on January 14, 1950, its official representatives remaining in China. The brutal treatment which many of these officials received at the hands of the communists and the difficulty which they experienced in attempting to leave China greatly increased American feelings of bitterness toward the Chinese communist régime. This recall of American officials was tantamount to severance of diplomatic relations, an act which formalized a cleavage over policy toward China between the United States and several friendly governments both in Asia and in Europe.

On January 19, 1950, Assistant Secretary of State George C. McGhee, speaking to the Annual Press Institute, applauded the British Commonwealth decision to develop an "economic program for South and Southeast Asia based on principles of self-help and mutual aid." The Assistant Secretary indicated that the United States would be willing to adapt its own efforts in furtherance of this program, later known as the Colombo Plan. To counteract the expressed view of Asian people that they had been neglected by the United States in favor of Western Europe, he assured the Asian people that the United States genuinely desired to encourage their nationalist aspirations and to assist them in surmounting their basic problems. Referring to the critical situation in the Far East resulting from events in China, he pointed up the need of the peoples of South and Southeast Asia for voluntary association with other free peoples of the world to increase stability in the area.

Still in January, 1950, Ambassador Jessup began a three-month fact-finding tour of fourteen Far Eastern countries. Purposes of the Jessup Mission were severalfold: to remind the Southeast Asian countries that they had not been forgotten, to make a first-hand survey of conditions in the area, to explore with the Southeast Asian governments ways and means in which the United States could help toward economic and political stability and security, and to review United States policy with the American diplomats in the field.

Ambassador Jessup's statements in the course of his tour are indicative of the concern which American policy-makers felt toward the Indochina situation. To Bao Dai in Saigon, he expressed the hope of closer relations between the United States and Vietnam. In hinting at impending American recognition of the three Indochinese régimes, he included Cambodia and Laos by name. Still on the subject of Indochina, he declared several days later in Djakarta that the United States had no intention of supporting colonialism in Indochina but was interested in supporting and assisting the national independence of Vietnam and other states. His statement clearly was intended to counteract the widely held Southeast Asian belief that United States recognition of the Bao Dai régime, regarded as a tool of the French, was tantamount to supporting French colonialism in Vietnam. In Singapore, on February 6th, Ambassador Jessup stated that the United States would view any armed aggression against Indochina as "a very grave matter." At the same time he hinted at the possibility of some form of emergency economic aid in view of the need of quick action to help save Southeast Asia from communism.

On February 7th, following long-delayed action by the French Assembly on agreements pertaining to a wider degree of self-government and independence for them, the United States formally recognized the three states of Vietnam, Cambodia, and Laos within the French Union. American recognition of the three states followed communist China's and the Soviet Union's recognition of Ho Chi Minh's Viet Minh régime by several days.

The Jessup Mission was climaxed by a Conference of American Ambassadors called by Ambassador Jessup on February 13th in Bangkok to search for an understanding of the conditions in the area and for affirmative steps to be taken by the United States in accordance with these conditions. Here at a three-day meeting at top level, diplomats in Southeast Asian posts had an opportunity to press their case for a strong American effort to curtail communist penetration in Southeast Asia. Discussions took place which ranged the entire field of American foreign policy in Southeast Asia. These included economic, political, and social problems of the Southeast Asian countries, the problems and potential of the Point Four program which at the time was before Congress, the matter of regional economic and security associations in Asia, implications of American recognition of Vietnam, Cambodia, and Laos, the war between France and the Viet Minh then in progress, the ramifications of a Japanese peace treaty, the problem of protecting Southeast Asia from communist aggression and subversion. According to a State Department communiqué, discussions at the conference "were conducted within the general framework of the announced policy of the United States to support the independence and nationalist aspirations of all Asian peoples."

Ambassador Jessup, returning to Washington at the conclusion of the conference with the vituperative Senator McCarthy baying at his heels, reported on March 29th to the Senate Committee on Foreign Relations, which was holding hearings on Southeast Asian aid, that in his view Indochina, Burma, and Thailand were priority problems. He advised sending military aid, especially small arms, to help support the anticommunist effort in Indochina; but in doing so he stressed the importance of economic aid and technical assistance rather than military aid. He urged that the United States make clear its purposes through an information and education campaign in Asia. On April 13th he reiterated his recommendations to the nation in a radio report summarizing America's Southeast Asian policy in six key points:

> The United States believes that every people has the right to be independent, to govern itself, and to work out its own problems in its own way. We have demonstrated this belief . . . in our relations with the Philippines, with the Republic of Korea and with the United States of Indonesia.
>
> The United States believes in the institutions of democratic government, and encourages the practice of democratic government wherever it is possible to do so. . . .
>
> The United States believes that free people who are determined to maintain their independence are entitled to military aid which will help them to remain free. . . .
>
> The United States, within the limits of its resources, gives economic aid, in the form of loans and technical assistance, where such aid is wanted and can help people to help themselves. An example of such aid is the recent Export-Import Bank loan to Indonesia. . . .

We shall continue to carry on a vigorous information program to make known the purposes and policies of the United States. . . .

We shall continue to work through the United Nations as well as through direct diplomatic channels to encourage the settlement of disputes that endanger peace and stability. . . .

Meanwhile, President Truman, on February 9th, was discussing with President Quirino the question of sending an economic mission to Manila. The Import-Export Bank, in a move fraught with political as well as economic significance, announced a $100,000,000 economic reconstruction loan to Indonesia on February 10th. And on February 14th, as President Truman was signing the Far Eastern Economic Assistance Act of 1950 in Washington, Soviet and Chinese officials in Moscow were signing a thirty-year Soviet-Chinese treaty of mutual friendship, alliance, and assistance.

On February 16th Secretary Acheson gave his ringing speech on "total diplomacy." "The only way to deal with the Soviet Union," said Acheson, "is to create situations of strength. Whereever the Soviet detects weakness or disunity—and it is quick to detect them—it exploits them to the full." American foreign policy, according to the Secretary of State, had to consist of two interrelated branches to meet the Soviet challenge. "First, we must be prepared to meet wherever possible all thrusts of the Soviet Union. . . . The second part of our foreign policy must be to create those economic, political, social and psychological conditions that strengthen and create confidence in the democratic way of life." He urged patience and self-discipline on the American people and close voluntary cooperation among the various branches of government and, in fact, upon all American national organizations in a concerted effort at "total diplomacy" to meet and defeat the communist menace.

The Asia calendar continued active through the month, the Department of State announcing on February 23rd its intent to send a special mission to Southeast Asia, headed by R. Allen Griffin, publisher of the Monterey (California) *Peninsula Herald* and former Deputy Head of the China ECA Mission. The objectives of the Griffin Mission were "to prepare the way for the most expeditious and efficient use of whatever technical assistance funds may become available for that area . . . to study the needs for possible projects throughout the area and also lay the groundwork for anticipated programs under the Point Four legislation."

It was at this point that American officials were beginning to express frankly their alarm at the possible weakening of Southeast Asian leaders to communist pressures owing to the "bandwagon psychology" which was developing in the wake of Chinese and Viet Minh communist successes. While reports were being circulated of substantial increases of Chinese aid to Ho Chi Minh and requests for large-scale American military and economic aid were being made by Vietnamese and French officials, there took place an inauspicious sequence of events which could and should have been avoided. A few days after the arrival of the Griffin Mission in Saigon to discuss American economic and technical aid with Vietnamese and French officials, segments of the American Pacific Fleet proceeded to pay a "goodwill" visit to Saigon, and war planes from the United States aircraft carrier *Boxer* took off on "goodwill" flights over northern Vietnam. This prankish display of United States military strength in the teeth of a discussion of American economic aid proved too blatant a reminder of the carrot-and-whip era of gunboat diplomacy to go unnoticed by either communists or noncommunists in Southeast Asia. In Saigon, large-scale protest riots broke out on March 18th and 19th, and Viet Minh forces fired on American warships in the harbor.

On March 15th Secretary Acheson made the first important public statement on the concept of the Truman Doctrine to Southeast Asia. In a speech before the Commonwealth Club of San Francisco, he applied United States policy in Southeast Asia in the context of the Truman Doctrine that "the United States must support free people who are resisting attempted subjugation by armed minorities or outside pressures."

In early April the Far East was high on the docket as John Foster Dulles, appointed as special consultant to the Secretary of State, began exploratory conversations to lay the groundwork for negotiating a peace treaty with Japan. Secretary Acheson, reporting on the issues of the cold war before the American Society of Newspaper Editors on April 22nd, amplified the complexity of the communist threat and repeated the call for unified and concerted "total diplomacy" by the American nation.

Still in April, the beleaguered overseas information program received a new lease on life following a postwar interval of congressional neglect and abuse, particularly directed to the enfeebled Voice of America. The first hopeful note came when a large number of congressmen, who had toured Europe in the summer of 1947 to see for themselves the conditions leading to Marshall Plan proposals, returned home sufficiently disturbed by the barrage of Soviet propaganda against the Marshall Plan to be ready to support an improved and expanded American information program. Permanent legislative authorization for such an overseas information program thereupon was provided by the Smith-Mundt Act of January 1948 which was expected somehow to produce dramatic results. After a year of vain waiting, a United States Advisory Committee on Information, in March 1949, recommended the appropriation of $36,000,000 for the fiscal year 1950, representing a substantial increase over the previous year, to help raise the Voice of America mumble to a roar. While this served to whet congressional expectations all the more on the prospective accomplishments of the information program and to increase earlier controversy on the message to be brought to the peoples of the world by the Voice of America, the Bureau of the Budget combined with Congress to dim any realities of expansion by cutting the recommended appropriation in half. This same story was repeated through the year 1949 into the first part of 1950. Then, President Truman speaking before the American Society of Newspaper Editors on April 20th scored a hit with the use of the phrase "Campaign of Truth."

"We must make ourselves known as we really are," he said, "not as Communist propaganda pictures us. We must pool our efforts with those of the other free peoples in a sustained, intensified program to promote the cause of freedom against the propaganda of slavery. We must make ourselves heard round the world in a great campaign of truth."

A catchword could scarcely solve many of the problems which the overseas information program was encountering, but the President's address tied to increasing congressional awareness gave new force to the overseas information effort and the burden of campaigning for truth.

On May 8th the Secretary of State, having conferred with the

French foreign minister in Paris, announced that the United States would provide economic aid and military equipment to the Associated States of Indochina and to France to assist in restoring stability to the Indochina states and to help them pursue their peaceful and democratic development. The statement revealed American recognition of the fact that France and the governments and peoples of Indochina held primary responsibility for meeting the communist threat in Indochina. It was soon backed by direct communiqués on May 24th to the French government and the chiefs of state of Vietnam, Laos, and Cambodia announcing inauguration of an American economic aid program and the establishment of a special economic mission to the Associated States to be stationed in Saigon. The first allotment for economic aid amounted to $23,000,000.

On May 11th the Griffin Mission, returning to Washington from its economic survey of Southeast Asia, recommended a program of $64,000,000 for economic aid to the area and a reported $30,000,000 for military aid. The Department of State decided against making the Griffin Mission recommendations public because they were still "in process of review, and negotiations with the governments concerned are being carried on."

In this same period, a Conference of Foreign Ministers in London provided Secretary Acheson an opportunity to clarify and coordinate American policy in Southeast Asia with the French and British foreign ministers. According to a statement released to the press on May 20th, Secretary Acheson had reviewed the entire Southeast Asia situation with Mr. Bevin and Mr. Schuman. In the discussions, recognition was made of Britain's and France's "legitimate interests" in Malaya and Indochina where, it was agreed, scarcely any further contributions could be expected for the total regional defense of Southeast Asia. The three officials also agreed that communist aggression in Europe and in Southeast Asia was linked and that appropriate measures to combat it would have to be made in those two vital areas of the world. When Secretary Acheson reported to Congress on the conference, he reiterated American recognition of French and British responsibility, stating that American aid to Indochina would be complementary to French efforts there and that, in the rest of Southeast Asia, American aid would be coordinated with the Colombo Plan of the British Commonwealth, then in process of formulation.

During early June 1950, Secretary Acheson told the Senate Foreign Affairs and Armed Services committees that the funds which Congress had provided for the general China area under the Mutual Defense Assistance Act of 1949 had enabled the nation's executive branch to initiate measures strengthening the noncommunist states of Southeast Asia and showing America's determination to support France and the states of the French Union in the struggle to preserve the freedom and integrity of Indochina. "Military aid," he said, "when such aid can be effective, is an essential element of our course of action."

President Truman on June 5th signed the Foreign Economic Assistance Act which authorized the third year of the European Recovery Program and which provided for establishment of the Point Four Program. The United Nations Technical Assistance Conference, scheduled to be held originally in 1949 but postponed because of the uncertainty of United States participation, finally followed from June 12th to 14th. During its session, the United States pledged to underwrite some $12,000,000, or 60 per cent, of the United Nations Technical Assistance program budget.

A NEW POLICY OUTLOOK

What is the import of this chronology of events, American policy statements, and American policy actions toward Southeast Asia in the first half of 1950? Certainly it is a reflection of the new American concern toward Southeast Asia, the growing American awareness of the area's importance to American security. It suggests in skeletal form the vigorous American effort which has been adopted to recoup in some measure the opportunities for influencing the course of events in Southeast Asia, forfeited in the initial postwar period, and to offset the effects of the earlier policy of limited interest and noninvolvement. More than anything else, perhaps, it presents the shadow of a new policy orientation beginning to assume form and dimension.

Throughout the cold-war period, the complex problems posed by communism seemed doomed to be regarded by a large segment of the public, Congress, and even government officialdom primarily in military terms. On this basis, military force seemed to be considered its sole effective counter weapon. Secretary Acheson's "cold war" and "total diplomacy" speeches tried in some measure to dispel this belief and to counter the oversimplified analysis which would seem to ignore the encompassing nature of communist tactics whose wedges are driven by psychological, economic, and political techniques as much as by any military strategy.

While valid and frequently repeated, the claim that the United States has served the interests of all noncommunist countries as well as its own by determinedly resisting communist expansion also has tended to oversimplify the problem of communism in Southeast Asia. Although the claim has given comfort to some noncommunist countries and raised denials in only a few, still the majority of noncommunist countries have not been prepared to subordinate their interests and policies to this overriding identity of aim, despite the moral pressure to do so in the view of many Americans.

Between 1947 and 1950, the communist threat in Asia was viewed by a less articulate minority segment primarily in nonmilitary terms. This reasoning was based on the premise that widespread discontent with the economic, political, and social order of things has given communism its strength as an ideological world force. Its obvious counteraction, therefore, lay in changing the conditions in which communism flourished rather than in relying on mechanical military solutions for problems whose character was essentially psychological. Applied to Southeast Asia, this analysis called for programs of economic, technical, educational, social, and political construction and for a general attitude of American participation in the Asian revolution.

Divided into these two general currents of thought, the lines of American response to the communist program never became so sharply delineated as to focus on one side to the exclusion of the other. In fact, people on each side admitted the validity of certain aspects of the alternate program, while in neither case were there available the requisite estimates of need or of assistance to support the advocated programs. Although no basic difference was represented in the broad objectives of the conflicting viewpoints, the serious division concerned the method of approach, emphasis, and techniques for pursuing these same objectives. The communist victory in China which made extensive use of military activities in its final stages—the "armed struggle" phase of the communist revolution—only served to emphasize these latter differences by strengthening the case on the one side and clouding it further on the other.

The proponents of a forceful and militant policy tended to stress, even overstress, United States capacity to impel other countries to follow the dictates of American foreign policy. By contrast, the Secretary of State and those officials who dealt directly with foreign governments were extremely conscious of foreign policy limitations, and felt the grave responsibility of decision-making at a time when only a thin and indistinct line could be drawn between hot and cold war.

During the first six months of 1950, the new policy orientation which appeared to be taking shape underscored the importance of removing the causes of communist appeal and success in Southeast Asia. Internal Southeast Asian conditions which admitted specific opportunities for communist penetration and subversion were the concern of the Case-Fosdick Mission, the Jessup Mission, and the Griffin Mission, as well as of the Secretary of State, whose interest in these conditions and in techniques for alleviating them were revealed in statements on the problem. New activity included efforts to make economic and technical aid, a vigorous information program, and educational and training programs key American activities in Southeast Asia, to score the similarity of interests between Americans and Asians, and to high-light American concurrence in the matter of helping the Southeast Asian peoples achieve their own goals in their own way. Policy-wise, the changing orientation seemed to accommodate the idea that the "containment" policy did not bear transferral from Europe to Southeast Asia in the same terms and that, instead, emphasis was to be placed on constructive programs for Southeast Asia which would make use of the positive elements ordinarily stated negatively in the policy of "containment." Strong opposition continued to come from the protagonists of military solutions to communist threats and from the hard core within the State Department's European division who resisted any openly anti-French line in Indochina. In addition, the venomous McCarthy campaign, without actually changing administration foreign policy, managed to weaken the general conduct of foreign affairs and to hamper positive readjustment of Far Eastern policy. Although in process of evolving by June, 1950, an American policy for Southeast Asia, guided by these concepts and attitudes, still had not emerged in fact.

The question of whether an earlier shift in American policy might have saved the day in Indochina, or decisively have altered the course of American relations with the countries of Southeast Asia, is difficult to resolve for several reasons. On the Asian side, few nationalist Southeast Asian régimes were committed wholeheartedly to the economic and political reforms which were needed to meet the communist challenge. On the American side, it is dubious that Washington entirely understood the depths of revolutionary fervor racking Southeast Asia or that, having understood, could have shifted American foreign policy far enough and fast enough to embrace the revolution in process. Nor is it probable that either Washington or the American people thoroughly appreciated the wide gap which existed between America's professed objectives and America's concrete policy actions in Southeast Asia or realized the extent of basic policy action which would have to be redirected to close that gap.

Despite these factors, there is no question that the United States was headed toward an active foreign policy, at least partially attuned to the conditions, needs, and aspirations of the people of Southeast Asia, and that, by mid-1950, the first steps toward joining the procession of human events in the area had been taken.

KOREA CHANGES EVERYTHING

On June 25, 1950, without warning, North Korean armies, which the Soviet Union had equipped, trained, and sponsored, initiated their frontal assault on the Republic of Korea.

The United Nations Security Council, called at once into emergency session, ordered an immediate cease fire in Korea and the withdrawal of North Korean forces. Two days later, on June 27th, it called upon United Nations members "to furnish such assistance to the Republic of Korea as may be necessary to repel the armed attack and to restore international peace and security in the area." That day, President Truman gave orders for American air and sea forces to support the South Korean troops and for the United States Seventh Fleet to prevent any attack on Formosa or any action from Formosa against the China mainland. The President announced substantial increases in military aid to the Philippines and Indochina and the dispatch of American military missions to Manila and Saigon. On June 30th he authorized missions by the American Air Force above the thirty-eighth parallel, the use of American ground forces in the Korean War, and a naval blockade of the Korean coast.

To the United States, the act of communist aggression in Korea indicated three important facts. First, the communists were willing to resort to overt international aggression—if they thought they could get away with it. Second, noncommunist military power was critically weak. Third, the distinct possibility of communist aggression elsewhere existed.

The Korean War had basic and instant effects on American policy. It caused the United States to begin a major rearmament effort and limited remobilization at home; in Europe, it caused the United States to prod Atlantic Alliance members to build up their military forces. In foreign policy generally, it added the impetus which resulted in the United States placement of military considerations at the front of every issue. By way of illustration, the United States originally gave Marshall Plan aid with the stipulation that none of it be used for military purposes. Less than a year after the start of the Korean War, the military effect of Marshall Plan aid was the overriding consideration in its allotment. By 1952 almost 80 per cent of American aid to Europe went in the form of military equipment, the rest in "defense support." Although this extreme policy emphasis never prevailed in Southeast Asia, as the Korean War progressed, American policy toward the area focused with increasing bluntness on questions of military strength while it pushed further out of scrutiny the importance of economic, political, social, and psychological factors.

United States policy toward Southeast Asia clearly indicated the same shift of emphasis. On July 5th the State Department sent a newly created military survey mission under John Melby to visit Indochina, Malaya, Indonesia, Burma, Thailand, and the

Philippines. The Melby Mission was expected to determine the military build-up possible in each of the visited countries, to recommend priorities for arms shipments, to discuss the composition of American military advisory groups which could be assigned to each country. In view of these purposes, the Melby Mission was received unofficially by the Indonesian government which thus registered its objections, and was forced to cancel its scheduled Burma visit when the Burmese government signified its opposition to military alignment.

On June 29th announcement was made of an American economic survey mission to the Philippines under Daniel Bell, former Under Secretary of the Treasury. The Bell Mission, issuing its report in October, strongly, yet objectively, condemned many aspects of Philippine economic and governmental administration and recommended far-reaching reforms as a requisite before any increase of American economic aid to that country. At the same time military aid to the Philippines continued in increasing amounts. To coordinate foreign information and psychological strategy, the Department of State on August 17th announced the establishment of a national psychological strategy board under the chairmanship of the Secretary of State to include representatives of the Departments of Defense, the Joint Chiefs of Staff, and the Central Intelligence Agency.

The Japanese peace treaty and the continued strengthening of Asian military and economic power were on the agenda when Dean Rusk, Assistant Secretary of State for Far Eastern Affairs, spoke on September 9th. "We shall view with sympathy any joint effort which the nations of Asia and the Far East might wish to make in behalf of the security or the well-being of the area as a whole," he declared.

Following this line, Congress added a substantial emergency defense appropriation to the Mutual Defense Assistance Program for 1950–1951, including in the additional allotment $303,000,000 for use in Southeast Asia and the Philippines and $75,000,000 for the general area of China. An additional $27,500,000 were earmarked for the Philippines, Korea, and Iran which had been included as a unit in the original appropriations. In the event of further aggression, the United States made a proposal to the United

Nations for a "Uniting for Peace" plan under which the General Assembly, to act quickly and effectively, could by-pass a Soviet veto in the Security Council.

From San Francisco, President Truman on October 17th called upon the free world to build up its defenses. He declared:

> Events in Korea have made it more apparent than ever that the evil spirit of aggression is still abroad in the world. So long as this is true, we are all faced with a clear and present danger. . . . The free men of the world have but one choice if they are to remain free. They must oppose strength with strength. This is not the task for the United States alone. It is a task for the free nations to undertake together. . . .

The President, turning specifically to Asian affairs, continued:

> Today, the peoples of the Far East, as well as peoples in other parts of the world, are struggling with the false revolution of communism. . . . In this time of crisis, we ask the peoples of the Far East to understand us as we try to understand them. We are not trying to push blueprints upon them as ready-made answers for all their complicated problems. Every people must develop according to its own particular genius and must express its own moral and cultural values in its own way. . . .

By October, Chinese communist troops had two new targets—Tibet and Korea. When communist Chinese extended their intervention in the Korean War to new dimensions soon afterward, it became, in the words of General MacArthur, a "new war" which precipitated a further American paradox. The inhibitions imposed by the United Nations clearly weakened American military policy in the Korean War, while military considerations, imposed by the stark realities of communist military capability, contrived to weaken American foreign policy both toward Southeast Asia and toward Europe.

On December 30th Secretary Acheson reviewed the events of 1950 and outlined policies for the coming year, 1951, in a covering statement: "We will redouble our efforts to build situations of strength to meet trouble wherever it threatens. . . . Economic aid will be carried forward—although re-directed where necessary to contribute to the military strength of the free world."

As the pattern of policy emerged by the end of 1950, its orientation was clearly in the direction of military defense. For Southeast

Asian peoples interested chiefly in the fulfillment of independence, in the development of internal economic systems, and in expansion of technical capabilities, America's military orientation had specific meanings. These included such possibilities as the following: (1) intensified pressure for overt alignment with the anticommunist alliance; (2) American aid as a diplomatic lever in the construction of a united front against communism in Asia; (3) the necessity for a stand in opposition to a brother Asian nation; (4) sacrifices in economic and public welfare programs in order to create, equip, and train modern military forces; (5) the construction of military superstructures on weak economic, social, and political foundations. Not all Southeast Asian leaders were willing to accept these implications.

6. THE SHAPE OF POLICY—KOREA TO MANILA

During the Korean War, United States policy operated in the Far East on a military-crisis basis. Scant opportunity existed for focusing on the delicate balance between military and economic measures in Southeast Asia or on long-range diplomatic problems. The Korean armistice agreements resulting from the political and military stalemate in Korea provided only a temporary respite which was followed almost immediately by a steadily deteriorating military situation in Indochina which soon reached crisis proportions. Despite unusually strenuous last-minute efforts by the French, and heavy matériel backing by the United States, the war against Ho Chi Minh's communist forces turned from bad to worse. With the dramatic defense and final collapse of Dienbienphu and the Indochina armistice agreements, another dismal chapter in the story of the war between France and the Viet Minh was concluded.

The Indochina armistice agreements were far from satisfactory from a United States policy stand; but, for the first time in several years, they did bring a measure of peace to Asia, however uncertain and temporary. The settlement also meant that, even though the Indochina crisis continued, its character had shifted from military to political and economic, providing relief from emergency military decisions and a chance at last for some long-range policy planning and programming.

At the conclusion of the Indochina armistice agreements, the United States moved quickly to create a collective security organization for Southeast Asia in the hope of preventing a recurrence of communist aggression in South Vietnam, Laos, Cambodia, Thailand, or East Pakistan. Terms were set in the Southeast Asia Defense Treaty, signed on September 8, 1954, at Manila.

From the period of the Korean War to the Manila Pact, the United States gave primary consideration in Southeast Asia to the need for building a protective bulwark against external communist aggression and, in doing so, based its policy in the area on four cornerstones. These were: (1) deterrence of aggression, (2) collective security, (3) economic and technical aid programs, and (4) support of noncommunist South Vietnam. The four cornerstones are prime considerations for an understanding of the many pitfalls and problems which beset American policy toward Southeast Asia today.

THE STRATEGY TO DETER AGGRESSION

The strategy to deter aggression is the pivotal point. Its strength is embodied in the concept of "massive retaliation" which emerged in President Eisenhower's second State of the Union Address, in January 1954, almost a year after he first laid the groundwork for it in his initial State of the Union Address.

At the time of the first address, in February 1953, the President declared that the problem of the United States was to achieve adequate military strength within the limits of "endurable strain" on the economy and that the amassing of military power without regard to economic capacity would be in the nature of defending the nation against one form of disaster by inviting another. In essence, the President's formula was the same one which friendly and allied countries in Asia and Europe were applying to their own situations.

Although the previous administration had grappled with the identical military versus political and economic theme, President Eisenhower's administration approached the subject with a different slant on the capacity of the American economy and of the American military role in any future Asian war.

For example, President Eisenhower's "new look" defense policy, the policy planned to gear the United States military budget to long-term requirements, envisaged "the development of an armed posture . . . supported year in and year out on a long-term basis," a concentration on mobile striking forces making the necessary economies in manpower and resources, full use of new weapons and techniques, and a national airpower "superior to that of any other nation."

Admiral Arthur Radford, Chairman of the Joint Chiefs of Staff, describing the "new look" to the National Press Club in December 1953, said:

. . . we plan force levels which provide us mobile, versatile, combat forces in readiness, and an adequate mobilization base. These strength levels will be of such magnitude that our allies can recognize both our determination to counter any aggression and our determination to support our national and international policies and commitments. At the same time, these levels will be those which are possible of attainment over the long pull.

The President and the National Security Council, by approving the 1954–1957 military budget estimates which included appropriations reduced in line with the long-term strategy, on December 19, 1953, endorsed the "new-look" program.

In his second State of the Union Address, President Eisenhower reported:

As we enter this new year, our military power continues to grow. This power is for our own defense and to deter aggression. We shall not be aggressors, but we and our allies have and will maintain a massive capability to strike back. Here are some of the considerations in our defense planning. First, while determined to use atomic power to serve the usages of peace, we take into full account our great and growing number of nuclear weapons and the most effective means of using them against an aggressor if they are needed to preserve our freedom. . . . Second, the usefulness of these new weapons creates new relationships between men and materials. These new relationships permit economies in the use of men as we build forces suited to our situation in the world today. As will be seen from the budget message on January 21, the air power of our Navy and Air Force is receiving heavy emphasis. Third, our armed forces must regain mobility of action. Our strategic reserves must be centrally placed and readily deployable to meet sudden aggression against ourselves and our allies.

Secretary Dulles, defining the administration's strategy in further detail, signified the foreign policy implications of massive retaliation:

Local defense will always be important, but there is no local defense which alone will contain the mighty landpower of the communist world. Local defenses must be reinforced by the further deterrent of massive retaliatory power. A potential aggressor must know that he cannot always prescribe battle conditions that suit him. Otherwise, for example, a potential aggressor, who is glutted with manpower, might be tempted to attack in confidence that resistance would be confined to manpower. He might be tempted to attack in places where his superiority was decisive. The way to deter aggression is for the free community to be willing and able to respond vigorously at places and with means of its own choosing.[1]

It was the Secretary's pronouncement that the basic policy decision of the United States was "to depend primarily upon a great capacity to retaliate, instantly, by means and at places of our choosing," as the best means of deterring attack and, in the event of aggression, as the best way of ensuring victory. He sounded two clear warnings by this policy statement: (1) in the event of aggression, retaliation could include the use of nuclear weapons; (2) retaliatory measures would not necessarily be confined to the point of aggression.

On the intent to maintain American military bases in Okinawa, the Secretary declared that this was necessary "to ensure adequate striking power to implement the collective security concept"; and, in line with President Eisenhower's earlier statement, he reiterated that United States military forces in the Far East would feature "highly mobile naval, air and amphibious units."

The work of providing the massive retaliatory power in the strategy to deter aggression is thus clearly assigned to the American forces. According to this scheme, an aggressor would encounter a two-pronged response. At the point of attack the response would be that of the local forces of the country under assault, buttressed by American material aid and, perhaps, naval and air support. This would leave United States forces free for retaliation "by means and at places" of American choice and from bases maintained for that purpose for dealing a series of massive blows designed to overwhelm the aggressor. Presumably at the realization that such retaliatory measures would outweigh any possible gain from an act of aggression, the potential aggressor would be deterred.

Following the "new-look" defense policy and this concept of

security through deterrence at the threat of massive retaliation, the process of integrating nuclear weapons into the American military structure as standard components of American military planning, equipment, and training was begun during 1954 and 1955. At the same time, American military manpower and budget levels were reduced. Theoretically, the resulting slack in the general security was taken up by heavy emphasis on the Strategic Air Command, guided-missile development, nuclear-weapons production, tactical atomic artillery, and tactical atomic bombs suitable for precision delivery on pinpoint targets. The heavy reliance on air-atomic power and tactical atomic weapons which is now being built into America's strategy to deter aggression is the natural outgrowth of a defense policy established on the premise of increased long-range security at less cost at a time of expanding American military commitments in the Far East. The circumstances offered no alternative in the planning by the Joint Chiefs of Staff other than that of exploiting to the full America's technical and scientific capacity for strategic and tactical nuclear warfare.

Partly as a result of the concern expressed by America's European allies, and partly as a reaction to American criticism, several officials have sought to "clarify" and further "explain" the massive retaliation doctrine. For instance, Vice President Nixon gave an explanation which did little to allay European fears. He said:

> Rather than let the Communists nibble us to death all over the world in little wars we would rely in the future primarily on our massive mobile retaliatory power which we could use in our discretion against the major source of aggression at times and places that we choose. We adjusted our armed strength to meet the requirements of this new concept and, what was just as important, we let the world and we let the Communists know what we intended to do.[2]

Chester Bowles, onetime American Ambassador to India, raising several pertinent questions about the "instant retaliation" doctrine in a *New York Times Magazine* article, issued a challenge for a "great debate" on the points involved in "what appears to be a far-reaching shift in our foreign policy." [3] He was answered by Senate Majority Leader William Knowland, in a clarification intended "to correct some of the erroneous impressions" which the senator felt were created by Mr. Bowles's article.[4] "We did not and would not expect to rely solely on the atomic weapon. The essence of the new policy is to develop a wider range of effective measures—economic, political and psychological as well as military —and thus be enabled to combat communism more effectively," Senator Knowland wrote. The doctrine "is neither a fundamental shift in the nation's foreign policy nor a refinement and restatement of past policies" but is "a departure from the policy of containment. . . ." Senator Knowland stressed the fact that the Kremlin would not be warned in advance of America's defensive methods and the character of American retaliation in case of aggression: "That part of our foreign policy which, in case of open aggression, calls for instant retaliation 'at places of our own choosing' means that if and when the United States national interest requires active resistance to further Communist aggression, reprisal would be appropriate to the area and objective."

Former Secretary of State Dean Acheson, joining the *Times*-article fray, questioned the effect of the doctrine on the Western Alliance whose unity had been so laboriously nurtured and built up in the previous administration.[5]

Despite the conflicting viewpoints, final clarification of the policy at the present date of writing must rest on Secretary Dulles's testimony before the Senate Committee on Foreign Relations. Characterizing the nature of the communist threat in a reference to the Soviet bloc, Secretary Dulles said:

> Its great strength is manpower, but also it is strong in terms of planes, submarines, and atomic capabilities. . . . The Soviet bloc also commands a political apparatus which operates in every country of the world, seeking to capitalize upon all of the discontents and unsatisfied ambitions which inevitably exist in greater or less degree throughout the free world. . . . The threat is virtually unlimited so far as time is concerned. . . . It operates in terms of what Lenin and Stalin called "an entire historical era." [6]

In the consideration of an American policy to meet the communist threat, Secretary Dulles declared that

> military defense must be within the capacity of the free world to sustain for an indefinite time without such impairment of its economic and social fabric as would expose it to piecemeal seizure from within by the political

apparatus of communism. The free nations should not attempt to match the Soviet bloc man for man and gun for gun. The best way to deter aggression is to make the aggressor know in advance that he will suffer damage outweighing what he can hope to gain. Thus an aggressor must not be able to count upon a sanctuary status for those resources which he does not use in committing aggression. To apply this deterrent principle the free world must maintain and be prepared to use effective means to make aggression too costly to be tempting.

The Secretary, strengthening the massive retaliation concept, held that the free world

must have the mobility and flexibility to bring collective power to bear against an enemy on a *selective or massive basis* as conditions may require. For this purpose its arsenal must include a wide range of air, sea, and land power based on *both conventional and atomic weapons.* These new weapons can be used not only for strategic purposes but also for tactical purposes. The greatest deterrent to war is the ability of the free world to respond by *means best suited to the particular area and circumstances.* There should be a capacity—I emphasize the word capacity—for massive retaliation without delay. I point out that the possession of that capacity does not impose the necessity of using it in every instance of attack. It is not our intention to turn every local war into a general war.[7]

Through introduction of the idea of a "selective" response to aggression and of scaling the character of retaliation to that of the aggression, the concept of massive retaliation is thus placed in a new light. No longer is the weapon of massive retaliation, with its implications of full and unrestrained use of strategic and tactical atomic weapons "at times and places of American choice" to be solely considered as a possible reaction to aggression; the weapon of measured retaliation is suggested as the more logical military reaction. Massive retaliation thus includes a measured retaliation in this double talk which presumably provides the United States a lozenge assortment of responses to communist aggression and a high degree of flexibility.

In further clarifying his retaliation doctrine, Secretary Dulles also depicted the role of local defense forces in threatened countries. He wrote:

In every endangered area there should be a sufficient military establishment to maintain order against subversion and to resist other forms of indirect aggression and minor satellite aggressions. This serves the indispensable need to demonstrate a purpose to resist, and to compel any aggressor to expose his real intent by such serious fighting as will brand him before all the world and promptly bring collective measures into operation. . . . For all these reasons, local defense is important. But in such areas the main reliance must be on the power of the free community to retaliate with great force by mobile means at places of its own choice.[8]

As a result of the 1955 Quemoy-Matsu crisis which helped place renewed emphasis on the possible use of tactical atomic weapons to frustrate any communist effort to occupy the islands, one new element was added to Secretary Dulles's retaliation policy formulation. Now it was best for the potential aggressor to be "kept guessing" about any possible United States intervention rather than to be warned completely and in advance about retaliation. There is an element of uncertainty in the new tactic—whether it is a manifestation of flexibility on the part of the massive retaliation policy or of indecision on the part of its protagonists.

COLLECTIVE SECURITY

If deterring aggression is the pivotal point of American security policy, then collective security is the wedge with which it can be driven. In Secretary Dulles's phrases, a collective system of defense is "the cornerstone of security for the free nations. . . . No single nation can develop for itself defensive power of adequate scope and flexibility. In seeking to do so, each would become a garrison state and none would achieve security." [9]

The idea of collective security, so basic to American foreign policy today, came into being with the Second World War, and has been pursued with vigor despite such disappointments as resulted from a misplaced faith in the collective security provisions of the United Nations Charter. Its policy tempered by experience with the limitations of the United Nations as a security organization, the United States now bases its security on a nearly worldwide network of regional collective security organizations.

Three premises underly United States concern for collective security. These are (1) that the stated objectives and actions of the Soviet Union and communist China are the major threat to world peace today; (2) that the unification of the noncommunist states of the world for collective self-defense makes peace more likely to prevail; (3) and that defense against communist aggression is a common task which should be shared by all members of the free world, each contributing whatever it can to the collective security. United States security policy today and, in effect, a large part of total American foreign policy are activated by this concept of collective security combined with the idea of deterrence of aggression by retaliatory power.

By March 1955 the United States was party to five different collective security treaties in Asia and the Pacific, each having some bearing on the security of Southeast Asia.

Construction of this complex network of security alliances began in late 1950 when, under the impetus of the cold war's sharpening issues dramatized by the communist conquest of China and the Korean War, the United States concluded that Japan should participate in the Pacific strategy for containing communism and maintaining security, and accordingly sent John Foster Dulles, then a State Department consultant, and a small cadre of associates to Japan to undertake diplomatic negotiations for a Japanese peace treaty and for a series of defense treaties with Japan, the Philippines, Australia, and New Zealand.

It took several months of careful negotiations to win over some of the reluctant Southeast Asian governments to the American view of a "peace of reconciliation" which Mr. Dulles deemed necessary for the collective defense of the area on the premise that Japan no longer posed a threat to Pacific security and was sufficiently repentant to become a participant in the treaty plans. Such states as the Philippines, Burma, and Indonesia, which had experienced the brutal Japanese occupation, presented special difficulties by demanding reparations payments far beyond the capacity of Japan's still crippled economy. Although refusing to attend the Japanese peace conference because of dissatisfaction with the reparations arrangements, Burma later reached a separate agreement with Japan on the basis of the "best deal possible," in the words of Burmese Prime Minister U Nu. The Philippines, Indonesia, and Thailand also concluded separate reparations agreements with Japan at a later date.

Of the fifty-five governments invited to attend the Japanese

Treaty of Peace Conference in early September 1951 at San Francisco, fifty-two accepted, and all save three, the Soviet Union, Czechoslovakia, and Poland, signed the treaty of peace.

Recognition that "Japan as a sovereign nation possesses the inherent right of individual or collective self-defense . . . and . . . may voluntarily enter into collective security arrangements" was given in Article 5 of the treaty. The provision that all occupation forces should be withdrawn from Japan within ninety days of the effective treaty date was set forth in Article 6, with one important qualification:

> Nothing in this provision shall, however, prevent the stationing or retention of foreign armed forces in Japanese territory under or in consequence of any bilateral or multilateral agreements which have been or may be made between one or more of the Allied Powers, on the one hand, and Japan on the other.

Parallel with the peace treaty negotiations, a bilateral security treaty was being negotiated between the United States and Japan, and this too was signed on September 8th along with a Tripartite Security Treaty between Australia, New Zealand, and the United States (the ANZUS Pact), previously negotiated. Just a week earlier, in Washington, the United States and the Philippines signed a mutual defense treaty in the roundup of efforts toward collective security in the Pacific.

From the viewpoint of the United States, the Japanese treaty constituted the most important of the three security treaties. It provided the right for the United States "to dispose United States land, air and sea forces in and about Japan," to be used "to contribute to the maintenance of international peace and security in the Far East and to the security of Japan against armed attack from without, including assistance given at the express request of the Japanese Government to put down large-scale internal riots and disturbances in Japan, caused through instigation or intervention by an outside Power or Powers." According to treaty provisions, no other country would be given military rights in Japan without the consent of the United States. Continuance of the treaty would be assured until agreement by the two governments that its purposes were satisfactorily assured by United Nations arrangements or "alternative individual or collective security dispositions." The United States declared its willingness to maintain armed forces in and about Japan in the interest of peace and security and to deter armed attack upon Japan with the expectation that "Japan will itself increasingly assume responsibility for its own defense against direct and indirect aggression. . . ."

By the terms of the Tripartite Security Treaty, Australia and New Zealand gained long-sought assurances of American support and assistance in the event of an armed attack. The three treaty participants declared "publicly and formally their sense of unity, so that no potential aggressor could be under the illusion that any of them stand alone in the Pacific area, and further to coordinate their efforts for collective defense for the preservation of peace and security pending the development of a more comprehensive system of regional security in the Pacific area." Although the ANZUS Pact bore some resemblance to the North Atlantic Treaty, its critical article, Article 4, was less definite:

> Each Party recognizes that an armed attack in the Pacific area on any of the Parties would be dangerous to its own peace and safety and declares that it would act to meet the common danger in accordance with its constitutional processes.

In seeking such assurances, Australia and New Zealand were motivated as much by suspicions of a resurgent militarism in Japan as by the threat of a communist attack.

The Mutual Defense Treaty with the Philippines followed the general pattern of the ANZUS Pact and, in fact, did little more than formalize already existing understandings of security ties between the Philippines and the United States. As President Truman said on April 18, 1951, "The whole world knows that the United States recognizes that an armed attack on the Philippines would be looked upon by the United States as dangerous to its own peace and safety and that it would act accordingly."

Although none of the four security treaties [10] contributed directly to Southeast Asian security, the pattern of United States long-range thinking is clear in statements on the development of a more comprehensive collective security system for the area. Again, the negotiation of a mutual defense treaty with the Republic of

Korea in 1953 and another with the Republic of China (Formosa) in 1954 extended the outer boundaries of American security concern in the Pacific even further.

The United States, though hoping in time to consolidate the network of bilateral and trilateral mutual defense treaties into a comprehensive system of collective security for Asia and the Pacific, nevertheless showed a hesitancy about hastening the process for reasons expressed at the time by Mr. Dulles:

> . . . it is not at this time practicable to draw a line which would bring all the free peoples of the Pacific and East Asia into a formal mutual security area. . . . Those Asian nations such as Indonesia and Burma which have just won liberation from Japanese aggression and political freedom from Western colonialism have hesitated to assume security relationships either with Japan or with the Western Powers. As a practical matter, in Indo-China and Malaya, assistance must be given largely through France and the United Kingdom, a procedure which many in Asia find repellent, as promoting "colonial imperialism." Some countries are as yet unable or unwilling to qualify for definite security arrangements under the Vandenberg formula of "continuous and effective self-help and mutual aid." Lastly, but perhaps, not least, is the fact that the United States should not assume formal commitments which overstrain its present capabilities and give rise to military expectations we could not fulfill, particularly in terms of land forces. The security treaties now made involve only islands, where security is strongly influenced by sea and air power. . . .[11]

Later, in the spring of 1953, under a new administration in Washington, and with a new title, Secretary of State Dulles visited India, Pakistan, and several Middle Eastern countries to ascertain, among other things, the extent of interest in a coordinated defense against communist aggression. Pakistan had for some time been expressing its interest in receiving American military aid within the terms of the Vandenberg formula, and coordinating defense measures with neighboring states in the Middle East. In India, already staunchly opposed to collective security in principle and practice, the effect of the agreement between the United States and Pakistan was greatly to increase tensions between India and the United States as well as between India and Pakistan. If any sparse hopes did exist for winning Indian cooperation over to collective security measures in Southeast Asia, however, an added damper was put on them by the mutual security agreement which the United States in time negotiated with Pakistan.

Still working toward security, and acting on the suspicion that the cessation of Korean hostilities would mean increased Chinese assistance to the Viet Minh forces in Indochina, President Eisenhower, on April 16, 1953, called for united action to check communist aggression in Southeast Asia. During 1953 and 1954, United States and European military and political leaders continued to meet and hold exploratory conversations on the subject; but no concrete proposals for collective security organization in Southeast Asia emerged from all the talk.

Throughout this period, however, the pressure for more vigorous collective security measures continued in the United States. The Chairman of the Senate Foreign Relations Committee, for example, in September 1953, recommended a "third great pact" for the Far East which would operate like the Rio Pact in Latin America and the North Atlantic Treaty alliance in Western Europe. The official attitude was more restrained. Its tenor was one of watchful waiting until the Asian nations directly concerned indicated their clear and widespread acceptance of collective security. Assistant Secretary of State for Far Eastern Affairs Walter S. Robertson expressed this policy in a talk on October 9:

> Those both here and in the Far East who have recognized the desirability of a common defensive effort in the Asian-Pacific area have looked to the United States Government to exert its influence in favor of such a pact. We continue to believe, however, that any effective Asian-Pacific organization must come about as a result of the Asians' own initiative, that it must wait upon a general appreciation among the Asians of the desirability of collective action in attacking their common problems. This is clearly not a field in which outsiders can usefully assert themselves. We do not wish to give the impression that we are trying to hustle or joggle our friends across the Pacific, because we are not. Any moves to be made in the direction of regional organization are clearly up to them.[12]

As Chinese communist aid was stepped up to the Viet Minh forces in Indochina, as French plans for early victory drew closer to a stalemate, as the collapse of anticommunist resistance in Vietnam became more certain, the official attitude began to waver during the first part of 1954. By degrees, because of the Indochina circumstances, the United States was being propelled into accepting a Southeast Asian collective security system which would gain less than full Asian support. A month away from the Geneva Conference on Korea and Indochina, the United States completed its policy turn so that it was vigorously espousing a Southeast Asian collective security system which would be formulated at the earliest possible opportunity by as many participants as possible.

During the anxious days of the siege of Dienbienphu, Secretary Dulles reiterated the President's warning of the previous year:

> Under the conditions of today, the imposition on Southeast Asia of the political system of Communist Russia and its Chinese Communist ally, by whatever means, would be a grave threat to the whole free community. The United States feels that the possibility should not be passively accepted, but should be met by united action. . . .

By the time the United States reached this point of dedication, however, and moved to translate proposals for a Southeast Asian collective defense organization into reality, Great Britain and France had become noticeably less enthusiastic. In an attempt to gain support for a united defense effort for Indochina and Southeast Asia, Secretary Dulles went to Europe for a series of talks. In London, following talks with Foreign Secretary Anthony Eden, Great Britain and the United States agreed that events in Indochina

> not only threaten those now directly involved, but also endanger the peace and security of the entire area of Southeast Asia and the Western Pacific, where our two nations and other friendly and allied nations have vital interests. Accordingly we are ready to take part, with the other countries principally concerned, in an examination of the possibility of establishing a collective defense, within the framework of the Charter of the United Nations, to assure the peace, security and freedom of Southeast Asia and the Western Pacific.[13]

In Paris, the talks with Foreign Minister Georges Bidault resulted in another communiqué, establishing the fact that the two governments

> recognize that the prolongation of the war in Indochina, which endangers the security of the countries immediately affected, also threatens the entire

area of Southeast Asia and of the Western Pacific. In close association with other interested nations, we will examine the possibility of establishing . . . a collective defense to assure the peace, security and freedom of this area.

Thus, shortly before the scheduled opening of the Geneva Conference, the only encouragement which Secretary Dulles was able to obtain from France and Britain was an agreement to "examine the possibility of establishing" a collective defense arrangement for Southeast Asia. It was Dulles's belief that at Geneva France's hand would be strengthened and that the future prospects of Vietnam, Cambodia, and Laos would be improved by conclusion of a formal arrangement for united action in Southeast Asia either before the Geneva Conference or, at the least, before the conclusion of any Indochina peace treaty. Because the United States already had made clear the fact that a prerequisite to any American intervention in Indochina was a "united action," pressure could only be brought to bear on the communist negotiators at Geneva by a collective defense treaty or a formal multilateral declaration.

Great Britain, having an eye to interests in Malaya, Singapore, and Borneo, was as anxious as the United States for a collective defense organization to protect Southeast Asia, but Foreign Secretary Eden differed with Secretary Dulles as to the probable political effects of ramming through a defense pact in the face of the Geneva Conference. In Eden's view, the good will and cooperation of the free Asian nations were needed for any successful collective defense system of the area. Eventually it was his hope that, through careful diplomacy, India and other neutralist states would be brought into an Asian defense pact or, at least, would be persuaded to take a sympathetic view of such a pact. Eden believed that hasty steps taken toward a defense alliance in an effort to exert pressure on the Geneva negotiations might have adverse political repercussions in India, Burma, and Indonesia and, possibly, might even eliminate a later opportunity to win their support for a collective security pact in Asia.

War-weary and discouraged, forced to the wall by political unrest at home and by the disintegrating military situation abroad, the French before the Geneva Conference looked only for some face-saving device by which the Indochina war could be ended.

Their negotiating position was so weak that their only hope for the leverage necessary to force a compromise with the communists lay in a pledge of allied or American intervention in Indochina in case of a breakdown in the negotiations. When the British refused to be a party to any allied pledge of intervention, the French encouraged the United States to make a unilateral declaration. Although Secretary Dulles wanted to give the French all the backing possible, he was restricted on the one hand by a lack of congressional support for intervention and, on the other, by a strong congressional segment which stood firmly against any concession, compromise, or negotiation with the communists.

In the end, the Indochina truce agreements represented a compromise for all parties concerned, even for the communists, who seemed to be settling for less than they were militarily capable of taking M. Mendès-France, the French premier who took office in the midst of the Geneva negotiations on a promise of peace for Indochina before July 20th, described the final settlements as sometimes cruel but necessary. British Secretary Eden believed that the Geneva Conference had averted the possibility of a third world war, but warned that the outcome depended on communist willingness to fulfill the truce agreements.

According to Secretary Dulles, the Geneva Conference "confirmed the need for unity" and demonstrated two important lessons: first, "that resistance to communism needs popular support, and this in turn means that the people should feel they are defending their own national institutions," and second, "that arrangements for collective security need to be made in advance of aggression, not after it is under way."

Because of an aversion to recognizing or guaranteeing communist gains, the United States was unwilling to sign the final Indochina truce agreements. However, since it was apparent that the settlement would have little meaning without it, the United States circumvented the dilemma by agreeing not to use force to upset the Indochina truce agreements and by guaranteeing noncommunist territory against communist attack. Against this background, it also moved swiftly to conclude a collective security treaty for Southeast Asia.

On September 8, 1954, just six weeks after the Geneva truce

agreements on Indochina, representatives of the United States, Great Britain, France, Australia, New Zealand, Pakistan, the Philippines, and Thailand signed the Southeast Asia Collective Defense Treaty (Manila Pact). By the provisions of the Manila Pact, the participating governments ". . . intending to declare publicly and formally their sense of unity, so that any potential aggressor will appreciate that the parties stand together in the area, and desiring further to coordinate their efforts for collective defense and for the preservation of peace and security," agreed, among other things,

> . . . by means of continuous and effective self-help and mutual aid, [to] maintain and develop their individual and collective capacity to resist armed attack and to prevent and counter subversive activities directed from without against their territorial integrity and political stability [Article 2].
>
> . . . to strengthen their free institutions and to cooperate with one another in the further development of economic measures, including technical assistance, designed both to promote economic progress and social well-being and to further the individual and collective efforts of governments toward these ends [Article 3].
>
> . . . to recognize . . . that any aggression by means of armed attack in the treaty area against any of the parties or against any state or territory which the parties by unanimous agreement may hereafter designate would endanger its own peace and safety, and agrees that it will in that event act to meet the common danger in accordance with its constitutional processes [Article 4].

In Article 8 of the Manila Pact, the treaty area is defined as "the general area of Southeast Asia, including also the entire territories of the Asian parties, and the general area of the Southwest Pacific not including the Pacific area north of Latitude 21 degrees 30 minutes N." This provision eliminates from the treaty area the territory of Formosa but includes in it the territory of Laos, Cambodia, and South Vietnam, three states restrained from becoming active participants in a military alliance by the terms of the Indochina armistice agreements. Attached to its signature on the Manila Pact is an "understanding" by the American delegation that the terms "aggression and armed attack" under Article 4 refer only to communist aggression. In the event of any aggression in the treaty area other than communist aggression, the United States agrees only "to consult" with the other Manila Pact members.

The basic commitment undertaken by the Manila Pact members under Article 4 is to recognize that armed attack against the treaty area would endanger their own peace and security and to act to meet the common danger in accordance with their own constitutional processes. This is a less specific commitment than the one made in the Rio Pact and the NATO Pact which employ the principle that an armed attack against one member of the security community is to be considered an armed attack against all.

Although not specifically obliged by the wording of the Manila Pact to commit military forces in the event of communist aggression or armed attack against the Southeast Asia treaty area, the United States has a strong moral obligation and a heavy political compulsion to do so. Because the successful practice of collective security requires not only a surplus of mutual confidence and understanding but also coordinated defense planning and a high degree of synchronization among the members of the security community in the realm of international politics, the Manila Pact provides for the establishment of a council to coordinate political and military affairs. This council, according to Article 4, consists of representatives of each of the Pact members who meet for "consultation with regard to military and any other planning as the situation obtaining in the treaty area may from time to time require."

ECONOMIC AID AND TECHNICAL ASSISTANCE

Begun in 1942 as a systematic program of Latin American aid, technical assistance provided such generally encouraging results as to contribute to a decision to expand American technical assistance to other economically retarded areas of the world. Accordingly, President Truman made it the fourth point of his inaugural address, on January 20, 1949:

> . . . we must embark on a bold new program for making the benefits of our scientific advances and industrial progress available for the improvement and growth of underdeveloped areas. . . .

I believe that we should make available to peace-loving peoples the benefits of our store of technical knowledge in order to help them realize their aspirations for a better life. And, in cooperation with other nations, we should foster capital investment in areas needing development.

Our aim should be to help the free peoples of the world, through their own efforts, to produce more food, more clothing, more materials for housing and more mechanical power to lighten their burdens.

When the Act for International Development which implemented the Point Four idea came before Congress as legislation, it evoked such heated debate that at one point a strong opposition was within one vote of killing it. Yet, eventually passing muster in June 1950, the Act contained an unusually specific statement of American policy toward underdeveloped areas despite congressional uncertainty as to the merit and need of a technical assistance program of global proportions and despite serious cuts in the Administration's appropriation requests:

It is declared to be the policy of the United States to aid the efforts of the peoples of economically underdeveloped areas to develop their resources and improve their working and living conditions by encouraging the exchange of technical knowledge and skills and the flow of investment capital to countries which provide conditions under which such technical assistance and capital can effectively and constructively contribute to raising standards of living, creating new sources of wealth, increasing productivity, and expanding purchasing power.

Although American spokesmen sounded a warning on the smallness of the contemplated assistance program, Southeast Asian governments, recalling the magnitude of American aid to Western Europe, generally believed that large-scale American aid was on the way. But if the Southeast Asian understanding of the amount of aid and assistance was exaggerated in one direction, United States interpretations of budgetary requirements for an assistance program of effective proportions was off in another direction. During congressional debate over the Act for International Development, its proponents vaunted the exploitation of American "know how" plus some simple and inexpensive implements as a means for accomplishing wonders in economically retarded areas at minimum expense. Even Secretary Acheson, testifying in 1950 before the

Senate Committee on Foreign Relations, declared that the contemplated technical assistance program

> by its nature . . . is not and never will be a big-money enterprise. It involves salaries and expenses of people—not vast purchases of machinery and raw materials. Its objective is to show other people how to meet their own needs, not to attempt to meet those needs ourselves. For this reason, the cost of technical cooperation will always be modest, compared with the cost of other types of programs.[14]

As finally approved by Congress, technical assistance was awarded a total appropriation of $35,000,000, $12,000,000 being earmarked as the American contribution to the United Nations technical assistance program. With the passage of the Act for International Development and the availability for use in Southeast Asia of some funds budgeted under the China Area Aid Act of 1950, the beginning of an economic and technical assistance program for Southeast Asia was made possible.

Although by its nature a technical cooperation program for underdeveloped countries is certain to be cheaper than an economic aid program to provide capital equipment, basic commodities, and funds, one very important point neither was stressed by the administration nor grasped by Congress. If it is to have real economic or political significance, technical assistance must be regarded as the first step toward making practicable large economic aid programs in underdeveloped areas.

Under the pressure of the Korean and Indochina wars, the essentially economic objectives of American economic aid and technical assistance to Southeast Asia soon gave way to more specific political and military objectives. In October 1951 the program was linked to military aid, rearmament, and collective security in the terms of the Mutual Security Act of 1951 whose stated purpose was

> . . . to maintain the security and to promote the foreign policy of the United States by authorizing military, economic, and technical assistance to friendly countries and to strengthen the mutual security and individual and collective defenses of the free world, to develop their resources in the interest of the United States and to facilitate the effective participation of these countries in the United Nations system for collective security. The purpose of . . . the Act for International Development . . . shall hereafter be deemed to include this purpose.

The critical shift in United States attitudes and philosophy of foreign aid is clear in any comparison of purposes and stated objectives of the Point Four idea and the Act for International Development with those of the Mutual Security Act of 1951. By 1951 the "bold new program" of helping others to help themselves achieve their own economic aspirations faded into the background to be dominated by new considerations of military strength and collective defense. In the pattern of the 1951 Mutual Security Act, American foreign aid programs came to be regarded primarily as a means of relieving weak economies of some of the burden of building military forces for mutual defense and, secondarily, as a means of bolstering the morale of governments in their resistance to communism. Economic aid became so increasingly blurred with military aid [15] and technical assistance became so linked in general purpose to the mutual security program that, by January 1954, Secretary Dulles could assert that "broadly speaking foreign budgetary aid is being limited to situations where it clearly contributes to military strength."

With the advent of the Eisenhower administration, several aspects of the 1951 foreign aid policy pattern have been changed. First, the new administration, seeking to make good its campaign pledge of a balanced budget, carefully combed for cuts the 1953–1954 budget inherited from its predecessor. The new administration, in reviewing the Mutual Security Agency records, decided that it could safely cut the foreign aid appropriation of 7.6 billion dollars recommended by Mr. Truman to 5.1 billion dollars and that it could use some of the 9.5 billion dollars in carry-over funds which had not yet been expended or obligated from previous appropriations to maintain a foreign aid program of more than 6 billion dollars. Over President Eisenhower's protest, Congress cut the appropriation of new money to 4.5 billion dollars. By using the device of drawing on carry-over funds, the administration through fiscal 1955–1956 was able to maintain a relatively constant level of foreign aid spending while Congress cut appropriations and looked forward to an early termination of all foreign aid.

The obvious dilemma took shape at the end of 1955 when the carry-over funds reached dangerously low levels and the pipeline of contracts for future delivery of military and economic aid equipment threatened to run dry. The administration, faced with the prospect either of having to reduce the levels of foreign aid or of approaching Congress for a considerable increase in foreign aid appropriations, indicated that it would ask Congress for an increase of about one billion dollars in the foreign aid appropriations for fiscal 1956–1957. This marked a considerable change in the administration's foreign aid policy, which had been represented in Congress as reducing foreign aid to a trickle once America's allies were armed with weapons on order. Following Secretary Dulles's statement in December 1955 that "both the economic and the military aid will need to go on for a considerable period of time at about the present level," Congress in general acted outraged and indignant.

A second major change in the Eisenhower administration foreign aid policy was the creation of the Foreign Operations Administration (FOA) under Mr. Harold Stassen to take over the functions of the Mutual Security Agency and also to absorb the Technical Cooperation Administration, previously under the Department of State.[16] The idea of creating the new agency and of relieving the State Department of foreign aid and technical assistance responsibilities, according to the President, was to permit the Department to concentrate on its basic diplomatic and policy formulation tasks. Undoutedly, some thought also was given to wiping the slate clean of the Truman administration.

Reflecting the growing urge of Congress to curtail and terminate foreign aid and, presumably, administration policy that "economic assistance on a grant basis should be terminated as swiftly as our national interest would allow,"[17] the Mutual Security Act of 1954 provided that the Foreign Operations Administration "shall cease to exist at the close of June 30, 1955."

Nevertheless, the FOA was succeeded on July 1, 1955, by the International Cooperation Administration, whose characteristics seem to reflect certain significant foreign aid policy changes. For one, under the reorganization, economic aid and technical assistance were assigned to ICA, while specific responsibility for military aid was given to the Department of Defense. For another, the ICA was integrated into the Department of State under the specific supervision of the Secretary of State, and consequently, unlike its predecessors, has no direct voice in Cabinet-level decisions. Placement of the ICA in the Department of State suggests that the United States Government may be planning to use economic aid and technical assistance as an arm of general diplomacy in a more direct and specific manner than it has in the past. The President's pronouncement at the time of the ICA activation that American foreign assistance programs should be a permanent part of governmental organization rather than a series of year-to-year and emergency-type operations in itself marks a significant policy change.

A third change in foreign aid policy under the Eisenhower administration was the shifting of the center of gravity of American aid from Europe to the Far East. For example, in 1952 Europe received about 75 per cent of all American aid funds, but by 1955 its allocation had dropped to 25 per cent, with 55 per cent assigned to the Far East. By 1956 the allocation to the Far East had been increased to 75 per cent. This new emphasis on the Far East was due in part to the closing out of economic aid to Europe, and in part to the heavy expense of military aid to Korea, Formosa, and Indochina. Although foreign aid budgets continued to be 75 to 80 per cent military in nature, the need to increase economic aid levels was being newly emphasized by the President and the Secretary of State by the end of 1955. Their statements to that effect, however, were not followed by any impressive increase in the economic aspects of American foreign aid operations.

Under the ICA, certain aspects of American foreign aid and technical assistance activities have taken on a distinctly Eisenhower-administration flavor. For example, beginning in 1953, administration leaders made clear their intent to trim economic aid and assistance to "long-haul" proportions just as they attempted to do in the matter of American defense policy planning. With the new program, the President requested and received a $100,000,000 contingency fund for his discretionary use in extraordinary situations. By the end of 1955, the ICA announced plans to hold back some 20 per cent of all economic and technical aid funds appropriated by Congress to create another emergency reserve fund totaling approximately $100,000,000. Presumably, the two emergency reserve funds provide an economic counterpart to America's security-through-retaliation policy in that they constitute a kind of "highly mobile financial striking force" to be rushed into areas of crisis or of imminent communist threats. Considering the nature of communist operations in underdeveloped areas, the idea of a reserve emergency fund which would fill the breach on the socioeconomic front in case of a communist break-through seems scarcely credible strategy. Somehow it smacks of reluctance on the part of the United States to undertake serious measures prior to a crisis in the economic affairs of the vulnerable underdeveloped areas of the world.

SUPPORT OF SOUTH VIETNAM

Because a communist victory in Vietnam posed a threat to democracy in all Southeast Asia, ever since the Korean War began the United States has supported anticommunist forces in Vietnam as a fourth bulwark of its policy toward the area. To this end, it bore more than half the cost of the total French and Vietnamese expenditure in the seven-year war with the Viet Minh, and since the armistice agreements has been extending large-scale aid and support to South Vietnam.

At the date of writing, declared United States policy is to extend all possible economic, military, and diplomatic aid to the southern Vietnamese zone in order to give the nationalist régime every possible chance for overcoming the tremendous internal problems and external pressures which it faces. The United States regards this policy, which it has maintained at considerable expense and in the face of many frustrations, as the only alternative to abandoning South Vietnam to the communists and to all the serious security and political consequences which such a disavowal could mean to South and Southeast Asia.

Although the United States probably did not intend that its effort to help Vietnam's nationalist régime survive, rally popular support, and overcome some of its major international difficulties should become so highly significant, it has come to represent an important test case for noncommunist methods in Southeast Asia as opposed to communist methods and achievements.

It took the United States almost three years—until the time in late 1949 when Mao Tse-tung's Chinese communist troops were knocking at the Indochina border—to recognize the dangers of the Indochina situation and two years more to back its recognition with arms and significant economic aid; but once the United States became involved in Indochina it increased its degree of implication with amazing rapidity.[18]

At first, the United States started off modestly enough in early 1950 by recognizing Laos, Cambodia, and Vietnam in anticipation of their full independence. Following the Griffin Mission's recommendations,[19] it agreed to extend aid to Indochina, and designated an American representative to work with the governments of the Associated States and the French high commissioner in Saigon.

The United States made its decision to extend aid to Indochina with some misgiving. In Vietnam, Bao Dai, the chief of state, commanded little popular support and was considered a French puppet, yet the French were unwilling to grant Vietnam and the Bao Dai government the full measure of independence and freedom necessary to rally nationalist support. American officials knew that any aid extended to Indochina through the French would open the United States to charges of supporting French colonialism and that the governments of the Associated States were not prepared to administer effectively American aid channeled directly to Laos, Cambodia, and Vietnam. But they hoped to persuade the French to hasten full independence and, by dealing as much as possible with the three Associated States, to help create conditions in which American aid could be given directly with reasonable effectiveness.

The United States intent was to act as an intermediary between the Vietnamese people and the French. On the one hand, it hoped to restrain Vietnamese eagerness for full independence until minimum economic, political, and military foundations were laid for it and, on the other, it hoped to keep continual pressure on the French to grant wider autonomy to the Vietnamese, Cambodian, and Laotian nationalist governments and to move those states rapidly toward full independence. Quite apart from the problems which European defense plans created for United States and French relations, this was a precarious game for the United States to play because the French were waging an extremely difficult war against Ho Chi Minh's communist forces not only to retain control of Indochina but also to forestall any chain reaction for independence among other members of the French Colonial Empire. The result was that too much pressure on the French to grant independence in Indochina could conceivably lessen their incentive to continue fighting the communist Viet Minh, but too little evidence of progress toward independence would fail to give the Vietnamese nationalists any incentive to commit themselves to the struggle.

For a few brief months the United States served as mediator between the Vietnamese and the French with some limited success. However, the American policy-makers failed to reckon with the full extent of French resistance toward any curtailment of their effective control over Indochina or with French determination to reject any outside influence on French colonial policies in Indochina. The French bargaining position was so strengthened by the urgency of the threat of Viet Minh success that the State Department by April 1950 reportedly recognized "the unique defensive role played in Indochina by the French and the importance of that role to the whole of Southeast Asia." [20]

The question of a Vietnamese national army caused one critical French-American disagreement. The United States felt that creation of such an army could serve several purposes. It could provide a manifestation of growing Vietnamese independence; in time, it could make feasible the withdrawal of French troops from Indochina to bolster defenses in Europe; and in addition it could reduce the colonial aspects of the war in Indochina. But the French, realizing that a national army would be an additional lever to force France out of Indochina, and also fearing that a Vietnamese army, once created, would turn against its colonial forces, steadfastly resisted any serious effort for its creation. Apparently France was well aware that maintenance of its status in Indochina depended on force of arms.

For the United States, the outbreak of the Korean War opened up a new set of considerations in Indochina. Without entirely forsaking the role of mediator, the United States decided to concentrate primarily on the military aspects of the Indochina situation, a position which meant a measure of retreat from the earlier anticolonial and pronationalist sentiments in favor of backing the

French military effort to defeat the Viet Minh. By its assumption of constantly greater responsibility for the French military effort, the United States soon spun itself into such a web of involvement in Indochina that inevitably it became the receiver of a bankrupt French policy which was recognized by many American officials to be wrong and destined for failure from the very start.

Of the strands of this web, the first is manifested in the "falling domino" theory of Indochina's relationship to the security of South and Southeast Asia. Although President Eisenhower first applied the domino analogy to Indochina in a press conference on April 7, 1954, American policy-makers from the start of the war in Indochina were concerned about the logic behind the theory. During a visit to Washington in September 1951, General Jean de Lattre de Tassigny, the French high commissioner and commander in chief in Indochina, stated that if Indochina fell to the communists, nothing would be in the way of stopping further communist expansion in Asia until Suez. A great deal of evidence supported this thesis, a favorite with the French in their representations for increased United States help in Indochina. For one, the French forces in Indochina represented the only modern anticommunist army in South and Southeast Asia. For another, a communist victory in Indochina following on the heels of the communist victory in China would be certain to stimulate the "bandwagon psychology" of many Southeast Asian leaders, and its strategic, political, and psychological consequences would increase greatly the problems of defending Southeast Asia. For these reasons, the United States concern for the security of all Southeast Asia as well as for Indochina obviously began to motivate its involvement in Indochina.

The fear of communist China's intervention in the war in Indochina provided a second strand in the web of United States involvement in Indochina. From the time in late 1949 when communist China's troops reached the Indochina border, the French first feared this possibility. Later, with Chinese communist intervention in the Korean War followed by the start of the Kaesong truce talks in July 1951, the French specter became a full-blown nightmare. During that period the Chinese not only had completed a railway line to the Indochina border but also had built up troop concentrations estimated at 250,000 in the South China provinces of Yunnan and Kwangsi, making it clear that Chinese communist troops and matériel could be released by any Korean truce or armistice to increase communist pressure on Southeast Asia and, specifically, on Indochina. It was already well known that China was the base for nearly all of Ho Chi Minh's arms and that the training and equipping of Viet Minh troops were taking place in South China. It seemed inevitable that any cessation of hostilities in Korea would mean a diversion of communist military supply and manpower from Korea to Indochina.

With this contingency in view, the French pursued two courses of action. First, they continued to press the United States for increased amounts and faster deliveries of military aid, and dispatched such distinguished emissaries as General de Lattre de Tassigny and, later, his successor, High Commissioner Jean Letourneau, among others, to Washington to dramatize the issue. Second, they played up the idea that the Korean and Indochina wars were a single military effort on two fronts in an attempt to get a specific American policy statement to that effect.

In the matter of the French pressure for more aid, the United States was sympathetic and cooperative but took the opportunity to encourage the French to grant greater authority to the governments of the Associated States and to hasten the development of national armies in Vietnam, Cambodia, and Laos. In the case of M. Letourneau's visit, for example, the United States provided additional aid with the stipulation that it be used specifically for building the national armies of the Associated States to a point where they could take over more of the burden of defense in Indochina.

On their second course of action, the French were unable to get specific American policy assurance until March 1953 when, on a visit from French Premier René Mayer, Foreign Minister Georges Bidault, and other high French officials, President Eisenhower and Secretary Dulles fully and publicly endorsed the French contention that the struggles against communist aggression in Indochina and Korea were "parts of the same pattern."

In the following month Laos was invaded by Viet Minh troops who pushed on to the outer defenses of Luang Prabang, the ancient Laotian capital, before they were forced to retreat by the monsoon rains. This incident was partially responsible for several American statements of solidarity with the French in Indochina and warnings to the communists to avoid any new adventures. For example, President Eisenhower on April 16, 1953, declared that "any armistice in Korea that merely released aggressive armies to attack elsewhere would be a fraud."

In anticipation of the Korean armistice, which came three months later, the United States and France issued a joint warning that "should the Chinese Communist régime take advantage of an armistice to pursue aggressive war elsewhere in the Far East, such action would have the most serious consequences for the efforts to bring about peace in the world and would conflict directly with the understanding on which any armistice on Korea would rest."

The strands of United States involvement drew tighter as sixteen nations made a joint declaration from Washington on July 27, a few hours after the Korean armistice agreements were signed at Panmunjom, specifically linking the Korean and Indochina wars. The sixteen United Nations participants in the Korean War joined together to warn that any revival of armed attack in Korea would meet prompt and unified resistance and that "in all probability, it would not be possible to confine hostilities within the frontiers of Korea." Finally, the nations declared, "we are of the opinion that the armistice must not result in jeopardizing the restoration or the safeguarding of peace in any other part of Asia."

With the Korean armistice, United States policy faced new difficulties in Indochina. Although the Korean peace paved the way for greatly increased American aid to France and the Associated States, it also provided communist China with the same opportunity to aid the Viet Minh. In the hope of speeding victory, the United States encouraged France to press military activities in Indochina more vigorously and to increase the participation and support in the struggle of the nationals of Vietnam, Cambodia, and Laos by giving those states full independence and by expanding their national armies. On its side, the United States was prepared both to grant great increases of military and economic aid to Indochina and to give vent to frequent expressions of "grave concern" for any sign of outside assistance to the Viet Minh in an attempt to deter Chinese intervention.

Needless to say, the political declarations of Washington, Paris, and London failed to frighten either the communist Viet Minh or the Chinese. Although Chinese troops did not enter Indochina in force as they did in Korea, Chinese technicians, advisers, and training missions were active in territory controlled by the Viet Minh, and a steadily increasing stream of military equipment from Czechoslovakia, Russia, and China poured across the Kwangsi-Tonkin border to reinforce the Viet Minh.

Although the Korean armistice coupled with French losses increased popular French opposition to the war in Indochina and strengthened the French desire for a negotiated settlement, the United States and France agreed to a final all-out effort to destroy the Viet Minh. This was the Navarre Plan, named for General Henri-Eugène Navarre, former chief of staff of NATO land forces in Central Europe who arrived May 1953 in Saigon to serve as commander of French Union forces in Indochina.

The Navarre Plan called for a vast increase in the recruitment and training of Vietnamese troops and an aggressive mobile offensive designed to bring victory in two years. To it were to be added two colonial infantry regiments transferred from France's NATO divisions, as well as the French battalion which had been serving in Korea. To ensure the plan, France expressed a firm resolve to fulfill its often-repeated promise of granting full independence to the three Indochina states. In Secretary Dulles's words, the plan was "to break the organized body of Communist aggression by the end of the 1955 fighting season and thereby reduce the fighting to guerrilla warfare which could, in 1956, be met for the most part by national forces of the three Associated States." To that end, the United States pledged to increase its 1953–1954 aid allotment of $400,000,000 by $385,000,000 which would be made available before the end of 1954.

The most difficult part of the plan was winning the support of the Vietnamese, Cambodians, and Laotians who long since had grown cynical of French pledges of independence. In the fall of 1953 France, negotiating with each of the Indochina states for independence "within the French Union," reached full agreement solely with Laos but attained sufficient agreement with Cambodia and Vietnam to put the Navarre Plan into operation. The French made it clear that the Navarre Plan would be their last major effort on their own responsibility and that its failure would mean the alternatives of a negotiated settlement with the communists or American entry into the war in Indochina.

By early 1954 the United States faced the problem of keeping the French and Vietnamese nationalists in the war, especially when within six months of its announcement the Navarre Plan bogged down, with the result that there was increased political pressure in France for a negotiated settlement. With close to one-third of their national budget expended on the war in Indochina and casualties over a six-year period equivalent to American casualties in Korea, many French saw little reason not to settle for a negotiated peace in Indochina as the United States had done in Korea.

The United States, holding the view that Indochina was even more vital to American and free-world security than Korea, spurned the thought of a negotiated settlement but was unwilling to commit American forces to the struggle except as retaliation in the case of Chinese communist intervention. It soon became clear, however, that a Viet Minh victory in northern Vietnam might not require Chinese intervention beyond the supply of arms and advisers. If Indochina had to be held, who would hold it?

Both in France and in the United States, the battle for Dienbienphu became the symbol in the public mind of French willingness to continue the fight. As part of the Navarre Plan to revitalize the war, the outpost of Dienbienphu, deep in Viet Minh territory and entirely dependent on airborne supply, had been seized and built into a major French fortress. From Dienbienphu, the French hoped not only to protect Laos and harass the Viet Minh rear but also to lure the Viet Minh into massed battle on open terrain where they could use French training, artillery, and air support to full effect. The strategy backfired.

Viet Minh General Vo Nguyen Giap patiently began to ring the fortress with the largest Viet Minh army ever assembled, with massed artillery and antiaircraft weapons brought from China, and, with his preparations completed, launched into a series of heavy assaults. The assaults, starting in mid-March, continued for eight weeks until a final mass Viet Minh assault overwhelmed the fortress on May 7th, the day before discussions on Indochina opened in

Geneva. The psychological effects of the fall of Dienbienphu both on the French and on the Viet Minh were decisive. General Giap immediately followed his victory with a major campaign to sweep the French from all Tonkin while the French, in Paris and Geneva, looked for some face-saving device with which to end the war.

On at least four earlier occasions, the French had placed important segments of their army in situations similar to Dienbienphu, but each time they had managed to extricate themselves, though suffering heavy losses. Dienbienphu differed from earlier situations only in that the French committed larger numbers of troops to a less tenable position and in that they were unable to extricate themselves from it. As dramatic and heroic as was the Dienbienphu defense, its defenders somehow symbolized the basic issue of the war. With the exception of a handful of special Vietnamese troops, an officer, and a noncommissioned French officer corps, most of the men who defended Dienbienphu so valiantly and bitterly were French colonial troops from Africa and the French Foreign Legion whose numbers constitute a high ratio of expatriate Germans.

During the months of March and April 1954, it was evident that the United States verged on entry into the war in Indochina. Since the events of those weeks remain shrouded in secrecy, the closeness of that decision probably never will be known.[21] General Paul Ely, the French chief of staff, arrived in Washington on March 20 and, reportedly, told President Eisenhower and his advisers that only American action could save the Indochina situation, that unless the United States acted to lift the Dienbienphu siege, France's only alternative was to negotiate a settlement with the communists. American leaders were divided in their opinions. Evidently such officials as Admiral Arthur W. Radford, Chairman of the Joint Chiefs of Staff; Vice President Richard M. Nixon, and Senator William F. Knowland favored intervention, while Secretary Dulles presumably favored it only if other powers, especially Great Britain, were prepared to join in, and then on a basis limited to air strikes if possible.[22] On March 29th Secretary Dulles went so far as to issue a call for "united action" in Indochina. Already based in the area were two American aircraft carriers carrying some two hundred planes with additional air power available in the Philippines.

During the first weeks of April, administration spokesmen

made several statements which were designed to prepare the American public for the possibility of intervention in Indochina. For example, Secretary Dulles on April 5th told the House Committee on Foreign Relations that the United States was determined not to let Indochina fall to the communists. President Eisenhower on April 7th characterized the fall of Indochina as the first in a chain reaction that, like a row of falling dominoes, could lead to the loss of all Southeast Asia. Vice President Nixon informed a Society of Newspaper Editors meeting in Washington on April 16 that Indochina was vital to American security interests and that if American troops were needed to hold the area the United States must face up to the situation and dispatch forces. The Vice President's statement, however, was categorically denied as government policy three days later by Secretary Dulles, who gave the press to understand that Nixon's declaration was personal opinion, not government policy, and that it was "unlikely" for American forces to be dispatched to Indochina.

United States decision concerned itself with three questions: Was united action possible? Could limited intervention by air power save Dienbienphu? What would the Chinese communists do?

Throughout the month of April, Secretary Dulles kept in constant touch with the British in the effort to gain agreement for joint military action in Indochina. But British reaction was clearly opposed to any such intervention. In a statement to the House of Commons on April 27th, Sir Winston Churchill said that there would be no British commitments to military action in Indochina in advance of the Geneva Conference results. Sir Anthony Eden, defending the British decision in the House of Commons, said:

> The United Kingdom Government has been reproached in some unofficial quarters for their failure to support armed intervention to try to save Dienbienphu. It was quite true that we were not willing to support such action. This was for three reasons which then seemed to be good and still seem to be good. Firstly, we were advised that air action alone could not have been effective; secondly, any such military intervention could have destroyed the chances of a settlement at Geneva; thirdly, it might well have led to a general war in Asia.[23]

While Secretary Dulles vainly sought united action to save the fortress, time ran out on Dienbienphu. Thereafter, the United

States focused its policy on strengthening France's bargaining position in any way possible at Geneva and, at the same time, on maintaining a measure of aloofness from any concessions made there to the communists.

The Indochina armistice agreements which were concluded at Geneva, July 21, 1954, provided, among other things, for the partition of Vietnam into northern and southern military zones at a line near the seventeenth parallel. Within fifteen days of the cease-fire, each side was to muster its troops in designated regroupment zones and by May 18, 1955, to evacuate them to its own zone. The seventeenth parallel was not to be considered a political or territorial boundary. The agreement provided "that as far as Vietnam is concerned, the settlement of the political problems, carried out on the basis of respect for the principles of independence, unity and territorial integrity, should permit the Vietnamese people to enjoy the basic freedoms, guaranteed by the democratic institutions to be established after holding general free elections by secret ballot." The general elections so specified in the agreements were to take place in June 1956.

The agreements prohibited the Indochinese states from allowing foreign military bases on their territory, with the exception of two minor French bases in Laos, and from joining any military alliance. The French recognized the independence and sovereignty of Cambodia, Laos, and Vietnam and agreed to withdrawal of all French troops from the territory of those states at the request of the governments concerned. During the regroupment period, civilians who wished to move from one zone to the other were to be "permitted and helped to do so by the authorities." The agreements made provision for an International Truce Commission composed of India as chairman, Poland and Canada, to supervise their execution.

After the dust of the armistice had settled, the United States found little cause for satisfaction in the situation which emerged in Vietnam. Although Indochina, the first domino, had not precisely toppled, practically speaking, half the piece had and the other half was wobbly. In South Vietnam, Premier Ngo Dinh Diem, an ardent nationalist and pro-American, assumed office in mid-June, but he had no organized following, little contact with the Vietnamese people, and no recent political experience. His greatest political assets were a reputation for integrity and courage and an unbroken twenty-year record of opposition to French colonialism.

The Vietnamese country after seven years of war was in economic, political, and social chaos, with the southern zone inundated by refugees from the communist zone who had to be fed, clothed, housed and, eventually, integrated into the economic and social fabric. Although the organized Viet Minh military units had withdrawn, they left behind as a heritage to the southern zone a network of communist agents and of thousands of village people who had lived under communist organization, indoctrination, and government, many of them happily, for several years.

Large segments of the countryside remained under control of such semiautonomous religious sects as the Cao Dai, Hoa Hao, and Binh Xuyen, whose private armies were estimated at upward of 40,000. The sects thrived on organized gambling and corruption built on a privileged position which the French had granted them. Although strongly and effectively anticommunist and, in a narrow sense, nationalist, they saw in Premier Diem a threat to their position. For the political stability of a government still in its formulative stages, the Vietnamese national army was an uncertain element, and Premier Diem could find tragically few nationalist leaders of experience and talent, free of the taint either of French or of Viet Minh collaboration to fill government and administrative posts.

By way of contrast, Ho Chi Minh, in the northern zone, was unrivaled as a popular leader. Along with his communist colleagues, Ho knew what was to be done and how to do it. More important, Ho and his leaders commanded a large trained and dedicated communist following, many of whom had extensive administrative experience at village and provincial levels, to serve as a government bureaucracy. In all their tasks, the Viet Minh leadership had the support of the battle-tested and high-spirited Viet Minh army, one of the largest in Asia. The Ho Chi Minh régime was thus able to consolidate its authority rapidly and, in the manner of communist China, to set about the tasks of ideological, political, and economic regimentation.

For the United States the facts were clear. Without American backing and cooperation, South Vietnam could have no chance for survival. Although at the time of the agreements, the prospects for constructing a democratic and viable South Vietnam to compete with the totalitarian régime in the north seemed dim, the United States had no acceptable alternative to helping Premier Diem and his nationalist régime meet the test of independence. Under terms of the Manila Pact, therefore, the United States guaranteed South Vietnam as well as Cambodia and Laos against external communist attack and undertook to help create a Vietnamese national army through a vast military assistance and training program and to help fashion a national political and economic structure through an extensive economic aid and technical assistance program.

7. PROBLEMS OF SECURITY

The future of Southeast Asia is menaced by two distinct yet interrelated communist lines of attack. These are the external threat of overt international aggression from communist China or communist Vietnam and the threat of internal communist penetration and subversion which could lead to successful communist insurrections or civil wars of "national liberation" within the Southeast Asian states. The intent of American policy is to help Southeast Asia achieve the greatest security possible against both threats.

From the start of the Korean War, the United States has deemed the communists' external threat to Southeast Asia to be the matter of most urgent consideration. For American policy, the result has been the decision to take on the essentially military task of constructing a protective shield around Southeast Asia first of all. The United States concept of placing military needs ahead of economic and other considerations implies, of course, that, as far as the Southeast Asia countries are concerned, the advantage of internal and economic progress is largely lost on them as long as the defensibility of these countries against aggression lies open to question and, in fact, as long as aggression remains a plausible threat. The reverse of this hypothesis also holds true: even a protective shield against external military threats loses meaning if, in the course of its construction, the Southeast Asian states within its bounds collapse from internal pressures.

Although communist doctrine generally does not advocate overt international aggression as the most practical means of expanding the area of communist-dominated territory, the possible use of the method in future communist moves must be taken into account. Three times in fifteen years the communists clearly have resorted to open military attack in their plot for world dominance —in the case of Finland, in the Baltic countries and Poland, and in Korea—and, in fact, if it were possible to argue the case of Tibet, whose sovereign legal status was questionable before the invasion of the communist Chinese, a fourth time might well be added to the list.

To the Chinese communist leaders, circumstances exist which could make resort to armed force against Southeast Asia appear practicable. For example, the possible removal or substantial reduction of the threat of United States retaliation conceivably could induce an attempt by communist China to duplicate the Japanese military feat of conquering Southeast Asia. Say that the United States, turning its attention elsewhere, were to become heavily involved with military commitments in another part of the world, such as the Middle East, the power vacuum which would result in Southeast Asia might indeed prove an irresistible temptation to the Chinese leaders. A negative happenstance would be for either the United States or communist China to drift or blunder into a situation from which it would be difficult to withdraw without open conflict. The events leading to the Quemoy-Matsu crisis in the winter of 1955 are a prime illustration of this type of happening. In view of the uncertain future status of Laos, Cambodia, and Vietnam, critical situations which would be difficult to keep under reasonable control are bound to develop.

Although it is a matter of speculation, there is always the possibility that the Soviet Union, for its own malignant reasons, might attempt to maneuver China into a war with the United States and that China, flushed by some sudden triumph or consumed by burning ambition, might need little prodding. For the Soviet Union, such an armed conflict, even of a localized nature, would have the several advantages of draining the United States of men, material, and resources, causing possible strains in the Western Alliance which would provide opportunities for increasing Soviet pressures on Europe or the Middle East, of increasing communist China's dependence on the Soviet Union in the event that any erring régime showed tendencies toward independent judgment and required hewing into line and, finally, in the wake of war, regardless of the military outcome, of precipitating economic, political, and social conditions which would be more conducive to the survival and spread of communism in Southeast Asia than of democracy. But if the Soviet Union is aware of these possibilities, so too are the Chinese communist leaders, who, it is assumed, will calculate their relations with the Soviet Union carefully before initiating or allowing themselves to be thrust into any major military operation in Southeast Asia.

In considering the potential of overt communist aggression against Southeast Asia, two important factors must be kept in mind: First, individually, no Southeast Asian country has sufficient military power to withstand a determined communist attack launched either by communist China or by communist Vietnam; second, of the eight noncommunist countries of Southeast Asia, only two are participants in collective security arrangements for the area—the Philippines, which is not immediately threatened, and Thailand. If Southeast Asia is to be defended against overt communist aggression, the United States must carry the major burden of defense.

Faced with this dilemma, how does the shape of American policy fit into the specific task of defending the security of Southeast Asia? Imposing in structure, with its four cornerstones of deterring aggression, collective security, supporting South Vietnam, and providing economic and technical aid, America's over-all security policy still must leave something to be desired when it obviously reveals consistent strains and cracks in its make-up and, in fact, has not succeeded in making the attainment of security against external communist aggression in Southeast Asia seem any less remote. The weaknesses and problems of United States security policy in Southeast Asia may be mirrored through three pertinent questions. Is United States strategy to deter aggression through massive retaliation credible to the communists? Does United States security policy provide for the possibility of limited or localized communist aggression? Is United States security policy directed toward the most dangerous threat to Southeast Asian security?

POLITICAL ALIGNMENT IN SOUTHEAST ASIA

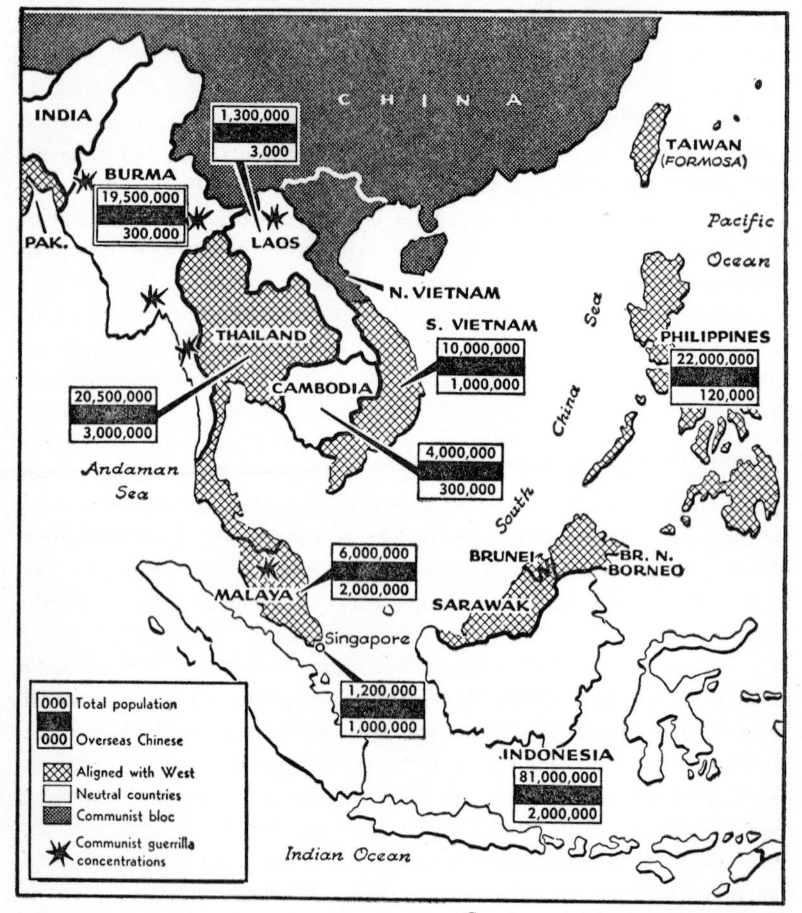

Courtesy of The New York Times

1. IS UNITED STATES STRATEGY TO DETER AGGRESSION THROUGH MASSIVE RETALIATION CREDIBLE TO THE COMMUNISTS?

Secretary Dulles and other ranking American spokesmen have stated repeatedly that an essential characteristic of the strategy to deter aggression is allied capability and determination to retaliate. The potential aggressor must be convinced that swift retribution is certain; he must "know in advance that he can and will be made to suffer for his aggression more than he can possibly gain by it."

Since there has been ample advertisement and dramatization of the American capability for massive retaliation, the communists presumably are well aware of American air-atomic potential and of the fact that aggression *could* result in retaliatory measures of a scale sufficient to outweigh any potential gains. In the minds of the communist leaders, the question therefore must read—*Will* the United States resort to strategic or tactical nuclear retaliation in case of armed attack against Southeast Asia? If the United States chooses to retaliate, where would she do it and under what circumstances?

When applied to Western Europe where United States commitments are clear-cut and American interests are historic and compelling, the massive retaliation doctrine is completely credible. So clear is it in Western Europe, where a formidable defense force stands ready to resist possible communist aggression, that the Soviets may seem to have no other recourse than the use of atomic weapons for any drastic aggressive move against Europe. In Western Europe there should be no communist doubts either on the seriousness of America's defense intentions or on the character of American response to any armed attack against the area. But in Southeast Asia, no such clear-cut commitments of a historical or traditional genesis appear to motivate the United States despite recently emphasized American interests in the area. In comparison with communist China and communist Vietnam's defense forces, Southeast Asia's local defense forces are far from formidable. With these prevailing conditions it may easily seem to the Chinese communist leaders that an attack on Southeast Asia could fail to provide compelling motivation for the United States to intervene in the area or to attempt massive retaliation. But their determination of United States reaction to a specific instance likely to precipitate retaliatory measures in all probability would be based on cautious appraisal of the American record, the state of American public opinion, and the potential reaction of America's allies.

Evidence of United States purposiveness as provided by the

record of recent analogous situations is inconclusive. In the case of communist aggression in Korea, the United States moved quickly and at first seemed to move decisively. But, in later months, the United States spurned the idea of expanding the Korean War geographically or strategically to include operations against mainland China or the use of "unconventional" weapons. In the case of Indochina, the American government demonstrated a high degree of uncertainty and confusion at the time of the Dienbienphu crisis. It was swayed by the desperate views of top American officials on the proper course of action and by the President's own statements that Indochina was essential to the security of Southeast Asia, and was, in fact, more important to American security than Korea. Yet, in the end, the President's decision was made against American intervention, a case neatly demonstrating the extreme reluctance of the United States to risk large-scale, perhaps massive, intervention, including possible use of American ground forces, in an attempt to alter the military outcome. The Quemoy-Matsu crisis of early 1955 is a more recent specific test of American intentions to employ the massive retaliation doctrine. Again, an impression of uncertainty and hesitancy owing to conflicting official views hovered over the affair, which resolved itself when the Chinese communists failed to pull off a threatened invasion of the offshore islands of Quemoy and Matsu for whatever reasons best known to them, including any possible concern over the effectiveness of the American massive retaliation doctrine.

Against the inconclusive record, the United States, however, has placed the clearly positive arraignment of its progress in integrating strategic and tactical atomic weapons into the American military establishment. The implication is that the United States intends to employ atomic weapons from the outset of any military engagement, providing conditions for the use of such weapons are militarily favorable.

Although the conviction seems to be growing in the United States that the communists have reached the outer limits of tolerable expansion in Asia beyond which there exists an invisible but clear line against trespass, this is not as apt to allay further communist depredations as may seem to be plausible, considering that any communist analysis of the effect of American public opinion on

American actions may arrive at different conclusions on the basis of contradictory evidence. For example, the United States chose to treat the earlier Japanese conquest of Southeast Asia with notes of protest and economic boycott, yet Pearl Harbor brought the United States finally into the Second World War. Though the Korean War precipitated action by the United States, it also quickly fatigued a large segment of the American public who came to regard American intervention in Korea as a terrible mistake. The Indochina and Quemoy-Matsu crises generated little public enthusiasm for American intervention beyond providing others with the implements of defense. On such bases, it is always possible for the communists to hypnotize themselves into believing that, in certain instances of communist attack in Southeast Asia, American public opinion would not stand for American intervention or retaliation.

Nor is the credibility of the United States strategy to deter aggression bolstered by an analysis of the attitudes of the major allies. The United States basic decision to seek security with her allies through collective and united effort—reaffirmed during the Dienbienphu crisis—presumably gives the allies opportunity to exercise influence on any decision to resort to massive retaliation. In Asia, Korea and Formosa are the only allied governments which, under any conditions, appear eager to support the United States in retaliatory measures against communist aggression, and Thailand seems ready to offer support under some conditions. In the case of Great Britain, a staunch and dependable ally, there is a basic difference not only in policies and objectives toward communist China but also in methods of approaching international problems, so that it is inevitable for the British to hold out as long as possible for negotiation, diplomacy, and compromise in any matter affecting Southeast Asia. In process of liquidating military commitments in Indochina and attempting to retain a sliding African Empire, France would seem to have little incentive for joint defense efforts with the United States in Southeast Asia. Count Australia and New Zealand in, but with limited resource and manpower contributions. The array of collective allied strength in all its disarray, rather than deter the communists, might produce the reverse effect, offering instead the glittering plum of an alliance cracked under the strain of making the decision for a united effort in Southeast Asia.

Taking the communist view then, it would seem that the United States intent to retaliate, massively or otherwise, in the event of an attack against Southeast Asia has not been established beyond a reasonable doubt by virtue of the American record or by communist estimates of American public opinion or by the evidence of allied support. From the American stand, the conclusion invites serious reflection: the doctrine of massive retaliation may lack the essential minimum factor of credibility to the communists.

For American security policy, the problem of establishing the credibility of this doctrine provides an all but impossible dilemma for American spokesmen who, using identical terms, must produce the desired effect on three different audiences. They must convince the potential communist aggressor of the seriousness of American intentions. They must inform the American public of American intentions and accompanying risks without inducing war hysteria or losing the voters at the voting booth. They must not alienate or frighten allies by the prospect of an impulsive or irresponsible American decision which could touch off a world-wide atomic war. The order is a large one, as is the dilemma, and neither seems capable of quick or easy resolution.

William W. Kaufmann, of the Princeton Center of International Studies, in his thoughtful critique of the massive retaliation doctrine suggests:

> We might do worse than to declare a moratorium on public pronouncements dealing with this subject. To the extent that the enemy requires further briefing about our intentions, there are other means and channels of communication which we can employ more effectively—and with less commitment and risk—than the open declaration.[1]

Apparently, Secretary Dulles has made use of closed channels of communication to convince the communists of the seriousness of American intentions. According to the highly controversial "brink of war" article in *Life* magazine (January 16, 1956), Secretary Dulles passed the word to Moscow and Peking through India's Prime Minister Nehru that the United States would carry its air attack into Manchuria and use tactical atomic weapons if the

Korea stalemate persisted and if the communists renewed hostilities during the peace negotiations. And again, he passed the word to Peking through Burma's Prime Minister U Nu that the United States meant business during the Formosa crisis in early 1955.[2] Whether or not these warnings actually averted war, as maintained in the *Life* report of the Dulles interview, can be known for sure only by the communists.

One thing is certain. Demonstrations of the seriousness of American intentions to defend Southeast Asia against communist attack would be more convincing than exhortations and warnings issued publicly or through neutralist intermediaries. However, an inherent limitation of the massive retaliation doctrine with its nuclear implications is that demonstration risks general war. Is it possible to demonstrate the seriousness of American intent in ways and by means avoiding the risk of full war?

It seems the only feasible demonstration of American intent is for the United States to achieve and maintain a clearly adequate level of defense preparedness deployed to meet any military move against Southeast Asia by whatever techniques and weapons the situation demands. But this is the very requirement the massive retaliation doctrine was developed to circumvent. Rather than military force deployed to meet a threat to Southeast Asia, the "new look" defense policy assigns the role of defense to "highly mobile naval, air and amphibious units" which at the present date of writing are still in the planning stage owing, in part, to defense economies.

2. *DOES UNITED STATES SECURITY POLICY PROVIDE FOR THE POSSIBILITY OF LIMITED OR LOCALIZED COMMUNIST AGGRESSION?*

As for the problems of "limited aggression" in present American security policy, the policy's antecedents bear inspection. Secretary of State Acheson's drive to create "situations of strength"—economic, political, and military—in areas of special weakness which cover the periphery of the communist bloc was intended to deter aggression and to create conditions in which the West might negotiate settlements with the communist world on a realistic basis. The Acheson policy regarded nuclear weapons as the last resort in case of war, and viewed the matter of building strength in areas of weakness as an alternative both to risking total atomic war and to inviting communist attack through local weakness. An integral part of American security policy planning in line with Secretary Acheson's thinking was the possibility of limited war with conventional weapons, an idea which Mr. Acheson has defended in these words: "If it is said, as it sometimes has been, that we cannot afford another war like Korea, the answer is that such a war is the only kind we can afford. Only a madman would attempt to avoid it by plunging into the unspeakable disaster of a world war." [3]

But if Mr. Acheson makes clear his defense of limited war, the fact remains that he has not been joined by a large number of Americans who, reacting unfavorably to the Korean experience, fell prey to the powerful political slogan "No more Koreas," implying no more limited wars. The Eisenhower administration, making use of the slogan, tied down its own future policy to a certain extent on the subject of limited war and thus was forced into developing the massive retaliation doctrine not only to deter communist aggression and offset communist strength in conventional armaments and manpower but also to offset the public reaction against limited war as well as to point up an internal political and economic decision to reduce defense spending. With the construction of the new security policy goes a de-emphasis of the effort to create situations of military strength in Southeast Asia along with its alternate premise of preparedness for limited wars by conventional techniques.

Secretary Dulles went to the root of present American security policy problems in Southeast Asia in a reformulation of the massive retaliation doctrine released to the press on March 16, 1954.[4] In discussing the doctrine the second time round, he emphasized the matter of "responding effectively on a selective basis." The new policy, he succinctly stated, "does not mean turning every local war into a world war," but it does mean that the free world "must not put itself into the position where the only response open to it is general war."

Applying America's strategy to deter aggression to the specific case of Southeast Asia presents serious problems both of proportion and of choice of retaliatory measures. For example, would the United States be willing to risk the consequences of massive retaliation to stop limited aggression or probing attack by the Vietnamese or Chinese communists against such areas as Laos or Cambodia, where America's vital security interests are merely peripheral? The answer is, probably not, because the interests at stake hardly justify the risk of turning the local war into a world war. In such an event the United States would seek a means of "responding effectively on a selective basis." But what selection of responses is available to the United States in the event of an attack on Laos or Cambodia?

In that part of the Manila Pact treaty area on the Asian continent, in East Pakistan, Thailand, Laos, and Cambodia especially, in the event of localized communist aggression the courses of American action are restricted by the inadequacies of factors for selective response in the area. American ground troops, "highly mobile" or otherwise, are not deployed for quick and effective counteraction. No major air bases are within range of tactical air power. And the effectiveness of American naval support would be reduced to near zero. The China coast could be blockaded and communication lines and supply concentrations in China could be bombed; but that kind of retaliation gives no assurance of stopping the aggression, and risks expanding it.

In the case of communist aggression against Korea, Japan, the Philippines, or Formosa, the United States has several choices. In addition to the extreme forms of retaliation, the United States can utilize a number of nearby army, air, and naval bases for retaliation purposes; it can gain a certain degree of support from the American navy because of the insular locations of the countries involved; and it can rely on considerable help from the growing local defense forces in each of these Asian states.

But a communist attack against Laos, Cambodia, northern Thailand, or Burma presents a very different situation. Actually, the United States would face a choice between massive retaliation as broadly outlined in the doctrine and a joint ground defense effort with the relatively weak Southeast Asian local defense forces.

A joint defense effort on the ground would probably be highly unpopular with the American public and would present difficult problems of transport, logistic support, and unfavorable terrain.

Viewed in combination with America's collective security commitments in Southeast Asia, the choices open to the United States cannot help being limited. In case of aggression or armed attack against the Manila Pact treaty area, the United States must honor its commitments under the Manila Pact precisely to the degree which the Asian participants expect. The United States must act quickly and decisively or else seriously curtail, if not destroy, the moral and political basis for American influence in the area. Only massive retaliation promises quick and decisive results.

It appears, then, that the flexibility of action cherished for purposes of a deterrent strategy may prove, in case of aggression, non-existent for purposes of a defense strategy.

The reluctance either to resort to massive retaliation in Southeast Asia or to commit American ground forces to meet limited aggression would seem to bring up one other consideration—the use of new tactical atomic weapons. If it were certain that the use of such weapons would not necessarily lead to a general war, cause the Soviet Union to become involved in the situation, or precipitate atomic retaliation, then it may be presumed tactical atomic weapons could logically be used in support of local defense forces to provide the necessary deterrent and defense against borderline cases of communist aggression. But there are three great gaps in this line of thinking. First of all, according to some military authorities, there is a certain amount of doubt over the value of using tactical atomic weapons for the mountain and jungle terrain of Southeast Asia or for communist military tactics in such areas. Second, the assumption that atomic weapons can be restricted, once they are used in some form, is a dangerous one. The unleashed power of atomic weapons can always lead to full-scale atomic war. Third, Asian political and psychological reactions to American use of any atomic weapons in Asia, tactical or strategic, could be so strong as to outweigh any tactical advantages gained by their use. Suspicious and resentful on the score of atomic weapons, many Asians harbor the belief that America's atomic weapons are "for use in Asia only." If the weapons were used in Asia, especially in a local Southeast

Asian war, not only would all suspicions seem to be justified but the use of such weapons could set off hysterical waves of hatred and anti-Americanism, undoing any good work wrought to that time.

The present defense scheme has still another serious weakness. With its de-emphasis of local defense forces and its strategy of massive retaliation, it implies an intention to trade Southeast Asia's territory for time in the event of a general or limited communist assault on Southeast Asia. The assumption follows that retaliation "at places of our own choosing" will force liberation of the sacrificed. For example, in case of a communist assault on Southeast Asia, it is believed that the Manila Pact allies may use the Kra Isthmus, the narrow neck of southern Thailand, as the main line of resistance because this vantage point would allow full exploitation of allied naval forces in the area. But such a strategy must afford limited satisfaction to the Southeast Asian government and people who are neither interested in suffering the fate of South Korea nor able to cope with the multitude of unprecedented economic and political problems which would result from the ordeal of occupation and liberation. Under the circumstances, it is possible that not only would communism suffer little loss as a political and social force but its appeal might even be enhanced.

Although in its application to Southeast Asia, American security policy fails to provide a reassuring degree of security, it is neither feasible nor desirable to repudiate its key aspects. The idea of massive retaliation plays an important role in American security policy in Asia. It cannot be abandoned even though it is not admirably geared to every type of security problem. If the communists were to launch any full-scale assault in an effort to conquer all of Southeast Asia, automatically American interests would be endangered to such an extent that an instant response would be justified, a matter which itself would prove massive retaliation a necessary American strategy.

It is principally in cases of limited or local communist aggression or of probing attacks against continental Southeast Asia, however, that the security policy fails to measure up and the doctrine of massive retaliation seems neither credible nor feasible. But here, fortunately, two deterrents, neither of them related to the United

States or to United States policy, serve to restrain the communists. In the first place, any act of overt international aggression, even with limited objectives, could easily unmask the communist intent to push all Asia into the communist camp. Since this might alert those countries which have based their policy on the vague hopes of neutralism, co-existence, and communist peace pledges to the real dangers of communism, consideration of the effect of any such revelation helps to deter military aggression. Say that the communist Chinese were to attack Thailand, Laos, or Cambodia, conceivably India, Indonesia, Burma, and Ceylon might be shocked into cooperating, possibly even affiliating, in collective security measures with the Manila Pact states. From the Chinese viewpoint, it must seem unduly problematical to arouse or frighten the Asian neutralist states prematurely, especially when a military effort in Southeast Asia contains many elements of risk and would attain merely an intermediate objective, even if successful.

This consideration has a logical concomitant in a second deterrent to communist military action. With less serious risks involved through tactics of infiltration, subversion, and insurrection from within, and with greater promise of success at relatively small expense, the communists can afford to pursue their objectives in other than external military ways. This poses another critical question left only partially answered, if it is answered at all, by American security policy.

3. IS UNITED STATES SECURITY POLICY DIRECTED TOWARD THE MOST DANGEROUS THREAT TO SECURITY IN SOUTHEAST ASIA?

Since the Korean War, American security policy in Southeast Asia has been focused primarily on the problems of meeting external communist aggression. Internal uprisings such as the postwar armed insurrections in Indochina, Burma, Malaya, Indonesia, and the Philippines, all of which were perpetrated and guided by local communists, do not fall into the category of "aggression" or "armed attack" within the meaning of the massive retaliation doctrine or the Manila Pact. Although American officials have long acknowledged the dangers of communist subversion in Southeast Asian states, the tendency has been to regard subversion in terms of long-range danger. If there were ever logic to support this view, it has certainly lost present meaning. Even more dire is the uncontrovertible fact that at the same time the United States has been preoccupied with building a defensive shield against external attack, the communists have been making great strides within several Southeast Asian states where they have concentrated on creating the proper conditions for eventual internal seizure of power.

The delegates to the Manila Conference and to the later Bangkok meeting of Manila Pact members, unanimously convinced that internal communist penetration and subversion was the most immediate and dangerous threat to Southeast Asia, expressed their anxiety through reminders in the Manila Pact. For example, Article 2 of the Manila Pact provides that the Manila Pact powers will ". . . by means of continuous and effective self-help and mutual aid . . . prevent and counter subversive activities directed from without against their territorial integrity and political stability." Article 4, paragraph 2, calls for immediate consultation by the parties whenever any party believes that there is a threat other than armed attack to the integrity, sovereignty, or political independence of any part of the treaty area. No obligation beyond consultation is contained in the paragraph, but the purpose of consultations is to agree on measures to be taken for the common defense.[5]

The implications of subversion which concerned the Manila Pact members were considered in their broadest sense as covering such a wide range of communist tactics, encouraged and supported by international communism, as infiltration of schools, government, security forces, social and labor organizations, propaganda, threats, sabotage, underground and front organization activities, organized civil disturbance, intimidation, terrorism, bribery, and conspiracy.

In stating the case before the Senate Committee on Foreign Relations during the Manila Pact hearings, Secretary Dulles said:

> To go on now to the question of subversion, as I pointed out, we deal with that in this treaty more specifically than we have with any other treaty. We recognize the danger more clearly. I must admit that the mere fact of

> recognizing the danger does not mean that we automatically have found a way to meet the danger. Subversion in that area is a very difficult thing to combat. It is virulent, it is well organized, it is effectively prosecuted by trained persons, and the task of meeting that threat will tax our resources and ingenuity to the utmost. . . .
>
> This threat is most acute at the moment in Vietnam, but, as I indicated, there are threats of the same character as to Laos, Cambodia, Thailand and Malaya; and Burma and Indonesia are not free from that danger.[6]

In seeking measures to counter subversive activities, Manila Pact members agreed to an exchange of information on the problems of subversion and on the potential use of various organizations and techniques for tightening internal security. They also agreed to periodic but discreet meetings of the eight participating powers to work out any plans for combating subversion on a multilateral basis. This need for discretion and secrecy explains in part the dearth of general public information on the subject, although the remaining explanation is that the United States and the Manila Pact powers are hard pressed to find feasible courses of action which promise a solution to the problems of subversion. For that matter, only time can show returns on such long-term objectives, and in that respect it is obvious that the communists, who have been actively pursuing their long-range subversive objectives for many years, are somewhere out in front.

The nature of the threat of subversion and of United States policy problems resulting from the threat may be illustrated by the present situations in Indonesia, Singapore, Laos, and Thailand.

In Indonesia the Indonesian Government has permitted the PKI to operate openly and at times has actively sanctioned its activities, as a result of which the communists have gained a vastly expanded organizational apparatus and membership in the country and maintain the prestige and opportunities which result from the placement of friends in high government positions. The party has indeed penetrated deeply the Indonesian labor movement and, in many areas, has even made inroads on the peasant population. This is a far cry from the disgrace which enveloped the PKI for a period of nearly two years following the abortive Madiun insurrection of 1948. The story of how the change was maneuvered is a study of communist opportunism and strategy.

While in hiding after the insurrection, the communist leaders devoted their energies to underground reorganization and future planning. Gradually, as 1951 wore on, Indonesian memories of Madiun seemed to grow sufficiently dim to permit increased above-ground activity. Owing to the organization of the Indonesian provisional government, the communist party controlled about twenty-five votes in Parliament, which allowed it to take advantage of a unique opportunity in 1952 to form an informal coalition with the PNI (Indonesian Nationalist Party), thus helping to form the Ali Sastroamidjojo government. In October 1954 the PKI fell heir to a more specific obligation from the Ali government when the Greater Indonesia Party resigned from the cabinet and left the PKI in the enviable position of holding the controlling votes in Parliament necessary to the Ali government's survival. Although the PNI leaders felt that they were clearly "using" the communist alliance at the outset, later developments would seem to render this belief somewhat suspect. The increased prestige and influence offered by affiliation with the Ali government not only left the communist party free to propagandize and organize without government interference, but also helped to increase the party membership from some 3,000 persons in 1948 to more than 150,000 in 1954, resulting in the polling of 6,000,000 votes by the PKI in the 1955 elections. Any comfort which the anticommunists may conceivably derive from the emergence of the PKI as only the fourth strongest party in Indonesia must be more than outweighed by the phenomenal growth in strength and influence which the communist party is enjoying, as well as its expanded capacity to precipitate trouble through its vast organizational network.

The PKI's present influence is especially marked in the Indonesian labor movement, where through control of a federation of more than thirty-five important labor unions (SOBSI) won over by propaganda, strenuous organizational activities, aggressive sponsorship of labor grievances, and agitation against unpopular foreign enterprises, it probably has sufficient power today to tie up Indonesian commerce and industry completely. Then there is the "people's militia" which the PKI attempted to organize in the spring of 1954 under the leadership of a communist-controlled organization of former guerrilla fighters called the "Perbebpsi" as a supplemental means for maintaining law and order. Although this proposal was defeated by the Indonesian government, the "Perbebpsi" reportedly are providing the core of communist local-action committees which are in process of being organized secretly among the workers and peasants.

Propaganda and education are well worn communist routes which the PKI has traveled extensively in Indonesia, infiltrating schools and social organizations, joining forces with communist China through an active student and cultural exchange program and, with seemingly inexhaustible funds, even building an imposing headquarters edifice on Djakarta's main street as manifestation of the party's new prestige and influence. The PKI as a result is again in a position from which it is possible to attempt an overt bid for power. That the party will make its bid goes without saying. The sole question is when and how it will do so.

Although speculation on future communist tactics in Indonesia is fairly profitless, some potentialities may be found in recent PKI activities. The new prestige and strength of the PKI may encourage its leaders to rely on a long-term propaganda and political campaign to gain control of Indonesia by way of the voting booth and parliamentary maneuver. At one point the party leadership seriously considered this strategy for Tan Ling Dije, who led the PKI from 1949 to 1953, was expelled from the party's central committee in October 1953 for advocating victory through parliamentary means only. The PKI's fifth national congress in 1954 was dominated by three new and youthful Moscow-oriented leaders—Aidit, Njoto, and Lukman. For a time their strategy appeared to be tailor-made to suit the requirements of an eventual urban-based proletarian insurrection in the traditional Moscow manner. But Soviet Communist Party boss Khrushchev in his speech to the Twentieth Congress of the Soviet Communist Party (February 14, 1956), with Aidit in attendance, may have reopened the possibility of parliamentary tactics for the PKI.

Although there is little question that the PKI has expanded and improved its underground apparatus, maintaining underground operations for the dual purpose of supplementing popular-front activities and of providing a refuge in case of difficulty, many Indonesians do not seem to regard communism as contrary to their national objectives or communist activities as subversive. Add to the problem the fact that a large amount of communist activity is carried out in full view of the Indonesian public and with government approval, and the fact that United States and Indonesian relations, although showing signs of improving, have been strained since 1951, and the limitations of United States policy for helping to counter communist advances in Indonesia become all too clear.

The case of Singapore illustrates the latent threats of communist subversion in its most dramatic form. Singapore, a Crown Colony whose economic activity is principally commercial or industrial, for some time has been promised increasing degrees of self-government though not independence by the British. A city where extremes of wealth and poverty are readily apparent, where the population is more than 80 per cent Chinese, half of them under twenty-one years of age, where the population not only has been inspired by communist China's recent accomplishments but also has indulged in a considerable amount of travel and student exchange with the area, a city where race tension is high, Singapore obviously was fertile ground for communist seeds of disaffection. And quietly, for a number of years, the Singapore communists have proceeded to the task of sowing them, using the usual tactics of propagandizing and organizing, of penetrating labor unions and, by reason of the unique existent situation, of infiltrating Chinese middle schools (the high-school and junior-college level) of the city. To date, the communists' full power in Singapore has not been demonstrated, but examples of their potential have proved sufficiently alarming. High among the samples are the Chinese youth of the city, whom the communists have welded into an effective tool for mob riots, terror, and civil disruption, a tool which they manipulated and controlled in the May 12, 1955, riots, a foreshadowing of the havoc which can be wreaked when the force of these thousands of hypnotized adolescents, grown to maturity, are unleashed upon the city. Less obvious but nonetheless deeply penetrated are the labor unions upon which the port and its industry depend. Let the communists manipulate this group and the commercial life of Singapore can be throttled.

If the communists were to decide on a reign of terror, could the British authorities or the moderate elements among the Singapore Chinese control the situation? The answer is dubious. Steps toward self-government in Singapore have led to election of a large left-wing representation responsive to the communist-led groups who control the latent forces of terror. The British would not seem to have it in their power to reverse the flow of events toward self-government without provoking widespread violence. British withdrawal would undoubtedly result in a communist-dominated Singapore. The seeming alternative of joining Singapore to the Malaya Federation with the promise of eventual independence would have the bizarre results of increasing communist infection of the entire Malaya Peninsula and of making the Malay peoples a minority in their own land.

If Singapore were communist-controlled or reduced to chaos and terror through communist inspiration, it obviously would have to be abandoned as the major Southeast Asian economic and military center, thus seriously impairing allied defenses under the Manila Pact. Even more serious, if Singapore were lost or reduced in importance to the allies as a result of communist subversion and disruption, it would mean that the international communist movement had effectively flanked the Manila Pact powers. Unhappy though the plight of Singapore may be, there is little that the United States can do to improve the deteriorating conditions.

In Laos, two governments are operating at the present time of writing—the communist-sponsored Pathet Lao government [7] and the legitimate Royal Laos government—a situation due partly to the *fait accompli* of preceding communist military actions [8] and partly to concessions granted Ho Chi Minh's and Mao Tse-tung's representatives at the 1954 Geneva Conference. Required by the Geneva agreements to regroup in the provinces of Sam Neua and Phongsaly, adjacent to the Chinese and Viet Minh borders, until a political settlement could be reached in Laos on the basis of free elections, the communists quickly used the provinces as a base within Laotian territory from which to exert constant pressure on the neighboring provinces as well as to establish a peasant-oriented communist régime.

The communist-inspired and -supported Pathet Lao leader Prince Souphanouvong, half-brother of Premier Souvanna Phouma of the legitimate Royal Laos government, boasted of the successful nature of communist infiltration into Laos in a Hanoi broadcast on February 23, 1955:

> In the heroic patriotic war of the Lao people against foreign aggression the Pathet Lao forces, shoulder to shoulder with the Vietnamese People's Volunteers, have reconquered from the hands of imperialist invaders half of the Lao territory and emancipated roughly half of the total population. Vast liberated areas were scattered in various provinces from the north to the south; worth noticing is that the three provinces of Sam Neua, Phongsaly, and Attopeu were entirely liberated. . . . The Pathet Lao forces which earnestly love peace have manifested their high concessionary spirit by agreeing to withdraw from their vast liberated areas scattered in 10 provinces to regroup in the two provinces of Sam Neua and Phongsaly.

Evidence of four primary characteristics of communist subversive strategy is revealed by the Pathet Lao situation. (1) Through the Pathet Lao, the communists use their device of forming a broad national united front in order to provide a base for the popular support which is vital either to an election victory or to a protracted armed struggle against the legitimate Laotian government. (2) Through the Pathet Lao, the communists establish a "liberated area" from which to eliminate the authority of the Royal Laotian government. (3) Strategically located, the communists gain the additional advantage of a "liberated area" so quickly and easily accessible to both communist China and Viet Minh territory, that full and unobstructed international communist support is assured. (4) With the status of the Pathet Lao government formalized by reason of the Geneva agreements, the communists are in position to make any future armed struggle appear to assume the character of a civil war.

Announcement of the formation of a "Thai Autonomous People's Government" in southern Yunnan Province was made by the Peking government, January, 1953.

The explanation of the organization of this new "People's Government" as an internal Chinese administrative arrangement granting cultural "autonomy" to the ethnic Thai peoples of South China scarcely holds water when viewed in relation to potential communist subversion and infiltration in the area. Take the following factors into consideration: (1) the area embraced by the new Thai Autonomous People's Government in southern Yunnan lies adjacent to the Laotian, Burmese, and Thai borders; (2) the ethnical relationship among the peoples of southern Yunnan, Thailand, and the adjacent border regions of Laos and Burma provides a convenient tool for communist penetration, a theory supported by former American Ambassador to Thailand Edwin F. Stanton in his declaration that "the Thai Autonomous People's Government has been created as an instrument to facilitate communist penetration into Thailand and Laos"; [9] (3) the recruitment of young Thai men and students for indoctrination and training in Yunnan and the distribution from Yunnan of communist propaganda designed to appeal to the less prosperous Thai peasants of northern Thailand and to some intellectuals and military leaders with a latent desire for a "Greater Thailand" [10] give explicit indication of the international purposes of the South Yunnan government; (4) the presence and pronouncements in China of former Prime Minister of Thailand Pridi Banomyong afford another clue to the direction which communist activity is taking.

The scheme would seem to be tailor-made for the now familiar pattern of infiltration, subversion, and "national liberation." The nucleus for a "national liberation" movement of a political sort is inherent in the combination of the Thai Autonomous People's Government, the lure of a "greater Thailand," and the attraction of a once popular and still influential leader (Pridi) as a rallying point, particularly with that leader ready to fall in with communist plans, as many Thai seem to think, in order to return to leadership in his native country. The base for organizing, training, and equipping an ethnic Thai "National Thai People's Liberation Army" would be southern Yunnan, where a "civil war" could conceivably be waged from across the border in the manner of the communist insurrection in Greece or Indochina.

During the Bandung Conference, Prince Wan Waithayakon, Foreign Minister of Thailand, expressed his government's concern over communist infiltration and subversion from South China. In his opening speech, Prince Wan said:

For it is a fact which in all responsibility I have to take into account, that Pridi Banomyong, a Thai politician, is organizing the training of Thai-speaking Chinese and persons of Thai race in Yunnan for purposes of infiltration and subversion in Thailand. I have also to know for certain the attitude adopted by the People's Republic of China in regard to the so-called persons of dual nationality in Thailand or, in other words, to the Chinese community of 3,000,000 in Thailand out of a population of 18,000,000. I might also mention the presence of 50,000 Vietnamese refugees in Northeast Thailand on the border of the Mekhong, the vast majority of whom choose to be repatriated to North Vietnam. In view of this situation as well as of the invasion of Laos by the Viet Minh forces in 1953 and also in 1954, Thailand has had clearly to face a threat of infiltration and subversion, if not of aggression itself.

Communist China's Chou En-lai, deprecating the idea that the Thai autonomous government in Yunnan was a threat to Thailand, responded that China had "no intention whatever to subvert the governments of its neighboring countries." Later, in a private conversation with Prince Wan, Chou offered to negotiate a nationality agreement with Thailand to end the problem of dual nationality of overseas Chinese in Thailand,[11] and claimed that Pridi was not in Yunnan organizing local Thai peoples but in Peking as a political refugee.

On the basis of these communist subversion-insurrection tactics in Indonesia, Singapore, Laos, and Thailand, several matters seem clear. First, no one type of countersubversion effort suits all cases because the situation in each of the four cases is in some measure unique. Second, the subversion-insurrection tactical situation is met neither by the massive retaliation nor by conventional collective security measures. Third, no effective deterrent operates to restrain communist subversive activities, and the communists are allowed to continue those tactics of internal subversion and insurrection which provide them the easiest and cheapest means for achieving their objectives with minimum risk.

In conclusion, United States policy does not appear to be focused on the major threat to Southeast Asia's security and independence. While internal communist activities represent the greatest danger in the Southeast Asian states, the United States rests the burden of its effort on protecting the area against the possibility of external international communist aggression. While the realm of economic, political, and psychological conditions is fraught with peril, the United States places its effort on military measures. The main road to security and strength in Southeast Asia, the best means of helping the Southeast Asian governments and people to withstand the pressures of internal communist subversion and infiltration, is the route of economic, political, and psychological support.

In designing any policy to meet the threats of communist subversion and insurrection, however, the following four major factors must be taken into account:

1. *The governments and people of Southeast Asia must provide the will, the initiative, and the direct action to overcome communist subversion in their own countries.* The internal competition for control of the governments and people of Southeast Asia is a struggle between communists and the legitimate nationalist leadership of the countries of the area. If the United States projects itself into this competition, either by policy or by attitude, in a manner which presents the problem to Asian people as a competition between indigenous communist objectives and American security or economic objectives, the people of Asia will almost certainly support indigenous forces. In the Philippines, Burma, Malaya, and Indonesia, the Southeast Asian people have demonstrated that they will reject communist leadership provided they are offered an acceptable indigenous alternative. Clearly a major problem for the United States is to devise ways and means of helping Southeast Asia to develop genuinely nationalist institutions and centers of authority which provide alternatives to communism acceptable to the Southeast Asian people.

2. *Communist subversive activities in Southeast Asia cannot be eliminated.* Since some degree of surreptitious communist activity exists in nearly every country in the world today, it would be a more realistic objective in Southeast Asia to attempt to reduce the effectiveness of communist propaganda and communist organization activity to an extent where they do not hamper the general economic and political development of the different countries or preclude maintenance of minimum standards of law and order. To this end, the levels of education and political sophistication could be raised, the quality of public administration improved, the area of public participation in local, provincial, and national government could be broadened, government public service and welfare activities could be expanded, corruption in government could be reduced,

and social, civic, professional, and youth organizations and activities could be encouraged. In most of these matters, the United States presumably could make an indirect but important contribution by providing advice, assistance, financing, and material when invited to do so.

3. *Communist subversion cannot be overcome solely by military measures.* Two purposes are being served by the United States provision of military equipment and training to Thailand, the Philippines, Vietnam, Cambodia, and Laos, and by the British military measures in Malaya. The purposes are (1) to strengthen the capacity of the aided states to defend themselves in case of attack; (2) to improve the capacity of the aided states to maintain internal law and order in order to counteract the more violent aspects of subversion. But as the Indochina War proved beyond a doubt, military force and coercion alone do not eliminate the appeals of communism or the effectiveness of communist propaganda and organization. Therefore, the equipment and organization for law enforcement is only the first and most elementary step toward internal peace and stability. Considering this limitation of military and police measures as a means of reducing communist effectiveness, it is interesting to note a number of promising steps taken in Southeast Asia of recent years with American and Manila Pact aid.

The Thai government, for example, in 1953 began to set up antisubversion schools, and since that time has sent antisubversion teams into the provinces to discuss techniques, progress, and latest developments in underground communist activity with local officials. It has also started organization of a 120,000-man home guard, along the lines of the Malaya home guard, for handling situations of subversion, in the hope not only of dealing more effectively with the situation but also of releasing elements of the regular army and police for normal duties. With the exchange of intelligence on subversive movements and maintenance of an area-wide check on the movements and activities of communist leaders under Manila Pact arrangements, with analysis and exchange of operational techniques for combating subversion on a multilateral basis, all Manila Pact governments and some Southeast Asian governments not parties to the Pact are benefiting by the extensive experience of the Philippines, Malaya, and Vietnam. Thus, an excellent countersubversion school in the Philippines receives students from Manila Pact governments and, in at least one instance, helped train several detachments of young army officers from a government that had not signed the Manila Pact. Other Southeast Asia governments are learning the lesson of President Magsaysay's experience in using the Philippine Army as a vehicle for winning good will and support in the countryside, an especially encouraging development because Southeast Asians in the past have tended to regard the army and police as their enemy, often for good reason. The new effort is directed toward improving discipline in the armed services and toward using the military as a constructive force to help communities rebuild homes, roads, bridges, to reestablish public services, and to help planting or harvest in disaster areas or in the wake of military operations along the lines of the Philippine Army Economic Development Corps.[12] The employment of the army in these ways is a long-standing communist tactic which the national armies at last are beginning to realize can be turned to their own uses. Thus, the cumulative impact of these newly adopted countersubversive measures of a military or quasi-military nature offers promise of relief from certain communist threats, although the measures in themselves by no means solve the existing problems.

There are several pitfalls inherent in any military aid program to help Southeast Asian states combat subversion or resist attack. In Thailand, for example, a military junta whose régime is less than democratic by any criteria has been helped to maintain political power by American military aid. This American policy has alienated unintentionally many members of the Thai civilian leadership élite who see the constant reduction of their chances to regain political control as the position of the military leaders continues to be strengthened by American military aid. When, in time, this civilian leadership returns to power, the question of *their* attitude toward the United States may well be an embarrassing one to answer.

4. *Communist subversion generally operates at a level of society at which the United States government cannot function ef-*

fectively. Although such American activities in Southeast Asia as the information program, the cultural and educational exchange programs may directly reach a segment of Southeast Asian nationals, American relations with the Southeast Asian states for the most part are confined to government levels. In contrast, communist subversion generally operates in defiance of national governments and at the grass roots of society, thus posing special problems for the United States as well as for the Southeast Asian governments. Because of the high degree of government centralization common in Southeast Asia and the growing intellectual and social gap between the people and the ruling élites, there exists in Southeast Asia at the lower end of the economic, intellectual, and social structure an untapped political vacuum which the communists seek to capture and divert to their own ends. This dangerous vacuum created by neglect of the peasants and working classes is recognized today by most Southeast Asian governments, which are attempting increasingly to extend the national government into the lives of larger numbers of people; but, after centuries of administrative and political concentration, the task is not an easy one.

The United States *can* play a direct role in combating subversion in Southeast Asia by a nonmilitary program to speed the general economic development and progress of the Southeast Asian states. Secretary Dulles has stated that "the people of Southeast Asia must be made to feel that their national institutions are in danger and they themselves are responsible for defending them." Mere statements to this effect will not accomplish the objective, no matter how highly desirable. How then to cause the Southeast Asian people to appreciate the communist danger to their institutions and traditions and accept the responsibility of meeting their problems head on? First of all, the Southeast Asian people must come to believe in their own future. They must be given evidence somehow in some way that they will be served better by noncommunist institutions than by communist ones. All around them they must see signs of the growth and advancement of *their* own nations. Primarily, they may only realize these visions; they may only read these signs in accomplished facts of their own economic and political progress.

SECURITY PROBLEMS IN SOUTH VIETNAM

Southeast Asian security rests to an uncomfortable degree on the outcome of the effort to construct an effective dam against expanding communist influence in South Vietnam. If South Vietnam can be made into a self-sufficient and dynamic state, then an important gap in the free-world defenses may be closed.

To this end, the United States has placed its confidence in the government of President Ngo Dinh Diem, beset as it is by a host of problems such as no other Southeast Asian government faces today. In its full extent, President Diem's government has the task, under extremely difficult conditions and in short order, of building, literally from the ground up, a national political, social, economic, and military structure in South Vietnam. Because it is paying most of the bills as well as because of the political symbolism which competition between northern and southern Vietnam represents, the United States exerts a great deal of influence on the Diem government and has a high stake in all that happens to it.

Taking over the reins of government in June 1954, Diem's first year in office was so wobbly that the republic's survival often was questionable. In view of the political and economic chaos which prevailed and the seeming inability of the Diem régime to establish its authority, the communists had every reason to believe that South Vietnam would fall like a ripe mango into their waiting arms.

First, General Nguyen Van Hinh, pro-French chief of staff of the Vietnamese Army, by an army mutiny in the fall of 1954 challenged the authority of Diem's shaky government, which, as a result, hung by a thread for several anxious weeks. Only pressures brought by the United States caused the French and Bao Dai to intercede, exiling General Hinh to France in November 1954, thus averting, at least for the time, a probable overt army coup. American pressures were primarily economic. Senator Mike Mansfield, reporting to the Senate Committee on Foreign Relations on a study mission to Indochina, recommended in October 1954, "In the event that the Diem government falls . . . the United States should consider an immediate suspension of all aid to Vietnam and the French Union forces. . . ." General Hinh is reported to have said: "I had only to lift my telephone and the *coup d'état* was on. But I was told that if it happened, the Americans would cut off all dollar aid." [13]

Next the Cao Dai and the Hoa Hao religious sects which, by reason of their private armies, controlled important sections of the countryside, and the Binh Xuyen, a powerful gangster group whose private armed force controlled rackets, gambling, narcotics trade, and prostitution in the Saigon-Cholon area, challenged the Diem régime in the spring of 1955 by launching a full-scale military attack on Saigon. In this severe test of strength, Diem somehow was able to persuade the leading Cao Dai generals to back the nationalist cause. Then, with the Vietnamese Army accepting his leadership despite disruptive efforts from Bao Dai ensconced in his home at Cannes on the French Riviera, Diem managed through several weeks of bitter fighting by the nationalist forces to foil the attempted coup, driving the Binh Xuyen forces out of the Saigon-Cholon area and breaking the Hoa Hao's grip over several important rural areas.

During the course of the brief revolt, Bao Dai challenged Diem's authority, thereby opening up delicate problems of constitutional authority and practical politics. In the end, Diem, whom Bao Dai, as chief of state, had appointed prime minister, was elected president in an October 1955 referendum despite Bao Dai's opposition, managing in doing so effectively to reduce Bao Dai's tenuous authority and prestige in South Vietnam. Although attempting to maintain a neutral position in the conflict of constitutional authority between Diem and Bao Dai, the United States fully supported the Diem government in its political and military efforts through the three crises.

Not that the quenching of the revolt means a resolution of the problem of the sects for Diem's government. Still at large are many members of the Binh Xuyen who retreated to the swamps along the Mekong River, where they continue to harass commerce and the neighboring countryside, and scattered bands of Cao Dai who maraud and live by banditry and extortion. Although probably incapable of challenging the government once again, the sects still retain a certain capacity to impede and harass provincial and local officials in their administrative duties.

In a very real sense, Diem's government, by meeting these three tests of its authority, reached its turning point. As it overcame each succeeding crisis, its position became strengthened, new nationalist spirit and patriotism were generated, loyalty of the national army was cemented, and Diem's personal prestige and standing received a tremendous boost. When President Diem followed the revolt of the sects by a rice-roots tour of central Vietnam, he evoked such spontaneous demonstrations of good will that his supporters were considerably astonished and cheered.

Having withstood the challenges to his government's authority, President Diem finally found himself in a position sufficiently improved to make it possible to tackle some of the difficult economic, social, and political problems of the country. By the end of 1955, the Vietnamese for the first time seemed to have a genuine nationalist government as an alternative either to Ho Chi Minh's communist régime or to a French-controlled government. The acceptability of Diem's government as such a continuing alternative for the Vietnamese people still will depend of course on its future performance in administration, reform, and representation.

Under frequent and severe criticism as undemocratic, arbitrary and corrupt during its first two years, the Diem régime from the very first faced a withering barrage of attackers who have waged an incessant campaign to obstruct its efforts, to discredit Diem, to undermine the role of the United States in Indochina and any idea that the régime can survive. Along with the communists in Hanoi, Peking, and Moscow and a number of Vietnamese nationalists and foreign observers, these critics have included many embittered French former *colons* whose attitude is based primarily on the bitter realization that their privileged position in Indochina nears its end. Rather than seek a *modus vivendi* with the South Vietnam government in a spirit of cooperation, many of these *colons* refuse to accept the facts of the situation and, in so doing, further alienate Vietnamese nationalists. Such tactics of obstruction and resistance have been especially prevalent at lower and intermediate bureaucratic levels and among private businessmen in Vietnam in a manner reminiscent of the disgruntled Dutch officials and merchants following Indonesian independence; but at the top official level, United States, Vietnamese, and French cooperation generally has been good. Senator Mansfield, reporting to the Senate Foreign Relations Committee in October 1955, found "a perceptible shift in French policy. Opposition to Diem, particularly on the part of French officials in Saigon, has subsided. In place of the undisguised hostility of a year ago, at least a degree of tolerance on both sides appears to be developing." [14]

Criticism can of course easily be leveled at the Diem government. The fact remains that the government of South Vietnam is not all it should be. It is by no means fully representative; it has taken arbitrary decisions; some officials have engaged in corrupt practices. As an ardent Roman Catholic President Diem, in selecting his advisers and administrators, has tended to favor the Catholic minority in Vietnam. He also has surrounded himself with a close group of officials, an inordinate number of whom are members of his own extensive family, and has shown a great impatience in his dealings with opposition nationalist groups and leaders. However, there seems to be cause for agreement among most Western observers that, under the prevailing emergency conditions, the régime's shortcomings in representative democracy are necessary. The gains which already have been made could easily be swept away by a period of governmental paralysis caused by factional bickering. It is unrealistic to expect that, in two years' time, an efficient, fully representative régime free of corrupt officials could arise like a phoenix from the ashes of French colonialism. Although the South Vietnam emergency requires strong central direction, the danger constantly remains that an arbitrary government will precipitate operation of the law of diminishing returns in the form of alienated Vietnamese intellectuals and leaders and resentful unrepresented groups. The real political test of the Diem government lies in the creation of political and social conditions in the country which will help to widen its representative base without critically sacrificing its effective leadership.

When South Vietnam held its first national elections for a 123-member National Assembly on March 4, 1956, some thirty members not government-sponsored candidates were elected to the Assembly despite boycotting of the elections by some Vietnamese opposition groups on the grounds that the election law was unfair. The Assembly proceeded to work on a constitution drafted by the Diem régime and giving the President wider powers than usually are associated with representative democracy. It was approved by the Assembly. Aware of the narrow margin of progress which stands between continued independence and possible national collapse, President Diem and his supporters concurred in the need for broader presidential powers to keep South Vietnam moving forward at a rapid clip. Nevertheless, President Diem faces a major challenge in this issue over the government's ability and willingness to expand its base of representation.

The Diem régime also faces the problem of winning the support and loyalty of the 80 to 85 per cent of the South Vietnamese people who live as peasants in the countryside. In order to bring the peasants into a closer relationship with the government, soon after independence Diem introduced land and tax reform measures, plans for village councils, and a system for provincial and local administration. Because of the lack of experienced officials and of know-how and will on the part of Vietnamese officialdom, however, the government was forced to hold up implementation of its plans.

More than on any other factor the survival of a noncommunist independent South Vietnam probably depends on the government's success among the peasant population. In many areas the stronghold of communist strength was and still lies in the countryside of South Vietnam. During the war in Indochina many rural areas of South Vietnam operated under communist rule and, according to reports, continue to operate under communist shadow governments. The communists took great pains to learn peasant problems and to gear their activities to peasant interests and fears. They brought the peasants hope for the future, gave them a sense of participation in government, administered a rough-and-ready justice, and protected the peasants from official corruption and extortion. Unless the Diem régime can top communist performance in South Vietnam's rural areas, its national government will rest on unreliable foundations.[15]

The United States effort in South Vietnam in large part has concentrated on the task of molding a modern national army. Using training techniques learned during the Korean War, American and French officers are working to create an efficient army capable of meeting any armed attack from the Viet Minh. Only the efforts of the national government, however, can assure the loyalty and spirit of that army, and only the degree of cooperation and support of the Vietnamese people can determine its effectiveness in meeting any attack or local uprising. At the time of writing, about 150,000 men constitute the national army with plans calling for a reserve of about equal size. Military reports from Saigon indicate that army morale and caliber are high and that rapid improvement of its leadership has been evident.

The United States also has made a major contribution to South Vietnam's struggle for stability by providing matériel and funds for the care and resettlement of some 800,000 Vietnamese refugees who took advantage of the terms of the Geneva accords to move to South Vietnam rather than to continue living in the north under a communist régime. Through 1955 the United States provided $56,000,000 for the refugee assistance and resettlement program. Some of the southern Vietnamese resent the large influx of northerners, many of them Catholics, because of a historic antipathy as well as because of the economic competition and the extensive financial aid which the refugees are receiving. Many virgin lands in the south still can and are being opened to the refugees, including Bao Dai's extensive royal preserve which, in the area around Dalat, was taken over in 1955 by the government. However, southern Vietnamese society will, in time, have to integrate many of the northern refugees who are neither equipped nor inclined to undertake the pioneer life of opening up new territories.

An important long-range problem for South Vietnam is the matter of finding its place in the international economy. Owing largely to the rice production in the Cochin-China delta area in the southern part of the state, for the past years a center of communist activities, Indochina, before the disruption of rice production and trade by the Indochina War and the Second World War, was the world's third largest rice exporter.[16] Although South Vietnam again undoubtedly can produce large rice surpluses for export, today's outlook in the international rice market is not such as to inspire it. All Asian countries have been striving for self-sufficiency in rice production with enough success that even Burma and Thailand are experiencing real difficulty in disposing of their rice surplus in free-world markets. For the South Vietnamese economy to provide an adequate and dependable level of foreign exchange without large-scale American assistance, South Vietnam will have to turn to light industry and economic diversification. Having many of the natural resources such as coal, iron, rubber, timber, zinc, lead, and phosphates, which are vital to the development of light industry, South Vietnam faces the problem of developing technically skilled manpower and accumulating capital to take advantage of its resources.

But the question which looms higher than saucers in the sky for Vietnam remains the matter of reunification of the two sides, North and South. The National Assembly elections of March 1956 in South Vietnam evoked strong protests as a violation of the Indochina armistice agreements from Hanoi, Peking, and Moscow. President Diem's government from the very beginning of its tenure clearly has opposed the terms for political settlement laid down in the Geneva accords which it did not sign. While accepting the principle of a political settlement on the basis of free elections as provided in the agreements, the Diem government has made clear its attitude, which it has not changed, on the impossibility of holding free elections under the conditions prevailing in the communist zone. The newly elected National Assembly as its first act sent a message denouncing the Geneva accords to the Manila Pact Council which was meeting at the time in Karachi, Pakistan. The message declared, "We do not consider ourselves as bound by the Geneva agreement, which has been signed against the will and in contempt of the interest of the Vietnamese people."

The communist government in Hanoi, supported by Moscow and Peking, on its side repeatedly has demanded that the elections be held and has called upon the French, who signed the Geneva accords, and the Armistice Commission which the accords established to supervise the armistice, to enforce the agreement's political provisions.

The United States bases its position in support of the Diem government on the fact that conditions for free elections do not exist in North Vietnam. The United States, which did not sign the Geneva accords, offered its guarantee against any effort to upset the accords by force of arms. In addition, by the Manila

Pact, it guaranteed the territory of Laos, Cambodia, and South Vietnam against any communist attack.

In the absence of agreement between the North and South Vietnam governments and among the big powers on a peaceful means of resolving the issue of reunification, the possibility invariably remains that the Viet Minh may resume hostilities in an effort to unify the country by force. A revival of hostilities could take several forms, any one of which would present the United States with difficult alternatives.

First and most likely in the event of a resumption of hostilities, the Viet Minh underground in the south could stage an armed uprising. To the communists, this would have the advantage of avoiding international complications by allowing the affair to seem an internal insurrection on the part of nationalists and patriots fighting for the right to decide their political future at the voting booth, as provided in the Indochina armistice agreements. In this situation, the many political, economic, and social advances of the Diem régime could be nullified and the country again plunged into chaos and internecine warfare. But if the Diem régime were to win wide popular support throughout South Vietnam, the result could be a collapse of the internal communist uprising in a repetition of the failures of the communist insurrections in Indonesia and Burma in 1948 which were lost because they were directed against independent nationalist governments. A revolt against an independent South Vietnam government also could have the reverse effect for the communists of stimulating nationalist unity and patriotism.

Second, the Viet Minh presumably could coordinate an invasion from the north with an internal communist uprising in the south. In such an event, the South Vietnam government would face even greater difficulties. Seasoned and battle-wise communist troops could prove more than a match for the fledgling South Vietnam national army; and the United States, together with the Manila Pact powers, would have to decide on a course of action. The alternatives here would be whether to throw full support to the Vietnamese nationalist effort or to limit intervention to providing supplies, naval and air support. The possibility that the Chinese communists would intervene on behalf of the Viet Minh undoubtedly would work to inhibit commitment of American ground troops in support of South Vietnam.

Third, the Viet Minh could launch an invasion starting out with Chinese communist troop support. Here, the Manila Pact powers and the United States would have a clearer decision to make, and probably would open up the prospect of the technicalities involved in the entire register of measured or massive retaliation.

It is also possible that as each succeeding communist effort begins to fail, hostilities could progress step by step, from an internal uprising in South Vietnam to Viet Minh intervention to Chinese communist intervention. But, unless the Chinese have concluded that they are ready for a full test of arms with the West, full-scale Chinese communist intervention is unlikely. In the last eventuality, the United States has, in fact, few alternatives. Its commitment to the survival of an independent, noncommunist South Vietnam and to an independent, noncommunist Southeast Asia is such a strong one that it cannot cast its support aside in the face of adversity and sacrifice.

In pursuing its policy in South Vietnam, the United States must steer its course between the Scylla and Charybdis of two policy attitudes. First, the United States must avoid assuming the role of successor to French colonialism in Vietnamese eyes while doing its utmost to ensure the survival and growth of an independent South Vietnam. Even though it is the disgruntled French former *colons* and the communists who assiduously play up the American colonialism theme, the United States must remember that the struggle for Vietnam is first and last a Vietnamese struggle. Though the United States cannot win the struggle, it can lose it by seeming to take over the power of decision which belongs of right to the South Vietnam government and to the Vietnamese people.

Second, the United States must avoid overemphasizing its support of Diem and his régime as opposed to its support of a Vietnamese national program. Events in other Asian countries over a period of the past several years have amply demonstrated the dangers implicit in permitting United States policy to rest on the political fortunes or personal proclivities of one man or government.

8. PROBLEMS OF ECONOMIC DEVELOPMENT

A combination of internal American political considerations and external communist military actions has partially obscured the fundamental importance of American foreign economic policy to the future of United States and Southeast Asian relations. In the next decade it is highly probable that the economic aspects of United States policy will prove more important to United States and Southeast Asian relations than any other aspect of United States policy both because rapid economic progress is the most basic aspiration and the minimum demand of every Southeast Asian government and because the internal socioeconomic front is a major focus of communist activities in Southeast Asia.

American policy therefore is left with the task of helping Southeast Asia's nationalist leaders and institutions progress toward their national objectives however possible within the general framework of democratic methods and values. But this is not to say that the United States can shoulder the responsibility for economic growth which Southeast Asians demand. For Southeast Asia the substance of economic progress cannot be imported; rather it must be generated from within the Southeast Asian societies. It is far more important for the Southeast Asian governments to stimulate their own economic growth and to foster social change than for the United States to set up any artificial or transplanted methods for economic development. Although by this token the United States can only play a marginal role in Southeast Asia's struggle for economic development, nevertheless the American contribution can prove to be the critical margin between economic progress and economic stagnation. Its importance, therefore, cannot be underestimated.

Because no adequate means exist for measuring economic development for Southeast Asia or for predicting its achievement through the use of various techniques, the measurement of economic status must remain as much a frame of mind as a statement of arithmetic. Too, even if the usual statistical indicators of national economic status (such as national income and production, life expectancy and literacy rates) presented valid bases for comparison, they still would be misleading when applied to Southeast Asia, where any statistical data not only is woefully inadequate and unreliable but fails to take into account such vital factors as distribution of national income, level of general welfare, local standards and values, or extent of subsistence farming as a way of life.

The close interrelationship of economic progress, political adjustment, and cultural change is a matter of prime importance. American foreign aid and assistance programs in Southeast Asia appear to be based on an expectation of the willingness and ability of the Southeast Asian governments and peoples to effect the political and cultural innovations essential for economic development, even though experience does not fully support the assumption. There is real question as to whether the Southeast Asian governments will be able to travel the difficult road leading to economic development by the techniques of democracy and representative government. For example, the majority of Southeast Asian governments are finding it difficult to make the necessary political decisions which will create conditions favorable to rapid economic growth, at times postponing essential reforms because they are too insecure to risk drastic corrective action or because government officials are involved.

A serious socioeconomic dichotomy which exists in Southeast Asia tends to split the population of the urban and rural areas into separate camps and adds to the problem. On the one side, the leadership élites, whose socioeconomic attitudes tend to run ahead of the pace of economic development, are concentrated in the cities, where they grow impatient and restive at the slowness of the process of development. On the other side are the mass of farm and village people with a resistance to socioeconomic innovation who lag so far behind their urban compatriots in interest and will for intellectual and cultural change that they constitute a drag on the rate of national economic development. A problem without solution at the moment, this socioeconomic gap between Southeast Asia's rural and urban peoples appears to be widening.

Since reform legislation and enforcement, socioeconomic attitude changes, political unity, and a national dynamism can only derive impetus from the peoples of Southeast Asia, it is clear that the United States cannot use a direct approach toward the political and cultural aspects of Southeast Asian economic development problems. However, the fact remains that United States activity in the economic sphere has great impact on Southeast Asia's political and cultural spheres. On an economic basis, it is always plausible that private American investment and American economic aid will stimulate indigenous capital investment, that American foreign trade policy will stimulate indigenous commercial activity and encourage the growth of local entrepreneur classes, and that American technical and educational assistance will introduce new attitudes and ideas in Southeast Asia. Through an effort directed primarily in the realm of economic aid and technical assistance, the United States can still help produce significant results and changes—at least in the short run—in Southeast Asia's cultural and intellectual attitudes.

There remain three basic economic requirements for economic progress in Southeast Asia: capital, international trade opportunities, and technical skill. In each of these areas, the United States can make impressive contributions to Southeast Asia's economic development.

CAPITAL FOR ECONOMIC DEVELOPMENT

The problems of accumulating capital for economic development in Southeast Asia are multitudinous. Low per capita productivity and income, nonproductive uses of the small margin of savings —for gold ornaments, religious and social festivities—exportation or hoarding of capital surplus by many Southeast Asians, dim the prospects for indigenous capital formation. Add to the situation the fact that the concepts of risk capital and of long-term investment are alien to most Southeast Asians, and the difficulties seem almost insurmountable.

Because of the unavailability of indigenous private capital, a strong inclination exists in Southeast Asia for economic development through government initiative, financing, management, and ownership. The Southeast Asian governments have a capacity to raise investment capital from tariffs, taxes, and government monopolies. In Burma and Indonesia the tendency to rely on government initiative for economic development is buttressed by an affinity for socialist types of economic organization. Elsewhere in Southeast Asia, where socialist theories have made little imprint, the tendency toward nationalized industry and government planning and regulation of the national economy rests on practical considerations. The reasoning is that the governments are the major source of capital accumulation, that they monopolize the services of the limited number of people who possess technical, financial, or administrative experience, that, as a result, the process of economic development is speeded up by economic planning and government regulation, and that time and resources are thereby saved. In the Southeast Asian view, the tasks of development are too urgent and the economic needs too great to leave economic growth to trial and error or to the caprice of individual initiative or to the free operation of the laws of supply and demand.

Although the prospects for capital formation within the Southeast Asian countries are limited, internal capital formation possibilities do exist which, if fully exploited, could contribute substantially to the development capital needs of the area. For one, there are sizable amounts of savings in the Southeast Asian countries which accrue to a small economic and social group, including many Chinese and Indians, but these savings are not reinvested to add to the national productive output. For another, there is a vast potential in the unused labor of the area. Although the Southeast Asian countries are not overpopulated, they do have sizable labor surpluses, especially between planting and harvesting seasons, which could account for sizable production increases and savings for capital formation, if mobilized and directed into village and cottage industries. For a third, there is the capital to be formed by an increase in the low per capita productivity of agricultural and industrial labor through the simple expedient of introducing minimum technological improvement. However, to make a technological advance a means of capital formation rather than a source of social unrest requires the availability of alternate employment which would absorb the manpower released by new machines or production techniques.

No reliable estimates have been made on the amount of capital which the Southeast Asian states can absorb effectively or which they need for a given rate of economic growth, but indications are that the effective limits have neither been reached nor approached. Although Southeast Asia's capacity to absorb outside capital is limited, thus far the need for outside capital still outstrips its available amounts.

In their need for capital, two sources of public loans are open to the Southeast Asian states. These are the United States Export-Import Bank and the United Nations International Bank for Reconstruction and Development. The Export-Import Bank, whose primary purpose of stimulating American exports is implicit in its name, usually requires that its loans be used to purchase American products. Even though political considerations shade its basic philosophy and often weigh in its operations, and though, since 1950, it has given increased attention to Asia's underdeveloped areas, at the present date of writing, the Export-Import Bank has authorized loans to only three Southeast Asian countries; Indonesia, the Philippines, and Thailand.

Except for three loans to Thailand totaling $25,400,000, the International Bank for Reconstruction and Development has provided no economic development capital for Southeast Asia. However, the IBRD has made a special contribution to the area through a series of valuable national economic surveys conducted in underdeveloped areas, including Malaya. In addition, by its consistent policy of requiring loan applicants to present sound development projects and by its policy of providing financial and economic experts to assist and advise governments of underdeveloped countries, the IBRD has helped to raise the general level of development planning in Southeast Asia and elsewhere. To the IBRD's total capital subscription, the American quota is set at 38 per cent, but in terms of paid-up subscriptions the American contribution actually has run as high as 86 per cent.

The limitations of the Export-Import Bank and the IBRD as sources of development capital for Southeast Asia stem both from their limited capitalization and from their generally conservative outlook. Both compute risk factors and extend loans on a basis of conventional banking practice. A specially important need or a soundly conceived development project justifies a loan only if prospects for repayment of principle and interest on schedule appear certain. Although both the Export-Import Bank and the IBRD are potential supplementary sources of capital, neither is in a position to meet the heavy capital demands of Southeast Asia or to risk the uncertainties inherent in the Southeast Asian economic scene.

In United States policy, the prospects of significant private American investment in Southeast Asia are poor, even though emphasis and hope have been placed on private American investment as a means of financing economic development in Southeast Asia and elsewhere. Despite frequent exhortations by American government officials and prominent reference in American economic and technical aid legislation favoring private American investment capital, the amount of private investment in Southeast Asia is small and gives no signs of significant increase. Furthermore, most private American investment in Southeast Asia is concentrated in extractive operations such as oil and rubber production rather than focused on Southeast Asia's over-all development needs.

There are numerous deterrents to increased private American investment in Southeast Asia. First, high risk factors, general political and economic instability, and governmental restraints in Southeast Asia turn American investment capital to other outlets more lucrative and more secure. Second, in some parts of Southeast Asia actual or latent hostility to foreign private investment exists. Third, the tendency toward planned economies and nationalization mitigates against private capital. Fourth, private capital generally is not attracted by the type of basic economic development needs, such as transportation, irrigation, power, communications and public utilities, which are vital to Southeast Asia's economic growth.

There is no way of circumventing the fact that private investors and banks are interested in secure and profitable use of their capital. Although the United States presumably might help increase incentives for private American investment in Southeast Asia, the countries which seek capital investments rather than the countries with surplus capital to invest or loan must originate the first and most important incentives. As a first step to attract foreign capital to their area, it is conceivable for the governments of Southeast Asia to make an intensified effort to muster and employ available domestic capital. Foreign investors are not likely to venture capital where domestic investors fear to do so. It is also possible for the Southeast Asian governments to attempt to eliminate, or at least to reduce, hostility and discrimination against private foreign capital by strengthening the legal status of foreign capital, giving assurances against expropriation or default of loans, reducing import-export quotas and duties and government regulation of business enterprise and exchange controls.

The reluctance of Southeast Asian governments to encourage or, in some instances, to permit foreign investment for the development of primary resources is an important obstacle to private foreign investment in Southeast Asia, whose explanation lies in colonialism and in the common Asian view that the Western colonial powers became rich by draining the Far East of raw materials.

In this area of primary resource development, a conflict of opinion exists which stems from a difference of interpretation in the kind of economic development which seems to be feasible for underdeveloped areas in the immediate future. The industrial nations tend to take the view that the economic development of underdeveloped areas lies within the

> framework of an international economy resting on specialization or division of labor in which underdeveloped areas will, for some time to come, continue chiefly as primary producers. Economic progress will unfold gradually for these countries. . . . Only as industrial skills accumulate and as literacy, public health, monetary-fiscal systems, commercial codes, etc., reach higher levels can these growing economies hope for significant increases in real incomes per capita.[1]

On the other side, the countries of Southeast Asia are interested in achieving national self-sufficiency and balanced economies to "perfect" their independence. They aspire as quickly as possible to modern industrialization, high living standards, and welfare states. The Southeast Asian leaders envisage goals requiring large amounts of capital which, in their terms, must come from abroad as long-term and low-interest loans and as grants-in-aid so as to prevent the further depression of domestic living standards during the early stages of economic development.

The facts of economic development in Southeast Asia in time may be expected to fall somewhere between the two conflicting views. Along with primary resource development, for example, American economic aid policy in Southeast Asia points up economic diversification and industrialization. Still, there is no alternative to the fact that, despite psychological blocks in Southeast Asia to intensified primary resource development, intelligent exploitation and marketing of raw materials is one of Southeast Asia's best means for raising capital and for accumulating the experience and skill which is necessary for the area's economic diversification and industrialization.

Three types of proposals have been made at various times for stimulating the flow of private American capital to Southeast Asia and other underdeveloped areas. These cover (1) schemes for American tax relief, (2) investment treaties, and (3) government insurance on private foreign investment. Although the American government has granted minor tax concessions to American companies operating in Latin America, it steadfastly has refused to consider any proposal of major tax relief a means of encouraging private American investment abroad. In the matter of investment treaties, since 1945 negotiations have established the legal status of American investment and commercial activities in ten foreign countries, none of them in Southeast Asia. The only such treaty in force between the United States and a Southeast Asian government today is the Treaty of Friendship, Commerce and Navigation concluded with Thailand in 1937. The proposal that the American government assume part of the risk of private American investment abroad through an insurance or guaranty scheme has been criticized as injecting government into private business and as decreasing the pressure on foreign governments to improve conditions for private investment. Under the Foreign Operations Administration, guaranties for currency convertibility and insurance against expropriation were available to American investors in seventeen foreign countries, but the only two Asian countries included in the scheme were Formosa and the Philippines. A fourth type of proposal has been made suggesting that new foreign investments be permitted rapid amortization in a situation similar to the one operating under American law which gives quick tax write-offs to American investments in basic materials development and in defense-production facilities in the United States.

Even if part or all of these proposals were adopted, there is little certainty that the flow of private American capital in Southeast Asia would increase to any significant extent because the proposals overlook two basic considerations. First, the development-capital needs of Southeast Asia exceed the available private capital supply. Second, private American capital will not increase in Southeast Asia until the political and economic groundwork is laid for secure and profitable investment.

However much the United States would like to have private American investment carry the major burden of development financing in Southeast Asia, it is forced to one major conclusion from past performance. Private American investors and businessmen are neither able nor willing to provide the capital to launch Southeast Asian economic development nor can they carry it through the critical initial stages of growth.

For the Southeast Asian governments, America's economic aid and technical assistance programs are their best hopes for the necessary outside aid in their struggle for economic development. For the United States, the opportunity to help the Southeast Asian governments and peoples achieve their economic development objectives through economic aid and technical assistance programs offers the best chance to influence political, social, and ideological developments in Southeast Asia.

ECONOMIC AID AND TECHNICAL ASSISTANCE

A great deal of the controversy on American foreign aid and assistance policies for such underdeveloped areas as Southeast Asia seems to stem from a confusion of United States objectives. There has been no formulation of clear and acceptable objectives, a matter which, until it is clarified, is scarcely likely to resolve key policy issues. What does the United States hope to achieve in Southeast Asia by economic aid and technical assistance? Spurred on by alarm over the spread of communism to offer such aid, United States policy actually conceived of economic and technical aid originally as the best means of hastening the vitally necessary process of raising living standards and improving economic conditions in the area. Progress toward achievement of Southeast Asia's economic aspirations, it was hoped, would create conditions advantageous to American economic, political and security interests.

Clearly, the attainment of "sound economic conditions and stable international economic relations" is at the core of American economic and technical aid. The further expectation is for the achievement of sound economic conditions to advance the cause of individual liberty, free institutions, and independence in the recipient states.

America's objectives in providing economic and technical aid, according to the conclusions of an International Development Advisory Board in June 1952, were:

> 1) To help the people of underdeveloped countries realize economic progress and political freedom which is the common aspiration of the common man wherever he may be.
>
> 2) To demonstrate that the democratic way is the surest way to realize this hope. . . .
>
> 3) To develop new sources of wealth and higher levels of productivity in order to strengthen not only the underdeveloped countries but the entire community of nations of the free world.[2]

With the realization of these objectives, the Advisory Board pointed out, the further spread of communism in the underdeveloped areas of the world might be avoided.

From statements of American officials, records of congressional debates, and provisions of economic aid and assistance legislation, it would appear as if United States aid and assistance to Southeast Asia were given in anticipation of such manifold blessings as the development of sources of supply for strategic materials, the expansion of American export trade, winning friends, opening the way for private American investment, the promotion of free enterprise, the encouragement of collective security, and the increase of military armament and mobilization capabilities in all underdeveloped areas. For a relatively small investment in Southeast Asia's economic development, this becomes a formidable listing of anticipated results, especially when it would look as if the idea of helping the recipient states achieve healthy indigenous economic progress were practically smothered in the crossfire of random American purposes.

The basic long-term objective of United States foreign policy in Southeast Asia is the growth of a series of independent, prosperous, democratically oriented and reasonably strong states in the area. Although this objective may never be fully realized, American interests are served by every step in that direction. And in that direction is the requisite of a vigorous economic development based on indigenous resources, motivated by the desires of the people, organized and emerging from Southeast Asia's national societies and cultures. It thus becomes evident that the logical rationale and justification for American economic aid and technical assistance to the area is a matter simply of economic growth and progress within the general framework of democratic principles.

Provided that the United States plays a straightforward and effective role in helping the Southeast Asian nations reach their development objectives, it is plausible that the United States may garner some worth-while political and economic by-products in the process of economic development. But these should be recognized in their true context as potential by-products, and not as objectives, so that the primary objectives may be realized without interference and so that friendly political relations may continue to be maintained between the United States and the Southeast Asian states.

Although it is a human reaction for Americans to hope to build a backlog of gratitude through aid and assistance, the fact is that such a concept misses the point of the American role in Southeast Asia's development struggles. The point is that American aid and assistance is intended to help create conditions in which the Southeast Asian peoples will develop a personal stake and a hopeful view in the destiny of their own nations. Mutual trust, confidence, and good will, rather than gratitude, may be expected to result from the experience of a partnership between peoples and governments working in pursuit of common interests for the common good rather than from the acts of allocating and receiving funds expressly for one thing or another, even in the name of democratic principles.

It is clearly impracticable to estimate with any degree of accuracy either the amount of American aid necessary or the period of time required to advance Southeast Asia's economic development to that point where it will be carried along by its own momentum, indigenous economic activity, and private capital. The only positive statement which can be made in this connection is that the process of economic development is long-range and requires greater amounts of outside economic aid than is at present being made available.

In principle, the United States Congress is reluctant to accept the idea of a long-term economic aid and technical assistance program in Southeast Asia or anywhere else. In United States practice, economic aid is regarded as an emergency measure to meet crisis conditions; technical assistance is considered a low-cost training program which should show dramatic results and become self-sustaining in a relatively short time. At each congressional session the question of cost and continuation of American aid and assistance is reopened and the administration in power is called upon to justify foreign aid and assistance operations by producing specific evidence of achievement and by presenting a case against the liquidation or curtailment of operations. Because the effects of economic aid and technical assistance are long-range, the important results being in the nature of intangibles, such as political and cultural impact, continuing justification for such aid often is difficult to formulate in concrete or statistical form. As a consequence, administration spokesmen, trying to improve their chances for obtaining necessary appropriations from Congress, tend to base their case on crisis conditions and a misleading relationship between military strength and economic development.

Sound long-term planning both by Southeast Asian governments and by American officials in charge of administering American aid continues to be hampered by the year-to-year uncertainty as to the size and continuation of American economic aid and technical assistance programs. To ensure the best possible economic development results for Southeast Asia, there must be firm assurance of the availability of American aid in amounts adequate to produce significant impact over longer planning periods. Probably a highly satisfactory arrangement would be for the United States to make aid and assistance commitments for periods of either five or ten years, thus facilitating both the planning and operation of economic development programs within a given period of time. When President Eisenhower proposed ten-year aid and assistance commitments in his 1956 State of the Union message, there was a wave of congressional protest. Nevertheless, the practical economic and diplomatic advantages of the long-term view of Southeast Asia's economic development needs and America's contribution to those needs are numerous and important.

From an American policy viewpoint, short-range activities of economic aid in Southeast Asia also are necessary in an effort to demonstrate the results of such aid to a large number of people as soon as possible. Short-run projects in the fields of national health and education and in such demonstrable programs as the development of roads, agriculture, and public facilities are political and psychological necessities in Southeast Asia. Through the initial stages of basic economic development, these lesser improvements help to nurture hope and confidence in the minds of Southeast Asians even though the core of economic development is contained in new production, new industries, new power sources, land reclamation, construction for irrigation and flood control and, above all, in changing economic and social attitudes. Again, this is not to change the focus from capital investment and the use of manpower and resources on basic long-term to short-term programs having an impressive amount of immediate political and economic gains. Rather, it is a reemphasis of the fact that short-run returns can be self-defeating, and that the Southeast Asian states need most of all to move toward a self-sustaining level of economic development in which American aid and assistance no longer will be necessary.

To Congress and the American public, the concept of technical assistance as a small and inexpensive operation penetrated deeper than its early advocates had intended. For the fact remains that any technical assistance program seeking to produce significant improvement in the economic status of two-thirds of the free world's population living in underdeveloped countries cannot be bought at bargain-basement prices, though the reverse need not follow either—that such a program should be on a "big money" scale comparable in any way to the size and extent of the European Recovery Program or the United States military aid program.

According to the Gray Report, a careful study of technical assistance and economic aid requirements made in 1950 by a specially appointed commission under the chairmanship of Gordon Gray, a "needed, feasible and effective program . . . would require funds of up to about 500 million dollars a year for several years, apart from emergency requirements arising from military action." [3]

The International Development Advisory Board, chairmanned by Nelson Rockefeller, confirmed this estimate in 1951 and further recommended that the United States contribute $200,000,000 to an International Development Authority which would be empowered to make grants to underdeveloped countries for partial financing of public works, and another $150,000,000 to the capital of an International Finance Corporation to encourage private investment.[4] The recurring $500,000,000-a-year figure runs about four times the average technical assistance appropriations made between 1950 and 1956.

One omission of both the Gray and Rockefeller reports was the failure to point out that over the short run technical assistance tends to increase economic aid needs. Technical assistance, supported by elementary economic aid, has little real meaning unless it can help lay the foundation for underdeveloped areas effectively to absorb larger amounts of outside capital, including the necessary economic aid, to put the economic development process over the hump and on a self-sustaining basis.

The question of relationship between the two kinds of aid—technical assistance and economic aid—has been the focal point for some of the controversy over the size of America's foreign aid programs. The tendency seems to be growing to consider technical assistance operations something apart from and, in some instances, only remotely related to economic aid. A House Foreign Affairs Committee special study mission reported in 1953

> that the economic supplementary aid programs, administered by TCA, are to a greater degree than desirable ECA-type assistance and not technical assistance in the sense in which the term was intended by the Congress. The study mission recommends that in considering the 1954 fiscal program

the "technical assistance" should be separated from the "economic support for technical assistance" (ESTA). By such a breakdown or separation the Congress could squarely meet and express its will as to the need and amount required for such "economic support for technical assistance," in order that the over-all program may be most effective. Thus, each type of aid could be considered and determined on its own merits.[5]

The Randall Commission report of 1954 reiterated the admonition that America's technical assistance program "need not and should not become a 'big-money' program and should not involve capital investments."

As long as the technical assistance and economic aid programs are coordinated and considered complementary aspects of a single over-all economic development process, perhaps it is as well to separate them for purposes of administration and appropriations. But it must be remembered that the plan of technical assistance, of helping to develop technical and administrative skill and knowledge, is a first step and only a first step toward economic development in Southeast Asia. Elimination of the acute shortage of trained and experienced workers, mechanics, managers, administrators, businessmen, bankers, engineers, chemists, industrial researchers, and the rest of the hierarchy is a top-priority problem to meet the objective of economic progress in Southeast Asia; but it is of little use and, in fact, may become an irritant to serious social unrest if, along with it, economic aid and capital investment is not forthcoming to provide employment for the newly trained technicians. In the same way, it is as poor policy to pour economic aid—capital and capital equipment—down the inexhaustible drain of a country before that country has technicians and managers available to use such aid effectively. Between technical assistance and economic aid for stimulating economic activity there must be close coordination. Between the two ingredients of economic development, trained technicians and capital equipment, a balance must be maintained.

BILATERAL VERSUS MULTILATERAL AID CHANNELS

Although the United States uses both bilateral and multilateral channels for foreign aid and technical assistance, the overwhelming emphasis is placed on bilateral government-to-government arrangements. For example, for the inclusive period 1952–1954, the United States pledged approximately $38,000,000 for multilateral activities through the United Nations technical assistance program, while it obligated ten times the amount, or some $380,000,000, for its own bilateral technical assistance activities.

Increased use of United Nations channels for extending American aid to underdeveloped areas has a number of important political and psychological advantages in its favor. For example, the governments of underdeveloped countries receiving United Nations aid, assistance, or advice have no fear of compromising their economic and political independence or of succumbing to foreign economic imperialism. In fact, it is possible for such Southeast Asian countries as the Philippines, Thailand, Burma, Indonesia and, more recently, Laos and Cambodia, as United Nations members, to derive a special sense of participation and control in receiving assistance through the United Nations because any feeling of obligation inherent in receiving direct aid is diffused by the multilateral approach, which permits the recipient government a degree of self-respect and independence that binational aid relationships make it difficult to maintain. Where American advisers may be inhibited by diplomatic factors, there is always the possibility that United Nations experts and advisers, because of these political and psychological conditions, may be able to impress governments receiving aid into making internal reforms and into maintaining higher levels of performance. In addition, the high prestige of the United Nations in Southeast Asia and the widespread feeling of the United Nations Charter as establishing the proper principles for international relations and of the United Nations Organization as providing the proper machinery for the conduct of international affairs add to the flexibility of the multilateral approach.

Supplementing these advantages of the United Nations approach to economic aid and technical assistance, Southeast Asian governments entering into direct foreign aid relationships with the United States often face important internal political disadvantages. Internal opposition groups, anticommunist as well as communist, often charge governments accepting direct American aid with "selling out to foreign imperialists" or "becoming agents of a foreign power." However unmerited these charges may be, they still manage to have a powerful political effect in nationalistic, colonial-conscious Southeast Asia. Such delicate political problems are involved in the acceptance as well as the grant of foreign aid, that it can happen that conditions proposed by the United States on loans and assistance would be rejected or resented by many Southeast Asian countries, whereas they would be accepted without political difficulty as United Nations proposals.

Again, use of the United Nations in giving American foreign aid and assistance has a certain number of operational advantages. For example, the international pool of technical and administrative talent which the United Nations can draw upon includes Indians, Danes, Swedes, English, Belgians, and French whose numbers and wide experience in dealing with the problems of economic development in tropical Asian underdeveloped areas far outstrip the small number of Americans having similar experience. A major American problem in the binational technical assistance program from the very outset has been to find, recruit, and retain such American personnel as possess the unique qualities of first-rate technical assistance experts or administrators.

On the other side are equally strong arguments favoring United States aid and assistance through direct government-to-government channels. From the American viewpoint, the United States, through the binational approach, is assured a large measure of control over the use of funds, matériel, and personnel which it has provided. It can use economic aid and technical assistance as an arm of American diplomacy, presumably to increase its negotiating power and to keep an avenue open for closer political, economic, and security relations with the recipient states. Through the binational approach, the United States also can rapidly redirect aid and assistance when necessary to countries under special economic pressures and can utilize the relationship as the only feasible channel for certain types of security aid which it considers essential. Because of these advantages and the fact that military aid, by its nature, depends on direct government arrangements, the United States Congress has indicated its decided preference for bilateral aid arrangements.

Because the United States government already contributes approximately 60 per cent of the total to the United Nations technical assistance program, Congress also has made clear its lack of interest in increasing the American contribution.[6] Clearly, it is undesirable for any single country to carry too great a share of the United Nations program. For example, if the United States were to direct its total or even a majority of its technical assistance outlay into the United Nations program, its resulting financial dominance of the program could eliminate many political and psychological advantages which accrue to the United Nations technical assistance operation as a whole.

In addition, from the American viewpoint, certain organizational and administrative characteristics of the United Nations Technical Assistance Administration are a disadvantage. For example, the UNTAA program operates on a project or functional basis through the UN's specialized agencies (such as the International Bank for Reconstruction and Development, the Food and Agricultural Organization, the World Health Organization, and the United Nations Educational, Scientific and Cultural Organization) in contrast to American technical assistance which, working on a country basis, is able to cut across such specific functional problems as health, education, and agriculture, to provide a balanced development program in accordance with the priority needs of the recipient countries. Although it is highly possible that the organizational framework of the UNTAA program could be adjusted to meet over-all country needs, provided there were adequate financial support behind it, the normally inhibiting factors which are inherent in multinational decision-making would seem to deny the kind of flexible and coordinated operations possible under a binational program. On the matter of administrative efficiency and economy, despite claims that the American programs are better administered than the United Nations ones, the basis for comparison between the two programs scarcely exists because both are so different in scope and general approach that they make any statements appear unreliable.

An integral factor in considering the relative merits of the two approaches to economic aid and technical assistance is, to be sure, the attitudes of Southeast Asian governments. In the Philippines, Thailand, and South Vietnam, United States aid is readily accepted on a binational basis without apparent serious political embarrassment or fear of any compromise of independence. This attitude is discernible for several reasons, including the fact that United States relations with the Philippines are well established, that Thailand, a noncolonial country, is relatively free of the fears and suspicions which beset formerly colonial countries, and that South Vietnam is not a member of the United Nations and has no alternate source of aid. Newly admitted to the United Nations, Laos and Cambodia undoubtedly are interested in United Nations technical assistance but also accept American aid in the absence of other aid sources of adequate size. From the American viewpoint, Singapore and Malaya are primarily British responsibilities, and therefore do not enter into the United States aid picture. In Indonesia, a limited American technical assistance mission has been permitted to operate, but the government has been reluctant to accept binational aid from the United States since its repudiation in January 1952 of a Mutual Security Agreement with the United States. Evidence of some dissipation of Indonesian reluctance toward aid brought an announcement in December 1955 of increased American aid to that country in 1956 from some $7,500,000 to more than $11,000,000. In Burma, United States binational aid was terminated in mid-1953 for political reasons, but aid offered through the United Nations continued to prove acceptable.

Justification exists for the recommendation that the United States can serve to advantage its own broader policy objectives and more specific economic development objectives by channeling a larger portion of American aid to underdeveloped areas through the United Nations. But it also appears logical for the bilateral approach to be considered a better comprehensive solution to the specific aid problems in Southeast Asia because the major disadvantages of bilateral aid operate after all in the political and psychological fields in only two of eight Southeast Asian states. Even if the United States were to divert half or all of its economic aid and technical assistance from a bilateral operation to the United Nations programs, it is questionable how much more United Nations technical assistance activity would result or filter through the United Nations political and administrative structure to Southeast Asia to benefit the area in any decisive way. The question, therefore, is not a matter of the choice of a channel of aid, because the need for both approaches to foreign aid and assistance is quite evident; it is, rather, a matter of proportion, the major limitation to a more extensive American participation in the United Nations effort being American unwillingness to contribute any more than its present 60 per cent appropriation to the United Nations technical assistance program.

In Southeast Asia the bilateral versus multilateral aid argument need not wind up in any such negative fashion as that of eliminating direct aid and concentrating on United Nations programs, but in a positive manner of improving the United States approach. Again, this can be accomplished (1) by clarifying the purpose and methods of United States aid and assistance to Americans and Southeast Asians, (2) by eliminating the security-team implications so often inherent in American aid, and (3) by conducting United States aid and assistance programs on a basis of a real partnership in progress with the Southeast Asian countries.

REGIONAL ARRANGEMENTS FOR ECONOMIC AID AND TECHNICAL ASSISTANCE

The regional approach to international problems, including those of economic development, has been one for which the United States has developed a penchant in recent years, resulting in part from the relative success of the European Recovery Program and its auxiliary the Organization for European Economic Cooperation (OEEC).[7] The Southeast Asia Collective Defense Treaty extended this concept to Southeast Asia. Participating governments unanimously agreed in preliminary discussions that the Manila Conference should consider cooperation for economic planning and development as well as for military and countersubversion planning and action. During the conference it was evident that Asian participants viewed the treaty organization as an opportunity for an expanded economic aid program in Southeast Asia. They believed that membership in the Manila Pact would give them certain economic benefits and that, in fact, the economic provisions of the collective security treaty would operate within the framework of a new organization on a basis of exclusiveness.

Although the United States hoped that other Asian nations would join the Manila Pact, it did not want any Asian nation to feel forced into security commitments by the use of economic pressures. Consequently, the United States took the stand at the Manila Conference that there should be no economic *quid pro quo* for becoming a member of the Manila Pact and that the principle of exclusiveness could not be applied to the economic problems of free Asia because each national economy in the area was interrelated. The United States view was that economic progress in the potential Manila Pact countries was closely bound to economic progress in such other countries as India, Burma, Indonesia, and Japan; therefore receipt of American economic aid and technical assistance was best determined by the economic advantages accruing to all rather than by Manila Pact membership.

In the matter of economic provisions of the Manila Pact,[8] it was not the intent of the United States to provide a framework for a regional economic development program because, among other reasons, the number of Asian participants in the pact were insufficient to constitute a "region" for purposes of economic planning and cooperation. But the regional approach to the problems of economic development in South and Southeast Asia remains very much alive in United States planning.

For example, as recently as May 1955 when he presented his 1956 foreign aid budget requests to Congress, President Eisenhower requested a $200,000,000 appropriation as a special regional development fund for Asia. The fund was to be used for a regional economic organization which would originate and evaluate regional development projects in fifteen Asian countries, titled for the purpose the "Arc of Free Asia." This appropriation request later was pared to $100,000,000 by Congress, which also placed a time limit on use of the fund through June 30, 1958. Through diplomatic channels United States representatives hinted that sympathetic consideration would be given to feasible and constructive regional development schemes on which Asian nations could meet and agree. When the Indian government, in line with this thinking, invited interested Asian nations to attend a conference at Simla beginning on May 9, 1955, the United States refrained from sending observers to avoid giving the impression of other than Asian decisions taken by the conference.

In a final statement issued after several days of deliberation, the

Simla Conference participants indicated their feeling that regional treatment could be accorded certain special projects for which additional funds would be welcome. However, they also agreed that it would be undesirable to earmark special funds for regional development projects at the time because regional projects would require more time to be brought to the stage of execution than projects involving only one nation. The Simla Conference demonstrated the fact that most Asian governments are uninterested in having a regional organization imposed between themselves and Washington as a channel for receiving American aid, fearing that such an organization would result in the loss of American interest and support for national economic objectives. It also pointed up a certain skepticism among the Asian nations toward their own regional planning and economic cooperation. In addition to economic nationalism, which played its part, other contributing factors in the Asian decision to reject regional development planning undoubtedly were the time element, the press of national needs in the Asian states, and the fact that the national economies of free Asia generally, excepting Japan, are competitive rather than complementary.

On the matter of a program for economic aid and technical assistance which successfully combines the bilateral and multilateral approaches, there is the Colombo Plan, a cooperative undertaking both by the advanced and by the underdeveloped countries of the British Commonwealth to share their resources for the economic development of South and Southeast Asia. Originally a Commonwealth development scheme which had its inception in January 1950 at a meeting of the British Commonwealth ministers in Colombo, Ceylon, the Colombo Plan remains open to other recipient and donor countries and, by 1955, numbered nineteen full members, including the United States.

Although retarded by inadequate financial support, the Colombo Plan enjoys high prestige and confidence among the Asian members. An indication of this was the October 1954 Consultative Committee meeting in Ottawa when, faced with problems of expanded membership, growing requests for technical assistance, and an increased need for long-term financing for economic development, the committee discovered Colombo Plan members divided on an American offer by Harold Stassen, Director of the Foreign Operations Administration, of increased American economic aid to Asian members of the Colombo Plan. Some Colombo Plan members favored the proposal, but Commonwealth members, for the most part, greeted it negatively. Not only did they feel that the Colombo Plan was their own construction but they also felt that the Plan owed its satisfactory operation to mutual confidence and understanding based on the explicit aims for economic development without qualifying requirements of economic, political, or security *quid pro quo*. It was their feeling that such advantages might be lost if the United States were to become too great a contributor to the Plan's direct operations. No definite American commitments followed Mr. Stassen's announcement, which apparently was misleading or misinterpreted.

Although sympathetic toward the Colombo Plan and a participant since 1951 in its Consultative Committee discussions, the United States prefers to work through its own technical assistance and economic aid programs, coordinating its efforts where possible with Colombo Plan activities.

The fact that India plays a dominant role in the Colombo Plan suggests one possibility for American restraint in supporting the Plan and, in reverse, for some Commonwealth misgivings of American support. "The head and center of the plan is India. In essence the Colombo Plan is really India's Five-Year Plan with the plans of the other countries as appendices. . . ." [9] Of all Asian countries, it is India which undoubtedly is most suspicious of American foreign aid motives. In turn, the United States considers that the development of other Asian countries deserves at least as much attention as does India.

Because of its prestige in Asia, the Colombo Plan merits United States interest as an alternate channel for effective economic aid to Southeast Asia. However, it does not necessarily require more active United States participation in the Colombo Plan for the Plan's techniques to be appraised for possibly valuable clues to any expanded American aid and assistance program in Southeast Asia.

CONDITIONS OF AID

One of the most controversial issues facing American foreign aid policy today is the extent and nature of conditions to be attached to American foreign aid and technical assistance. On the one side, the legislative branch, seeking to define and proscribe foreign aid operations as exactly as possible, holds the view that the United States ought to lay down conditions on aid to the states receiving it. To congressmen of this view American economic aid seems a legitimate means for exercising influence and direct pressure on the political, economic, and security decisions of other governments.

The executive branch, whose aim in foreign aid policy is to retain maximum flexibility and operational freedom, takes the other side—that a minimum of conditions for receiving foreign aid should be written into American foreign aid legislation. Not that the executive branch is opposed to using foreign aid as a bargaining point in negotiation with foreign governments. Rather, it feels that over-all American diplomatic interests as well as the general operational efficiency of the foreign aid program are best served by allowing the State Department and the foreign aid operational agencies freedom to negotiate in each specific case any conditions to be attached to American aid. In general, officials of the executive branch seem to be more aware than their colleagues in Congress of the limitations and dangers inherent in treating American foreign aid as a weapon in political negotiations.

Witness to this tug-of-war between the American legislative and executive branches are the newly independent governments of Southeast Asia which, sensitive to a point of no return on the subject of any encroachment on their political independence, eye critically any conditions attached to American aid which could conceivably provide opportunities for outside interference in their internal affairs.

The conditions attached to American foreign aid are of two general kinds. The first, ordinarily attached to grants of technical assistance, is designed to assure employment of American aid with maximum efficiency and minimum waste. In principle, this type of condition is considered unobjectionable and, for the most part, is accepted with minimum difficulty. An example of American foreign aid legislation imposing conditions of this sort is the Mutual Security Act of 1954 (Title III, Section 302) which requires that a recipient nation:

1) pay a fair share of the cost of the program;

2) provide all necessary information concerning the program and give the program full publicity;

3) seek to the maximum extent possible full coordination and integration of technical cooperation programs being carried out in that nation;

4) endeavor to make effective use of the results of the program; and

5) cooperate with other nations participating in the program in the mutual exchange of technical knowledge and skills.

The second type of condition is intended to exact specific political, economic, or strategic *quid pro quo* for American aid and assistance. In the Mutual Security Act of 1951, for example, recipient governments were required to take adequate steps to mobilize their industries for mutual defense and to gear their fiscal, budgetary, capital, political, and military resources to the Act's objectives. The sensitive Southeast Asian governments tend to read into conditions of this sort potential American interference in their domestic affairs. No matter how carefully these conditions are phrased, they seem to arouse suspicion on the part of the recipient states and to provide a convenient weapon for political opposition groups within those states to bludgeon the government. Even when Southeast Asian governments have been led by need into accepting American-imposed conditions along with American economic aid, they obviously have been reluctant to do so.

In the case of grants of military aid, a close security relationship between the two countries concerned is presumed and, as should be expected, calls for the attachment of more specific conditions. For example, the Mutual Security Act of 1954 in Title I (Mutual Defense Assistance) lists eleven specific "Conditions of Eligibility for Assistance."

The practice of using one legislative act, the Mutual Security Act, to include the practice of all types of American aid may serve as one source of consternation to Southeast Asian governments. For example, the general purposes of military assistance, laid down in the Mutual Security Act of 1954, are "to authorize measures in the common defense, including the furnishing of military assistance to friendly nations and international organizations in order to promote the foreign policy, security, and general welfare of the United States and to facilitate the effective participation of such nations in arrangements for individual and collective self-defense." By committing themselves to this particular set of conditions governing one type of aid, it is possible that some governments may fear that they also are binding themselves to other conditions set up in the Act for the receipt of other types of aid.

In general, American technical assistance is given free of conditions having political and security overtones. As a result, such aid has built up considerable good will and confidence in Southeast Asia to the point where technical assistance operations have even been possible in such a sensitive country as Indonesia. Constant pressure to forsake this long-term advantage for fancied short-run political gain is evidenced in such statements as the conclusion of a Southeast Asian Study Mission report by a 1954 House Foreign Affairs Committee Study: "The communist threat has grown more menacing. To meet it places a heavy drain on our resources. Such sums as we can grant for technical assistance must go to those who are standing on our side even at the expense of aid to those who are neutral." [10]

Congress has made no secret of its preference for giving military aid and its reluctance for continuing to give economic aid.[11] The 1954 Mutual Security Act, offering a way to meet this dilemma on the matter of needs versus congressional reluctance for economic aid reclassifies foreign economic aid of the ECA type as "defense support aid," and this brings it within the terms of Mutual Defense Assistance. The effect of course is to bind the receipt of economic aid to the same set of conditions as apply to the receipt of military aid, which would seem to stack the cards even more heavily against those states needing economic aid but loath to align themselves openly to any one side as a result of the gratuity. But this reclassification of economic aid as "defense support" is offset again in part by an additional category of aid called "development assistance" whose conditions are far less stringent than those applied to the military aid category. In the "defense support aid" and "development assistance aid" categories up to the present, appropriations have been about equal.

In matter of practice, the congressional record has been far better than its reputation for attaching conditions to foreign economic aid and technical assistance operations. The latter impression has been based on Asian misunderstandings and misapprehensions created by extreme proposals in Congress even though they were never adopted. Such proposals have had an unfortunate way of being widely circulated and, as might be expected, have caused irreparable difficulty and prejudice among the Asian people long in advance of any legislation to the contrary.

The attempt to use American aid and assistance in diplomatic negotiations to exact political concessions also damages the basic purpose of economic development. Although diplomats in the field may be strongly tempted to hold out the plum of economic aid and technical assistance as a lever to achieve certain immediate political objectives and, in some cases circumstances may even justify such connivance, use of American aid and assistance in bargaining reduces its long-range effectiveness.

Now that the ICA administers economic aid and technical assistance under the Department of State, the tendency may exist for the purposes and long-term effectiveness of American aid for economic development to be subordinated to short-run purposes of political bargaining. But the warning nonetheless remains that attaching political conditions to American aid or using American aid as a diplomatic lever undoubtedly are self-defeating expedients.[12] To believe that specifically American interests can be pursued through aid programs based on mutual interest only reflects confusion or dissension in the American understanding of reasonable foreign aid objectives.

The situation is summarized succinctly in the Randall Report:

> All American military, economic, and technical aid to other countries is rooted in the national interest of the United States. Such aid is acceptable to other countries only if it serves their national interests. The fundamental basis on which all foreign aid operations should rest, therefore, is mutual interest. Mutual interest cannot be created by pressure and can be destroyed by coercion.[13]

INTERNATIONAL TRADE AND ECONOMIC DEVELOPMENT

To help finance their economic development, the Southeast Asian governments are anxious to utilize the channels of international trade to expand their export earnings.

In doing so, however, they come face to face with four inhibiting economic factors which have operated to cause an unstable and generally unfavorable trade balance in the area. First, Southeast Asian foreign-exchange earnings are almost entirely dependent on the export of two or three products. Second, their export products for the most part are subject to unsettling price fluctuations on the international market. Third, the difficulty of marketing such a major export crop as rice has resulted in the accumulation of large surplus stocks in Burma and Thailand. Fourth, there is a limitation to the free-world trade outlets for a number of Southeast Asia's exports.

The following figures, given in percentage of total export by value, illustrate the extremely narrow base of the export trade of the Southeast Asian countries: rice provides 75 per cent of Burma's total export by value; rice provides 55 per cent of Thailand's export value; rubber and tin provide 80 per cent of Malaya's export value; rubber, tin, and petroleum provide 75 per cent of Indonesia's export value; and copra, sugar, and hemp provide 75 per cent of the Philippines' export value.

As a result of the economic specialization which confronts them at the present stage of their economic development, the Southeast Asian countries must depend for their economic well-being and progress on a capricious international market price and demand for their few key export products which in turn scarcely provide them an adequate or a stable level of foreign-exchange earnings for economic development.

This economic insecurity resulting from price fluctuations was graphically illustrated during the Korean War. During the early months of the war, the price of such strategic materials as tin and rubber increased so rapidly because of the greatly increased demand that the price of tin at one point rose 300 per cent over prewar levels, and during the years 1950 and 1951 Indonesia, Malaya, and Thailand experienced unprecedented prosperity. On the assumption or in the hope that the boom would be permanent, the three Southeast Asian countries expanded production of rubber and tin, increased government welfare services, raised wage scales, and geared their import regulations to a continued high level of foreign export earnings. By 1952, however, they faced a drastic drop in the international market prices of tin and rubber, the price of rubber falling 35 per cent between mid-1952 and mid-1954, the price of tin dropping 40 per cent in the first half of 1953 alone. For Southeast Asia it was a disillusioning experience which drove home the reality of their economic vulnerability, reinforced their determination to hasten economic self-sufficiency, and increased the temptation to expand trade with the communist bloc.

In Burma and Thailand, where economic progress depends on rice exports, since 1953 the situation has been steadily worsening. Prior to that time, from the end of the Second World War on, Thailand and Burma were able to take advantage of a rice seller's market to maintain a favorable balance-of-payments position and, being able to market all the rice they could produce at favorable prices, strained to increase their rice production. By 1953, however, India, Indonesia, the Philippines, and Malaya, having greatly expanded their rice and wheat production to the point where the first three countries had become almost self-supporting in rice, began cutting down their import needs. The United States, another rice producer which had been steadily expanding production in the postwar period, became a major rice competitor to Burma and Thailand for the rice markets of Japan and Korea.[14] The result was that Burma and Thailand began accumulating large rice surpluses, especially of the lower grades of rice, which they could not market despite the lowering of government rice-export prices.

Left with this loss in government revenue and the worsening of their trade-balance situation, the Southeast Asian governments find themselves under intense economic and political pressure to expand their trade with the communist bloc. Thus, when Soviet party leaders Khrushchev and Bulganin visited Burma in December 1955, it should not have been surprising that the two countries concluded a trade agreement by which the Soviet Union offered its materials and services to "assist and cooperate" in developing agriculture, irrigation, and industry in Burma in exchange for "convenient quantities" of Burmese rice. Under the terms of the agreement it is estimated that the Soviet Union will take as payment for services rendered approximately half of Burma's rice exports.[15]

The unmarketable rice surpluses, which have been accumulating in Burma and Thailand, present the United States with a difficult political and economic dilemma. On the one side, the United States is anxious for Burma and Thailand to find free-world outlets for their surplus rice; on the other, the United States includes in its economic and technical assistance objectives the need for food-deficit Asian countries to increase their agricultural production in order to increase their living standards and to decrease the amounts of foreign exchange which they must spend on food imports. Compounding the dilemma is America's own growing rice production and the political necessity for finding a way to dispose of rice surpluses in the United States. It would seem in this case as if American economic policies, both foreign and domestic, were in direct competition with American political policies.

Although it is encouraging from a Southeast Asian viewpoint to survey the free-world export outlets for rubber and tin on a long-range basis,[16] immediate needs for these two key Southeast Asian products are limited. Synthetic rubber, South American tin, and the development of tin substitutes are keen competitors for the American market. The Western Europe market, while growing, until recently offered Southeast Asia only limited foreign trade benefits because of currency-exchange problems. At the present time, the world's major deficit area in rubber, tin, and oil is the Soviet bloc. From this rundown, it is clear that any attempt on the part of United States policy to restrict trade contacts in these strategic materials between Southeast Asia and the communist bloc must be augmented by suitable alternate export outlets. Otherwise it is too easy for other Southeast Asian countries to follow the lead taken by Ceylon, which, faced with acute rice-import needs and an unmarketable rubber surplus on which she was unable to conclude any suitable rubber export agreement within the free world, contracted with communist China to trade rubber for rice.

Southeast Asia's marketing and distribution systems must be strengthened and the grade and quality of the area's export products must be improved before any further work can be done toward solving Southeast Asia's four major foreign trade problems. Other proposals which have been made for meeting the problem of fluctuating price and demand for Southeast Asia's exports include international marketing agreements, the establishment of an international price parity scheme, and the negotiation of long-term purchase agreements. On a short-run basis any of these proposals could be helpful, if they were translated into reality.

But, for any practical solution, Southeast Asia's export and foreign exchange problems require long-range developments. Southeast Asia's outlets can be increased by continued economic growth in the free world, and Southeast Asia's dependence on one or two items can, in time, be reduced by continued economic diversification. These are the two long-range solutions toward which American economic and technical aid is directed. In the final analysis, however, any early improvement in the trade situation depends more on liberal international trade conditions, especially in American practice, than on any other factor.

CONCLUSIONS

Without attempting to minimize the difficulties of economic development in Southeast Asia, it is as well to recognize the salient fact that the Southeast Asian countries possess some significant assets which, if properly employed, can bring economic progress and improved living standards within their reach.

First of all, the Southeast Asian countries contain the natural resource potential which is vital for national economic growth and development. Second, most of the countries have a start in transportation, communication, and industrial facilities which can be expanded to serve basic economic development needs. Third, when adequately motivated, the Southeast Asians are capable of energetic and sustained activity even though their tropical climate may not be suitable to the economic pace of Detroit, Manchester, or Tokyo. Fourth, devoted to the objective of economic development, Southeast Asian governments are open to outside suggestion and assistance provided the latter is offered by trustworthy sources and in a manner which does not arouse antagonism. Fifth, the Southeast Asian nations suffer neither the grinding poverty of such other areas as the Middle East nor the debilitating population dilemma of such countries as India.

If it is possible to raise living standards and to register significant economic progress anywhere in Asia within the framework of democratic methods and principles, the best opportunities would seem to lie in such favorably endowed states as Burma, Indonesia, Thailand, and the Philippines. There is no better area than Southeast Asia to test the theory that economically underdeveloped countries can attain their economic objectives under conditions of the modern world without resorting to communist techniques of force, human regimentation, cultural and social coercion, intellectual corruption, and dictatorship.

However, the pace of such Southeast Asian events as Indonesia's growing communist strength, Burma's increasing contacts with the communist world, Thailand's and the Philippines' uncertain economic progress, Indochina's critical economic and political conditions, and Malaya's unrest would seem to indicate that political and psychological opportunities are slipping for noncommunist solutions to the socioeconomic problems of the area. Unless the United States moves rapidly on the Southeast Asian scene with vigorous, broad-minded and long-range policies oriented to the area's economic, social, and political currents, it may miss all opportunity effectively to influence Southeast Asia's economic development.

On Southeast Asia's economic development, United States policy is faced with six major conclusions:

1. United States foreign aid and technical assistance objectives should become matters of such complete agreement that they are compatible with Southeast Asian national objectives and also are properly understood both in the United States and in the states of Southeast Asia. Too often American policy objectives in underdeveloped areas have appeared to be matters of controversy or multiple purpose dangling on lines of political expediency rather than on fixed and secure guidelines for action.

As long as vital American interests are served by Southeast Asia's economic growth and progress, justification exists for American economic aid and technical assistance. When, in the final analysis, it becomes clear that the fundamental and ultimate objective of American aid to Southeast Asia is the achievement of economic development in Southeast Asia within the context of free, humanitarian, and democratic principles, then the logic of the continuity of aid lies revealed. This is aid geared to need, aid given to avert rather than to meet Southeast Asia's political and economic crises. In the light of this overriding objective, such issues as bilateral versus multilateral aid channels, technical versus economic aid, loans versus grants, private versus public investment become reduced to manageable questions of the relative effectiveness and the reasonable American capacity to help.

2. United States national interests and objectives in underdeveloped areas can be secured only through a sustained, long-term effort of major proportions. If the United States is seriously to help the Southeast Asian governments toward economic development, it must conceive and execute technical assistance and economic aid programs on a basis of five- or ten-year planning periods. Year-to-year programs are neither suitable to the conditions in Southeast Asia nor to the magnitude of the threats to American interests and objectives in the area.

Because the outside capital necessary for Southeast Asian economic development scarcely is forthcoming from private American investment, despite wishful thinking on the subject, a major part of it must come from the American government in the form of long-term loans at low interest and grants-in-aid. The alternatives are for the United States to risk the consequences of economic stagnation in Southeast Asia or for Southeast Asian governments to turn to communist sources of aid and influence.

3. The United States should adjust the balance between military and economic aid to Southeast Asia. Taking into consideration the fact that the external military threat to Southeast Asia is real, that American military aid to the Philippines, South Vietnam, Cambodia, Laos, and Thailand contributes to the common security, helps to provide strength to maintain internal law and order, and lends an additional factor of deterrence against external aggression; and that building military strength in Southeast Asia is a necessary ingredient of American policy, overemphasis on military

aid still overlooks four basic factors. These are: (1) economic strength is considered by Southeast Asian governments to be a more immediate and urgent need than military strength; (2) military aid, although providing the means, does not provide the will for national defense; (3) by building military establishments which the Southeast Asian economies cannot support, American military aid becomes self-continuing and, by this same token, also increases the need for larger and more effective economic development programs; (4) Southeast Asia's independence probably faces greater internal political and economic threats than external military threats.

For all these reasons, it seems not only practical but essential for the United States to revise its ratio of total aid to Southeast Asia on the basis of internal social, political, and economic dangers rather than on the possibility of international communist aggression. To free American economic aid from the conditions imposed by Title I of the Mutual Security Acts, a greater portion of it should be classified as "development assistance" and less should be categorized as "defense support."

4. The United States should expand its effort on Southeast Asia's socioeconomic front. Community development schemes already have demonstrated that it is possible to introduce innovation and to stimulate social change at the village community level in Southeast Asia, although on a national social level it is another problem, the major difficulty being that integrated national societies have not yet been fully developed. In the latter case, a long-range impact on Southeast Asia's socioeconomic development may be felt by American support of national projects which Southeast Asian governments and private organizations have developed for the purpose of creating national societies and national institutions for group expression. The county-agent concept, which brings farmers into communication with one another and with their government, may well be one of the United States' most significant contributions to Southeast Asia on this cultural-sociological level which, generally speaking, is the first to feel the impact of technical assistance.

5. The American concept of technical assistance is the most imaginative and vigorous aid policy which the United States ever has advanced for underdeveloped areas, specifically for Southeast Asia. American technical assistance operations have won the con-

fidence of Southeast Asia's governments and people and have earned for themselves a high level of prestige. The United States should not squander impressive psychological advantages for short-term political purposes but should guard them carefully and use them as the framework of building a reinvigorated and expanded American program to help the Southeast Asian countries attain their national objectives of economic growth and progress. The Southeast Asian technical assistance programs should be increased substantially in size and scope and should be backed up by development assistance funds and by capital equipment which would be adequate to bridge the gap between the capital investment potential and the capacity to absorb investment of the Southeast Asian countries.

A series of fixed-term plans for national development which the Southeast Asian governments could work out and execute in partnership with the United States could serve as the first phase of an offensive on the internal economic problems of Southeast Asia based on the technical assistance approach. Understanding and support for these development plans by the Southeast Asian people would minimize the risks of government instability. In situations where bilateral partnership arrangements by their very nature would seem suspect, it would be plausible for an international committee of experts or an international development authority to function advantageously as part of a planning and operating agency.

6. The United States should not underestimate the fact that the way in which America conducts itself and the way in which Americans conduct themselves in seeking to aid Southeast Asia is every ounce as important as the measures which the United States takes to help Southeast Asia.

9. PROBLEMS OF AMERICAN DIPLOMACY

THE RETURN TO DIPLOMACY

Three recent developments on the international scene today substantially increase in importance the diplomatic aspects of American relations with the underdeveloped areas of the world in general and more specifically with Southeast Asia. Military in character, the first development is an outgrowth of Soviet progress in the field of nuclear weapons and guided-missile research. Even to the most ill informed, it is becoming increasingly evident that if the United States and the Soviet Union have not already reached the point of atomic stalemate, where each is capable of destroying the other, they are fast approaching it. Like the United States, the Soviet Union already appears to be planning and acting in terms of the capacity for instant and massive retaliation. In Churchillian terms, whether or not the "balance of terror" may serve to prevent general war is a matter of knowledge beyond present limits. What it does do is to telescope the communist and anticommunist worlds into uneasy proximity and a state of competitive co-existence where both may be expected to intensify efforts to gain their objectives by economic and diplomatic means. The effectiveness of American diplomacy in Southeast Asia is a key part of this struggle.

The second development, economic in nature, also takes on tangible import. When in 1955 the communists began to use their economic power as an instrument of diplomacy, all manner of repercussions were felt around the world. In the Middle East, for instance, the Soviets agreed to supply arms to Egypt in exchange for Egyptian cotton and negotiated to exchange industrial equipment and technical assistance with Syria for Syrian cotton.

This changed foreign economic policy moved on to Asia where the Soviets contracted in India to build, on terms laid down by the Indian government, a 1,000,000-ton steel mill at Orissa and, finally, during the late 1955 visit of Soviet party leaders Bulganin and Khrushchev to India, Burma, and Afghanistan, reached new highs of activity in Soviet promises and commitments to each one of the visited countries. For Afghanistan, the Soviet leaders promised a long-term loan of $100,000,000 (whose method and means of repayment were not made public) to pay for technical asssistance, machinery, industrial equipment, and capital goods from the Soviet Union. For India, the Soviet Union agreed to supply industrial equipment, machinery, one million tons of steel and other goods over a three-year period in exchange for Indian raw materials which it was hoped, together with official Soviet-agency expenditures in India, would balance the account. For Burma, the agreement was to provide technical assistance and to cooperate in developing agriculture, irrigation, and industry in exchange for Burmese rice exports to the Soviet bloc. Swimming in the current of activity with underdeveloped areas, the Soviet Union also proposed economic, technical, and even military aid to other Middle East, Latin America, and Southeast Asia countries, including an offer to buy rice from Thailand and to build an atomic power plant in Indonesia.

Although based on trade and loans rather than on economic and technical aid grants, the new Soviet move into the sphere of economic and technical assistance activities in underdeveloped areas has engendered considerable excitement and interest in South and Southeast Asia. In the United States, as seasoned an observer as Walter Lippmann was moved to comment that the altered Soviet foreign economic policy was an event of historic significance comparable to the Soviet's breaking of the American monopoly on atomic weapons. Although the Soviet Union's internal living standards can be sacrificed by the Soviet leaders for external political purposes to create surplus goods for export, it remains to be seen whether or not the economic strength of the Soviet Union will support a major foreign economic aid and technical assistance program. However, if the Soviet entry into the field of economic and technical assistance actually provides the underdeveloped countries of the world a choice of aid opportunities for economic development, then American diplomacy is taxed with a complex and new competitive situation.

The third development which increases the importance of American diplomacy and skill in Southeast Asia is the political need, corollary to the new Soviet foreign economic policy, to ease any existing tensions between the United States and the states of Southeast Asia. To offset the experimental Soviet program of a "soft" policy to Asia, heralded by such postures of international diplomacy as a series of top-level visits between communist and noncommunist Asian leaders and meetings purportedly to explore means of reducing international tensions which produce only momentary and false lulls in the cold war, the United States must be prepared to work more vigorously than ever in the diplomatic realm as well as in its foreign trade and aid policy. Although it is too early to measure the success of the communist's experiment with economic aid and technical assistance and with international diplomacy characterized by good will and reasonableness, there is no mistaking the fact that, very soon after the Geneva Conference, the Soviet actions were taken to influence the neutral states of the economically underdeveloped areas and America's allies. The Soviet Union obviously has launched a major drive, which the United States can scarcely ignore, to isolate the United States, by economic and political means, from the uncommitted neutral nations of the Middle East, South, and Southeast Asia.

In response to the challenge, the United States must consider the paradoxes of maintaining a system of collective security alliances and a reasonable level of defense preparedness among its allies through a period of communist tactical peacemongering, of improving relations with the neutralist states, more eager than ever to read innocent purpose and good intent into the slightest Soviet or Chinese compromise or relaxation of hostile posture.

By no means a final answer, a reduction of the major sources of political tension existing between the United States and the states of South and Southeast Asia should be a minimum first step toward these ends. Although they do not operate to an equal extent in the relationships between the United States and each of the Southeast Asian countries, the three major diplomatic issues which cause friction are (1) colonialism, (2) neutralism, (3) and American objectives and motives. Collectively, these issues indicate the scope of the task which confronts American diplomacy in Southeast Asia today.

THE ISSUE OF COLONIALISM

Time has not yet eroded the jagged emotional edges which the newly independent states of South and Southeast Asia still possess as a result of their colonial experiences. For both leaders and people, anticolonialism remains a burning international issue. Even though a few Southeast Asian leaders are particularly to blame for playing up the colonialism motif for internal political purposes, either to rationalize shortcomings of their own governments or to rally public support in time of internal crisis, the fact remains that the issue of ending colonialism is one of the major political principles guiding the foreign policies of Asia's newly independent states. Between the United States and Indonesia, Burma and India, colonialism is a specific diplomatic issue. Between the United States and Thailand and the Philippines, no such problem exists for reasons already cited. So far, colonialism has not reared itself in United States dealings either with Malaya or with the new states of Indochina.

To the United States and to the once colonial states of Asia, colonialism in the world today rates decidedly different appraisals and attitudes, as is evident in any comparison of West-East views on several aspects of the problem.

1. American spokesmen tend to point out that the Western colonial powers in the ten years following the Second World War granted complete political independence to more than 600,000,000 people who now constitute twelve new independent nations. Asian anticolonialists consider that the vast postwar liberation of colonial peoples was long overdue and, except in one or two cases, believe that it resulted from successful colonial revolts rather than from any sympathy by the colonial powers for the cause of independence.

In the Asian view, the fact that millions of people in a large part of the world still live under Western colonial bondage is the important one.

2. American officials tend to stress the dangers and risks of premature independence. "When we exercise restraint," Secretary Dulles stated, "it is because of a reasoned conviction that quick action (on independence for colonial areas) would not, in fact, produce true independence. Indeed, in some situations hasty action would spell confusion and division which would be the transition to a captivity far worse than present dependence." [1] To this the Asians reply that delayed independence is riskier than premature independence. Besides, they ask, what right have the colonial peoples to decide the timing of independence? The claim that colonial powers are "not yet ready for self-government or independence" has an old and familiar ring to Indians, Burmese, and Indonesians.

3. Speaking for the United States, Mr. Dulles assures the anticolonial governments: "The United States is using its influence to promote self-government. We do so more than is publicly known, for in these matters open pressures are rarely conducive to the best results." [2] As the Asian powers see it, the United States is *not* using its maximum efforts to force the issues of self-government and independence for colonial peoples. Worse, through its military and economic aid programs to Western Europe, the United States has made it possible for the colonial powers either to hold colonial areas which they would have lost otherwise or else to delay independence in other areas, such as Indonesia. Despite protestations to the contrary, the United States, by its economic, military, and diplomatic support of Britain, France, Holland, Belgium, and Portugal, in effect, has adopted a procolonial policy in the eyes of many Asian powers.

4. In the United States view, the issue of independence for colonial peoples is complicated by international communism, which seeks to use nationalism and resentment of colonialism as a device for absorbing colonial peoples into the communist system. The communists, who loudly denounce the West for colonialism, since the end of the war have extended their new and more terrible form of colonialism to embrace more than 600,000,000 people. But, in the Asian view, the risk of communism is increased by the post-

ponement of independence. If colonial people turn to communism to achieve independence from Western rule, as they did in Vietnam, then the Asians declare the fault lies with the Western colonial powers. In any case, communism appears to them to be no worse a fate than Western colonialism.

5. American officials play up America's anticolonial history and the American Revolution as the first revolt from colonial rule, emphasizing the idea that the United States is the world's foremost advocate of self-government and independence for dependent peoples. The anticolonial Asian governments see this only as evidence that the United States has lost touch with its revolutionary history, that it has become reactionary and alarmed by any change in the *status quo* which might seem to threaten its own way of life. They see how the United States has buttressed North African and Mediterranean colonial régimes and has established in the colonial possessions of European allies military bases which are a powerful hindrance to the progress of subject peoples toward self-determination.

6. American spokesmen seek to assure anticolonials that the era of Western imperialism is at an end and no longer constitutes a major threat. At the same time they attempt to convince Asian and African peoples that international communism is a new form of imperialism which is more dangerous to their independence than anything ever known before. To this the Asians answer is that they will believe Western imperialism is finished when all peoples are free from Western colonial rule and not before. On the representation of communism as a new form of imperialism, this is rendered suspect to them by the feeling that the West, especially the United States, may be developing a new form of economic imperialism under the guise of economic and military aid programs. Because governments which accept such aid, especially military aid, become dependent on its continuation, these governments soon fall under the significant, if not baleful, influence of the United States. Today's influence, so the argument runs, may be the basis for tomorrow's domination.

Add to this wide area of mutual misunderstanding Asian suspicions of the United States as a land full of race prejudice and a nation with an atomic superiority complex, and there is little wonder for the strain in American relations with a number of South and Southeast Asian governments.

American policy-makers are confronted with a difficult task in handling the dilemma posed by the issue of colonialism. As Secretary Dulles describes it:

We ourselves, as the first colony of modern times to win our independence, have a traditional sympathy with the peoples of the world who are trying to win like independence for themselves, and we would like very much to take a leadership ourselves in the program for winning independence. It is not always easy to reconcile our natural desires and aspirations in that respect with the equally important task of maintaining relations of trust and confidence with our European Allies who traditionally are the colonial powers. This is one of the great dilemmas which the United States foreign policy faces at this time, and I must say it creates at times and places dilemmas which I do not find lend themselves to any very satisfactory answer.[3]

In Mr. Dulles's description, one important consideration to the dilemma is omitted. More is at stake than the United States' "natural desires and aspirations" to take a leadership role in the present African-Asian independence struggles. The United States is compelled by political considerations to play an active role, its entire political relationship with the newly independent states of Asia and Africa being involved, for one thing. For another, American attitudes toward the present independence struggles are molding the shape of political relationships with future millions of independent peoples all over the world.

Too many contradictory factors must be taken into account to provide any clear-cut answers to the colonialism paradox. As each colonial issue arises, American policy-makers, while keeping one eye on the maintenance of the best possible relations with the Asian and African powers, the other on the need for a certain standard of order in the transition from a colonial status to independence, also must juggle three balls in the air for American security purposes —NATO unity, the United Nations political situation, and communist activities.

For American security and for international stability in general, it is extremely important that issues of self-determination, self-government, and independence in colonial areas be timed to permit adequate political and economic preparation. Otherwise the risk of an expansion of the areas of disorder in the world provides too great an opportunity for the communists to move in and extend their curtain of human and national bondage. By any objective evaluation, it must be recognized that there are colonial peoples so inadequately prepared and ill equipped for self-government or independence that it would be a disservice to them and to the principle of self-determination to grant them either objective prematurely.

In its concern for the proper timing of independence, the United States comes into direct conflict with most Asian and African powers, especially India, which, acting as leading spokesman and strategist on issues of self-determination, stands for the principle of immediate liberation of subject peoples. The communists, using the issues of nationalism and Western colonialism, fall in with this guise of a liberating force and apparently have taken in Mr. Nehru, whose complete unconcern for the realities of international communism is evidenced in his words that "anything that comes in the guise of a liberating force is . . . welcome."

As for the NATO alliance, the United States considers its unity, strength, and spirit the most important single foreign policy objective. As a result it tries to avoid meddling in the colonial affairs of any of the major colonial powers—Britain, France, Belgium, Portugal, and the Netherlands—all of which are key members of NATO, and have strong feelings about their colonial policies. On such policies, little difficulty remains between the United States and Britain. Great Britain, withdrawing from India, Pakistan, Ceylon, and Burma in grace and dignity, has applied its lesson of granting independence in time to the African Gold Coast and the Sudan. In its other African colonies and in Malaya, it is pushing forward rapidly with training and preparation for self-government and independence.

Within the NATO structure, colonial policy is a thorn in United States relations with France. Although the colonial issue in Indochina finally has been resolved, it was done in a manner highly unsatisfactory to France, the United States, and to the peoples of Indochina. On questions concerning other parts of the French Empire, French West Africa, Morocco, Tunisia, and Algeria, where the colonial issue remains a burning matter, France does not hesitate to use her geographic importance to any NATO defense plans as a foil for parrying United States pressures for more liberal French colonial practices.

The stresses and strains of American policy toward colonial questions are especially apparent in the United Nations, where Assembly votes on colonial questions often are subject to diplomatic pressures and bargaining. In the political caucusing on issues of self-determination, trusteeship, and human rights, the United States seems to wind up quite generally on the opposite side from India, leader of the Asian-African grouping.

In general, the United States expresses sympathy for the principles of self-determination and self-government but holds no fixed policy toward colonial questions in the United Nations. Prevailing political considerations in the United Nations, in NATO, or in the French government apparently qualify the extent to which the United States is prepared to uphold these principles in actual practice. The United States approach seems to consist of broad statements supporting the principle of self-determination followed by actions in which political considerations weigh more heavily than the avowed support of principle.

To India, Indonesia, and Burma, which place anticolonialism above anticommunism in their foreign policies, the United States appears only too ready to compromise the principles of self-determination, self-government, and independence. On the United States side, American officials are troubled by the almost complete tolerance with which India and Indonesia view Soviet conduct and the intolerance which they express toward American views on communism, colonialism, and human rights. In the frequent complaints over communist imperialism and communist denial of fundamental human rights voiced in the United Nations, India has never once sided with the West. Rather, in such discussions, India either abstains from participation or else sides with the Soviet bloc by taking the offensive that complaints over Soviet malpractices are distortions of the real question of colonialism.

Certain general characteristics, all of them antagonistic in some degree to the views of India, Indonesia, and Burma, are observable in the American treatment of colonial questions in the

United Nations. First of all, the United States attempts to avoid public conflict with its European allies, and this is interpreted as a procolonial policy by most Asian and African nations. Second, as a result of unhappy experience in the Indonesian Case when the United States attempted to serve the best interests both of the Netherlands and of Indonesia as mediator and managed to antagonize both sides, the United States attempts to stay out of disputes between colonial powers and dependent peoples. Third, the United States places more faith in direct peaceful negotiations between colonial powers and dependent peoples than in any other means of settling colonial disputes. A case in point is the United States vote to place Morocco and Tunisia on the United Nations agenda, then the vote to remove them from the agenda as soon as direct negotiations between France and the two protectorates showed some signs of progress. Fourth, the United States consistently upholds Article 2, paragraph 7, of the Charter, which provides that the Organization shall not take up matters essentially within the "domestic jurisdiction" of member states. Thus, the United States vote against including discussions of Algeria on the United Nations agenda was based on the fact that under French law Algeria administratively is an integral part of the French Republic. The "domestic jurisdiction" clause also has influenced United States policy in the United Nations toward questions of human rights, trusteeship, and racial problems in the Union of South Africa.

American officials are acutely aware of the communist campaign in Asia to pin the label of colonialism or imperialism on every American move. When colonial issues arise, the opportunity which they may give Moscow and Peking to advance their program of intensifying Asian and African distrust for American motives must be weighed carefully by American officials. A case in point where United States policy was not best served for that reason was the Bandung Conference of April 1955, first suggested by Indonesia's Prime Minister Ali Sastroamidjojo, and sponsored jointly by Indonesia, Ceylon, Pakistan, Burma, and India.

Purposes of the conference were to promote good will and cooperation among the nations of Asia and Africa, to consider social, economic, and cultural problems of the countries represented, to explore the possible contributions which the participants might make in the promotion of world peace, and "to consider problems of special interest to Asian and African peoples, for example, problems affecting national sovereignty and of racialism and colonialism." [4]

Here, in the lovely resort city of Bandung in the highlands of central Java, was provided just the right opportunity for the anti-colonial powers to dramatize the issue of colonialism. As host, Indonesia's President Sukarno opened the conference on April 19th by reminding the colorful assemblage of delegates representing twenty-nine countries [5] and more than half the world's population that the calendar date was the auspicious 180th anniversary of the ride of Paul Revere, a first dramatic incident in the first modern war of subject peoples against colonial domination—the American War of Independence.

Although the conference condemnation of Western colonialism was a foregone conclusion, the question of censorship of communist imperialism remained an open one. Without any prearranged agenda for the six-day meeting American officials feared that China's Chou En-lai, supported by such influential neutralist leaders as India's Nehru, Indonesia's Ali Sastroamidjojo, and Burma's U Nu, would take advantage of the opportunity to convert many conference participants to the view that the only real menace to the peoples of Asia and Africa is the Western white man's brand of colonialism or imperialism.

Privately, the meeting was viewed by key American officials with considerable distaste as a situation in which the United States had nothing to gain and much to lose. Fearful of conference results, the United States assumed an attitude of official aloofness, which, if not downright hostile, certainly failed to offer either sympathy or support to the conference nations. Although Manila Pact members, meeting in Bangkok a few months earlier, voted to send the organization's good wishes, the United States itself sent no official greetings to Bandung, managing by this act to snub twenty-eight nations in order to snub Chou En-lai. Two days before the opening of the conference, President Eisenhower, in a statement timed for effect on the Bandung conferees, announced that American foreign aid operations would undergo a major reorganization, and held out the prospect of increased and long-term Asian aid. Both the snub and the offer of money to assuage Asian and African suspicions played into Chou En-lai's hands.

Nevertheless, communist imperialism, along with Western colonialism, was attacked by a number of delegates, including General Carlos Romulo of the Philippines, Mohammed Ali of Pakistan, Prince Wan Waithayakon of Thailand, Ali Amini of Iran, Fatin Rustu Zorlu of Turkey, Fadhil el-Jamali of Iraq, and Sir John Kotelawala of Ceylon, who insisted that any conference condemnation of colonialism include both evils.

General Romulo, making a thinly veiled reference to international communism in his opening address, said: "It is perilously easy in this world for national independence to be more fiction than fact. Because it expresses the deepest desire of so many people in the world, it can be unscrupulously used as a shibboleth, as a façade, as an instrument for a new and different kind of subjection."

Iraq's Dr. el-Jamali made the strongest statement on communism, scoring it as a "subversive religion" with which the communists "confront the world with a new form of colonialism much deadlier than the old." Squarely facing Chou En-lai, and drawing thunderous applause at the end of his speech, he declared, "Today the Communist world has subject races in Asia and Eastern Europe on a much larger scale than any old colonial power." [6]

Ceylon's Sir John Kotelawala, perhaps the most effective speaker of all, urged that the conference condemn communist colonialism along with Western colonialism. Challenging the Moscow version of co-existence and denouncing communist subversive activities in Asia and Africa, he pointed out that the communists "have not attempted to disguise the fact that their ultimate and constant aim is to weaken and undermine the legally constituted governments of our countries so that at the appropriate time we can be transformed into satellites of Soviet Russia or Communist China." [7]

The delegates, agreeing to a compromise formula after heated discussion, condemned colonialism "in all its manifestations." In the final communiqué, "Declaration on Problems of Dependent Peoples," the Asian and African states agreed:

1) In declaring that colonialism in all its manifestations is an evil which should speedily be brought to an end;

2) In affirming that the subjection of peoples to alien subjugation, domination and exploitation constitutes a denial of fundamental human rights, is contrary to the Charter of the United Nations, and is an impediment to the promotion of world peace and cooperation;

3) In declaring its support of the case of freedom and independence for all such peoples; and

4) In calling upon the powers concerned to grant freedom and independence to such peoples.

The official American attitude softened only after it was clear that the currents at Bandung were running strongly against communism and that Chou En-lai could not run away with the conference. By then, however, the effort to recoup through friendliness the political and psychological stature which had been lost by earlier uncertainty and hesitation was too belated for any diplomatic gains. Too, the omissions of government policy were only underscored when private American citizens and groups sent personal greetings for the success of the conference in an attempt to make up for the diplomatic deficiency.

Under the circumstances, the United States is finding it difficult to win any wide public appreciation for its colonialism dilemma. It may be, as many American officials maintain, that the kind of free-wheeling uncompromising policy which colonial peoples expect of a standard bearer in the cause of self-determination and independence is not permitted by virtue of America's far-flung economic, political, and security responsibilities; but it remains of maximum importance for American relations with Asian and African nations in general and specifically with India, Burma, and Indonesia, that there is both understanding and respect for the United States position on colonial questions. On the United States' part, the friction generated over the colonialism issue in relations with India, Indonesia, and Burma may be reduced in several ways.

For one, the United States can assume a less ambiguous position on the colonialism issue. By attempting to parry the force on each side of the dilemma, the United States has come to grips with neither side. For instance, when colonial issues have been in the foreground, the United States has avoided any open embarrassment of the colonial powers while, at the same time, under cover of diplomatic privacy, officials regularly have pressed for the adoption of more liberal colonial policies and the hastening of early self-government and independence for colonial peoples in London, Paris, The Hague, and Lisbon. In some measure, the colonialism dilemma stems from an unwillingness to do publicly what is attempted privately for the cause of self-determination, self-government, and independence for colonial peoples.

Like his predecessor Mr. Acheson, Secretary Dulles seems to feel it is more effective to influence colonial powers through an indirect approach than by direct open pressures. However, from the outward evidence, America's indirect and private pressures on the colonial powers seem to have had little influence on their colonial practices. French colonial policy is a prime example of this. Despite six years of continual pressure by the United States to grant independence to the Indochina states, the French government failed to act, parrying American pressures with threats to torpedo the European Defense Community, until it was forced by military realities to grant independence to Laos, Cambodia, and Vietnam. By that time EDC had been dropped through France's failure at ratification, and the United States was left with the reputation in many Eastern countries of supporting French colonialism in Indochina.

This same diplomatic game, it may be assumed, is being played today over French stakes in North Africa, with American diplomatic representatives seeking more liberal French colonial practices in the area and the French ignoring the exhortations in one way or another.

Neither the confidence nor the cooperation of Asian and African powers is to be won by this private pressure without public acknowledgment of a policy toward liberalization of colonial practices. Although United States policy more firmly and actively sides with the colonial peoples in their struggle for self-government and independence than appears, the United States is wasting valuable diplomatic ammunition and reducing the effectiveness of its influence by failing to acknowledge openly its appeals and gestures on behalf of self-government and independence.

A second way in which the United States can reduce friction over the colonialism issue is to be certain that American officials exercise more intelligent diplomatic restraints in any public utterances on the sensitive colonial issues. Such a release, for example, as the joint statement on December 2, 1955, of Secretary Dulles and Portuguese Foreign Minister Paulo Cunha that Goa was one of the "Portuguese provinces in the Far East" should be avoided on the basis of possible emotional reactions which the pronouncement can unleash regardless of its legal correctness.[8] When the statement was made, it apparently was intended to point up the fact that the Soviet Union was inciting India to take Goa by force. The Portuguese-American statement followed Soviet communist party leader Khrushchev's declaration during his India tour that Goa should go to India and that India has the "right to oust" the Portuguese. The statement was violently denounced by the press in Singapore, Burma, Indonesia, and Ceylon, as well as India.

Although it is after the fact, it remains self-evident that if any American statement had to be made on Goa—and that need is dubious—the United States should not have made it jointly with the Portuguese foreign minister and should not have used terms which would seem to prejudge the status of Goa.

A third way for the United States to reduce friction over colonialism is to establish more firmly its position in support of the principles of self-determination, self-government, and independence for colonial peoples. Although American officials often reiterate American sympathy for these principles, their words somehow seem to fall on deaf ears. An illustration of this was the Philippine-sponsored joint proclamation of September 8, 1954, on self-government and independence for colonial peoples to which the American delegation eagerly agreed along with seven other Manila Pact members. The approved Pacific Charter as a result pledged the Manila Pact members to "uphold the principles of equal rights and self-determination of peoples" and to "strive by every peaceful means to promote self-government and to secure the independence of all countries whose peoples desire it and are able to undertake its responsibilities."

In the words of Secretary Dulles,[9] the Charter was supposed to prove "the most momentous product of the Conference," but since then little has been heard of it.

The need therefore clearly remains for the highest American

authority to issue a strong, clear-cut American policy statement, which comes down squarely as a matter of principle and policy on behalf of self-government and independence for colonial peoples. It is important that the United States' stand on the colonial issue be clearly defined for the colonial powers as well as for the people under colonial rule.

As a fourth method of alleviating the same friction, it is up to the United States to begin building its public record of sympathy and support for the principles of anticolonialism. As a starter, the United States should make every effort to close the gap between principle and practice in its policy over the colonialism issue, resisting any attempt by the colonial powers, especially France, to drive wedges of unrelated political considerations into American policy.

The United States should continue to approach each colonial issue on its own merits, in each case weighing the principle of self-determination against the readiness of the peoples to assume the responsibilities of independence. On the basis of a record which is sympathetic toward the principles of each case and which is untarnished by political premises and so exhibits fairness of judgment, the United States obviously would be in a better position to use more effectively its influence for orderly progression toward self-government and independence. The dangers and risks of premature independence are well enough known to the governments of India and Burma, despite India's extreme statements on occasion, that there is every possibility for the United States to be met halfway by these and other nations of the East provided United States integrity were above question in its avowed support of principle.

THE ISSUE OF NEUTRALISM

No diplomatic issue is so fraught with danger for United States relations with South and Southeast Asia as the conflict of views on neutralism and collective security.[10]

Although the United States, India, Burma, and Indonesia are fully agreed on the critical need for maintaining peace in the world, their agreement begins and ends there. The United States uses the principles of strength and collective security to pursue peace, while India, Burma, and Indonesia attempt to reach the same objective through compromise and positive neutralism. Each side seems to admit that the concepts of collective security and neutralism are diametrically opposed, but each side is convinced that its position is logical, just, and unassailable.

India, the leading advocate and spokesman for the neutralist "third force," feels that the United Nations provides ample machinery for collective security if the big powers would only use it. Because, however, big-power harmony is the most important ingredient of peace and because the lack of big-power agreement on any collective measures to deter or to punish aggression merely serves to increase the risk of war, India also feels that American efforts to build and organize for collective security continue to increase the war risk. It is India's contention that the United States would do more for peace by concentrating on conciliation and compromise for settling disputes and easing tensions rather than by building up military strength and by organizing such alliances as NATO and the Manila Pact. Furthermore, in following India's righteous line the United States would cease antagonizing both the Soviet Union and communist China.

This is excessively unrealistic reasoning, according to the United States, which began organizing for collective security outside the United Nations only after failure to establish a United Nations military force under the Charter provisions, only after organization of the East European satellites into a political and military bloc by the Soviet Union, and only after the failure of repeated efforts for negotiation with the Soviet Union. The United States has learned through hard experience that, despite its utterances, the communist bloc will resort to negotiation and compromise only when it is confronted by strength and that any adoption of the Indian neutralist position not only would indicate acceptance of an inverted analysis of the causes of war but also would mean one thing only: capitulation to Soviet demands.

A contradictory analysis of Moscow and Peking's international intentions obviously lies behind the sharp cleavage in viewpoints. The Moscow-Peking protestations of peace apparently are convincing to Sukarno, Nehru and U Nu, who seem to ignore the contingent fact that the communists' desire for peace is limited by communist-dictated terms—that is, a communized world amenable to Moscow rule.

The neutralists tend either to ignore or to dismiss the role of neutralism in communist doctrine, as set down by Mao Tse-tung's classic statement:

> To sit on the fence is impossible: a third road does not exist. We oppose the China of the Chiang Kai-shek reactionary clique who lean to the side of imperialism; we also oppose the illusion of a third road. Not only in China but also in the world, without exception, one either leans to the side of imperialism or to the side of socialism. Neutrality is mere camouflage and a third road does not exist.[11]

As for communist doctrine, Moscow and Peking both consider neutralism an untenable position but recognize the fact that the uncommitted middle powers stand between the so-called "imperialist" and "socialist" camps. Communist tactics tend to veer from ignoring the neutralists, to assailing them bitterly to courting them diligently. At the moment, in order to drive a wedge of distrust between the United States and the Asian countries, the Soviet Union and communist China seem to be wooing neutralists in tactics which deemphasize the true communist view toward neutralism and which high-light concepts of peaceful intent, coexistence, conciliation, and common interest.

Chou En-lai employed this tactical barrage to considerable diplomatic advantage at the Bandung Conference, where he worked to identify China with the South and Southeast Asian states as a "fellow-Asian nation" and stressed his eagerness to find issues of agreement and ideas of common interest for all Asian and African nations. "We have to admit," Chou declared, "that among our Asian and African countries we do have different ideologies and social systems. But this does not prevent us from seeking common ground and being united. . . . On the basis of our common points we should try to understand and appreciate the different views we hold."

Appreciation of noncommunist views and social systems is scarcely long-established communist policy but, without forsaking any of his negotiating skill, Chou En-lai scored his diplomatic triumph at Bandung by playing on the theme.

Another important dimension to the neutralist view lies in the conviction of such countries as India, Burma, and Indonesia that, by policies of nonalignment and noncommitment to either side, they can serve the cause of peace, acting as intermediaries between the communist and noncommunist blocs. On such questions as atomic-energy control and disarmament in the United Nations, the Indian delegation often has been cast in the role of intermediary who has sought to find compromise positions acceptable to the Soviet Union and to the United States. In the matter of the Korean and Indochina peace negotiations, India found itself as a neutralist playing an especially prominent part to secure the peace. With this background, neutralist governments have become attached to the idea that, geographically, they are ideally situated and, morally and politically, they are ideally qualified to serve as bridges for conciliatory and peaceful traffic between the communist and noncommunist world. On its side, the United States is more anxious for dikes which would hold back the flood of communism rather than bridges for communist traffic.

In tackling this dilemma of diplomatic engineering, the United States seems to be left with two broad approaches. In the first approach, it can place top priority on the maintenance of its collective security alignments, fortifying anticommunist morale and American prestige in such friendly countries as South Korea, Taiwan, the Philippines, Thailand, and Pakistan, even at the cost of alienating the neutralists, on the premise that it is better to retain certain friends than to risk their loss by courting others which are staying determinedly outside any anticommunist alignment in any case.

Or, in a second approach based on the assumption that the neutralists cannot possibly be won over to the anticommunist side, the United States can actively encourage the neutralist group in its chosen course. Although this second approach could create problems, it could have the advantage of reducing tensions in American relations with India, Burma, and Indonesia and would not necessarily result in destroying the systems of collective security previously built.

At the moment, as might be expected by the extreme courses represented in the two possible approaches, United States policy falls somewhere in between, closer, however, to the first position than to the second. Irritation and impatience toward the neutralists are evident in the attitude of American officials and congressmen to count those not with the United States as against the United States, and in American foreign aid policy too, which is heavily weighted in favor of states willing to align themselves on the anticommunist side.

President Eisenhower in a Christmas address (1954) attempted to straddle the fence on the neutralist issue. "The times are so critical and the differences between these two world systems so vital and vast," he said, "that grave doubt is cast upon the validity of neutralist arguments. . . ." Nevertheless, "we shall continue faithfully to demonstrate our complete respect for the right of self-decision by these neutrals." The President's emphasis was laid clearly on that "grave doubt" of neutralist arguments; but, the United States by that time having exhausted every feasible means to persuade or pressure the neutralists, especially India, to align themselves, if not actually, then psychologically with the anticommunist nations, his statement that the United States would respect the neutralists' self-decision was little more than admission of failure to sway the neutralists from the policy of nonalignment.

American efforts to contain and reduce the spread of neutralism by and large have had adverse political and psychological effects in the neutralist countries. First, the Indians, Burmese, and Indonesians have only become more convinced of the rightness of their course. Second, the same countries have become more suspect of America's principal interest in them as pawns in the struggle against communism. Third, these countries have come to nurture their belief that the United States neither understands nor approves of their political, social, and economic revolution nor of the problems presented by it.

In addition, America's antineutralism has played into communist hands by exposing American foreign policy to an enveloping "peace offensive" which the United States is neither psychologically nor politically prepared to counter quickly and effectively.

Consider India's position. Pakistan, the country which India considers its greatest threat, stands to obtain military equipment from the United States as the result of a military aid agreement.

Under the clouds of a steadily deteriorating relationship with India, the United States acts in concert with Britain to form collective security organizations in Southeast Asia and the Middle East, and almost every issue before the United Nations tends to bear some trace of the East-West conflict of opinion. Enter Khrushchev and Chou En-lai into this situation with smiling faces and arms outstretched, speaking of co-existence, common interest, mutual respect, profitable trade, economic and technical aid without strings, normalization of relations and peace.

The two approaches to the neutralists—communist close harmony as opposed to American scolding and finger waggling—have the obvious effect. Between the United States and India, Burma and Indonesia the rift widens, while among the Soviet Union, communist China, and the neutrals there is a closer drift.

Differences in China policy serve as another source of cleavage between the United States and the neutralists. The neutralists feel that Chiang Kai-shek is a feudalist discredited by his own people and that the Kuomintang is a lost cause. Although communist China's rapid rise to power may provide them with some deep-seated fears for the future, for the present their sympathies lie with the communist revolution in China so far as it leads to modernization, industrialization, improved living standards, and rejection of Western domination. The neutralists of India, Indonesia, and Burma also have a strong feeling that the United States policy of nonrecognition of communist China, coupled with support of Chiang on Taiwan, is unrealistic and a major source of tension in the Far East. They resent the fact that the Kuomintang representative sits on the United Nations Security Council and wields a potential veto over other Asian powers.

From United States experience in recent years, it seems clear that the neutralist attitudes of India and Burma can only be changed by Soviet or communist Chinese conduct and not by any American persuasion or inducement. The same holds true of the militant nonalignment policy of Indonesia, with the added difficulty that, in recent years, the Indonesian governments have been far more tolerant of internal communist activity than India and Burma.

The alternative is clear. Without a reasonable opportunity to win over the neutralists from their chosen course, United States policy and attitude must adjust to reality. That is to say, the United States need not become an active champion of Asian neutralism, a policy which may have merit under certain circumstances; but, to profit by the situation, it should take a more tolerant and sympathetic view of the neutralist policies of India, Burma, and Indonesia. The following considerations provide a reasonable basis for this alternative.

First, "independent neutralism" is the key to Indian, Indonesian, and Burmese foreign policies, a position which the United States cannot change but which the vital interests and security requirements of the United States can endure provided it is genuinely independent. Responsible, independent neutralism in India, Burma, and Indonesia is not inconsistent with America's objective of stopping the spread of communism; but it is intolerable to Moscow and Peking, which eventually regard all nations as enemies unless they are satellites.

Second, a completely bipolar world involves real risks. A certain flexibility with the international political alignment serves a useful purpose as a safety valve, but any excessive leanings toward the Soviet pole, either as a result of American antineutralism or in response to communist wooing, naturally would have serious implications for American security and world peace.

Third, the United States must prevent any disintegration of the free world's defense preparedness or collective security arrangements while seeking to accommodate neutralism in India, Burma, and Indonesia. Not an easy task because of the incidence of incipient neutralism in neighboring countries, this can be accomplished only by progress toward political and economic partnership which would supplement the security partnership established by the Manila Pact. In the final analysis, little security exists in a collective security alliance which cannot stand the strain of a neutral neighbor.

The continued deterioration of American relations with India, Indonesia, and Burma is precisely what would suit communist purposes best and what the United States should avoid, permitting neither its own policies nor those of the Soviet Union and communist China to isolate the neutralists from the West. The United

States must strive with every means at its disposal to rescue its legitimate differences of opinion with the neutralists from the morass of antagonism into which they have fallen.

The United States, without serious damage to its role as major partner in NATO and the Manila Pact, in positive and specific terms can:

1. drop its "stand up and be counted" approach to the neutralists;

2. modulate the pugnacious statements toward the neutralists and their viewpoint which its officials often tend to make;

3. increase its support to nationalist causes before the communists move in on them; and

4. pay greater respect to areas of common agreement and concentrate on widening the area of economic and political partnership with the neutralists.

AMERICA'S OBJECTIVES AND MOTIVES

The United States is failing at the task of winning Asia's confidence and of transmitting the best aspects of Western democracy to Asia. On every side evidence exists that American objectives and motives are misunderstood.

Secretary Dulles, referring to this misunderstanding in a somewhat self-righteous mood, attempts to point up American sincerity of motivation:

> The role of the United States is often misconceived. . . . It is not readily understood that a nation should take so enlightened a view of its own self-interest that it does much for others without seeking for itself any extension of its political power or national domain. Our motives are sometimes openly suspected. That does not make it any easier for us here at home to pursue a steady course. However, I hope and believe that we shall continue in our traditional way . . . we shall persist in helping others to help themselves gain peace and security and better standards of life in larger freedom.[12]

In contrast to the problems of developing and implementing foreign policy, the formulation of foreign policy objectives is usually considered to be a relatively simple task. Why, then, are American objectives in Southeast Asia a problem?

First, a characteristic of objectives is that they tend to build up expectations of achievement which can be attained in fact only in the very long run, if at all. The governments and peoples of Southeast Asia are impatient to achieve their own objectives, especially the more pressing ones of economic development, increased standards of living, and international prestige. In the formulation of its objectives, the United States has sought to accommodate many of the ambitious aspirations of the Southeast Asian states, but progress toward the realization of these objectives has been slow. The disappointment and the impatience of some Southeast Asian governments and peoples have caused some loss of confidence in the sincerity and, in some instances, the ability of the United States to help them achieve quickly the necessary improvements. In such circumstances, the attraction of the programs and stated objectives of the communists tend to increase in Southeast Asia.

Second, American objectives in Southeast Asia are a problem because they are so often misinterpreted and misunderstood. Sometimes this is due to the work of malicious groups hostile to the United States; sometimes it is due to the lack of a clear and appealing presentation. In either case, the conduct of United States foreign policy becomes more difficult.

Third, problems are also created when America's policies seem to contradict stated objectives. Obvious contradictions between America's objectives and policies create doubts and suspicions in the minds of many Southeast Asian people. The argument of practical or strategic necessity is not a compelling one to those who do not see threats and policy alternatives from the viewpoint of the United States.

Fourth, important problems develop out of conflicts between objectives considered as priority objectives in the estimation of the United States and those considered as their priority objectives by the governments and peoples of Southeast Asia. The problem of conflicting objectives is acute between the United States and some of the states of Southeast Asia primarily because of differences of opinion regarding the nature and source of the major threats to international peace and security.

Since 1950 the basic theme of American objectives in Southeast Asia clearly has shifted from that of helping Southeast Asians to help themselves achieve their own aspirations to one of resisting communism through military preparedness and collective security. The shift reflects America's concern for the dangerous imbalance of power in South and Southeast Asia revealed by the Korean and Indochina wars and the increasing tension between the United States and the Moscow-Peking Axis.

The urgency of the threat of communism in Southeast Asia or elsewhere and the need for the development of military strength throughout the noncommunist world are not questioned. But, it is suggested, the emphasis on anticommunism and military strength as objectives in the peculiar economic, political, and psychological conditions prevailing in Southeast Asia might do more harm than good to America's search for security. If, in fact, American objectives in Southeast Asia continue to be characterized as anticommunism and dominated by military considerations, the United States may meet increasing resistance in Southeast Asia for at least three reasons:

1. Anticommunism does not have the appeal or the urgency in Southeast Asian states that it does in the United States.

2. The governments and peoples of Southeast Asia consider anticolonialism and their own internal economic development as objectives at least as important as anticommunism.

3. A period of "soft tactics" by the communists, based on appeals for peaceful co-existence, nonaggression, and normalization of trade and diplomatic relations, will leave United States objectives and policies with little attraction for the peoples and governments of Southeast Asia.

Though American officials unanimously agree that the "battle for the minds of men" is a most important aspect of the current international struggle, the United States is neither winning nor, for that matter, holding its own in the battle for the minds of Southeast Asians. Of American diplomacy's three major weapons—military, economic, and ideological—relatively little emphasis has been placed on the ideological and little success has been achieved by it. While the United States pours out money on military and economic efforts, the popular image of the United States remains woefully distorted and the gulf of misunderstanding between the United States and Southeast Asia appears to widen and deepen.

In the realm of ideas, the United States has concentrated on the activities of the United States Information Agency and a Department of State exchange-of-persons program. From its inception in 1948, the United States information program seems to have been handicapped by inadequate budget allowances, by congressional suspicion, by rapid personnel turnover, and by uncertainty in its message and approach to Southeast Asia. The program, operating through such media of mass communication as press, radio, publications, circulars, libraries, and mobile motion-picture units, in the course of a few years already has undergone three major shifts in orientation and direction. The first phase to give a "true picture of America" in order to counter communist anti-American propaganda managed to impress on Southeast Asian minds meaningless images of superhighways, supermarkets, electric kitchens, and whirring industrial wheels coupled with what can only be described as a superunbelievable materialistic standard of living. If it would have called forth any specific reactions in Southeast Asia, the obvious ones would have been envy and dissatisfaction.

In the second phase, or 1950 shift, the program turned to a "campaign of truth" against the communist world, which left the feel of gigantic American bombers, marching men, and an America hypnotized by the threat of communism. Although the program at times helped to offset some international communist propaganda, to Southeast Asians it also seemed to imply that the United States, in its concern for communism, had forgotten their problems, needs, and aspirations.

At the present time the United States information program is in a third phase, in an attempt to associate the United States with the aims and aspirations of the Southeast Asian governments and peoples. This approach seems to hold some promise for the future, although it needs some effective and imaginative implementation and also must overcome a great amount of misunderstanding before it can possibly record positive progress.

The exchange of persons serves as the second major United States program in the ideological struggle in Asia. Thanks to the Fulbright Act, the Smith-Mundt Act, State Department funds, the

Mutual Security Administration, the Foreign Operations Administration, and the Military Aid and Assistance programs, several thousand Southeast Asians and Americans have made reciprocal visits to one another's countries as students, teachers, technical experts, cultural, intellectual, and political leaders and, above all, as ambassadors of good-will hoping to understand one another and the peoples of the countries visited.

As means for winning friends and influencing alien peoples to American ideas, both the United States information program and the exchange-of-persons program serve an important function, deserving of far greater support and sympathy than is generally allotted to them by Congress. But both programs are limited in scope and import in several ways. For one, only a relatively small number of people tend to benefit directly from the programs. Second, emphasis given to the written word by the information program seldom reaches below an intellectual élite "target group," and never competes with indigenous communist agents waging their campaigns directly in the villages and cities. Third, most Southeast Asians who read any meaning at all into information activities recognize the information program as propaganda, which has the net result of bringing important but not maximum returns on officially spoken and written United States messages and reports. Although the exchange-of-persons program seems to lie closer to answering the problem of an effective program in this field, its results often are unpredictable and its impact also is restricted.

To combat communism on an intellectual plane, some enthusiasts have advocated that the United States greatly expand its information program and launch an intensive "ideological crusade" for the mind of Asia. A titillating idea, this recommendation is of dubious practical merit because it is based on an assumption that American concepts, philosophy, and social institutions, that is, American ideology, can be made to prevail in Oriental minds. Environment and history shape culture and ideology and manifestation of them in the social, philosophical, intellectual, religious, political, and economic realms, which would seem to indicate change could only take place through transplantation in limited amounts and over long periods of time. Even then the end product might well be quite different from the original or even from the one desired. Today the two strong forces of nationalism and an indigenous cultural renascence motivate large numbers of the Southeast Asian peoples and governments. Both of these forces, which after all are directly opposite to a great American ideological crusade, should be encouraged rather than countered.

Indonesia's President Sukarno, speaking May 19, 1955, on the occasion of the forty-seventh anniversary of the Indonesian nationalist movement, reminded the world of this need to accommodate Asian nationalism. "So long as the American nation does not realize that the Asian and African nations are living in an era of national sentiment, national ideal, an era of national aspirations, so long as the American nation does not realize all of this, then every dollar spent by America to help Asia and Africa to bring freedom and justice to Asia and Africa will be of no value."

In fact, a vulnerable point at which to attack communist subversion in Southeast Asia might well be communism's ideological crusade. Through sympathy, encouragement, and appreciation for Southeast Asia's national ideological and cultural aspirations, the United States in time could conceivably pierce through the mask of communist imperialism—the doctrinaire and inflexible ideology concealed in the guise of nationalism.

In suggesting that the United States refrain from any ideological crusade in Asia, the implication is not that the United States lose its interest in transmitting ideas or influencing the beliefs in Southeast Asia but rather that it exercise an ideological influence within the context of Southeast Asian national aspirations and ideological and cultural patterns. The United States information program should be built around the four cornerstones which are the foundation of the Asian revolution—national independence, economic progress, national and human dignity and equality, and peace. Only to the extent that the United States is in fact associated with these four principles can it expect to evoke a sympathetic response and win the confidence of Southeast Asians.

Before formulating its statements of purpose and policy in Southeast Asia, it is highly important for the United States to understand what is in Southeast Asian minds. Perhaps the greatest significance of the Asian-African Conference at Bandung was the opportunity it presented to the United States to listen, carefully and sympathetically, as the representatives of the nonwhite, economically retarded majority of the world expressed their deepest convictions. It was unfortunate that the United States gave an impression of fearing what it would hear rather than of wishing to listen and learn.

At the present time the United States channels its information program almost entirely outside Southeast Asia's national societies in the effort to bombard the nationalistic armor of the Southeast Asian states with propaganda pellets. If it is to increase the effectiveness of its influence on Southeast Asian thinking and beliefs, the United States clearly must supplement its information and exchange-of-persons programs by a special effort within the Southeast Asian psychological environment, working with the Southeast Asian people toward achievement of their national aspirations.

In the realm of ideas, the technical assistance program is one conceptual framework which may allow for a point of entry toward this end. With the existent tendency of evaluating the United States technical assistance program primarily in economic and statistical terms, its potentialities for transmitting social and political ideas have been largely overlooked. To the recommendation that the technical assistance program be expanded in size and scope for economic reasons, there can now be added the recommendation that the program be extended for important social and ideological reasons.

Does the United States seek an atmosphere of personal rapport for the exchange of ideas which it cannot devise through its information program? Then watch Americans and Southeast Asian nationals wade together through rice paddies discussing methods of irrigation, fertilizers, seed; watch them sit together in a village market checking over means of controlling malaria, of improving cottage industries, of overcoming seasonal unemployment. Does the United States wish to prove its interest in Southeast Asia's economic future? Then let American technical experts continue to roll up their sleeves and work with Southeast Asian officials in helping to plan, organize, train, and build for their economic advancement.

It is not a matter of turning the United States technical cooperation programs into propaganda operations but rather of establishing a sound working partnership for the benefit of each party where each of the peoples concerned can exchange ideas and exercise a mutual influence.

For the United States to take full advantage of the opportunity to improve understanding of American motives and methods through the relationship of technical and economic cooperation, there will have to be an adjustment of certain congressional attitudes and of the techniques of technical cooperation. (1) The principle of foreign aid and technical assistance as a long-term aspect of American diplomacy in Asia will have to be accepted. (2) Both the idea and the fact of a working partnership with Southeast Asian governments and peoples will have to be established. (3) The economic and technical operations will have to be manned, for the most part, by career service people who are trained and experienced to look beyond the immediate technical aspects of their tasks to the equally important social and intellectual impact of their activities and behavior, a requirement which would seem to suggest the need for a permanent career service for technicians trained as diplomats, or for diplomats trained as technicians.

Historically, the traditional diplomatic functions of representing, observing, and reporting have been distinct from the newer operational diplomatic functions of economic and technical aid activity. Once the principle of foreign aid and technical cooperation as a long-term arm of American diplomacy is accepted, then the concept of merging the operational and representational functions follows naturally. In consolidating its economic and political arms of diplomacy to meet the different diplomatic instruments necessitated by changed world conditions, the United States already has taken two important steps. They are the merger of Foreign Service and Department of State personnel and the reorganization of economic aid and technical assistance operations under the aegis of the Department of State. A third step might well be the organization of a career foreign service corps of technical officers who would be capable of carrying out the dual task of representing American interests in Asia and of operating in a technical capacity to transmit American democratic ideas at a level of Asian societies which seldom before has been exposed to these ideas.

10. TEST FOR TOMORROW

Southeast Asia's future is a mosaic of uncertainties. Throughout the area revolutionary currents are running strongly; political, cultural, and ideological patterns are fluid. Southeast Asian governments, probing the structure of international society, are seeking their place in that society, yet remain undecided on a philosophical framework and a technique for economic development and growth. The Southeast Asian countries maintain divided attitudes toward Western colonialism, neutralism, collective security, economic co-operation with the Western powers, and communism in its internal and external aspects.

The over-all picture of Southeast Asia consists of a series of small, weak nations sandwiched between the two major Asian powers of communist China and neutralist India, engulfed by perplexing internal economic, political, and administrative problems, split by sharp social and ideological distinctions. The picture shows an in-between area exposed to heavy pressures and to lures for joining its lot to international communism, to Asian neutralism, or to a free-world alliance of Western democracies.

In a Southeast Asia whose future is so precarious, what can the United States anticipate? Under the prevailing revolutionary conditions, what can United States policy reasonably hope to accomplish?

Certainly it is not reasonable for the United States to assume that Southeast Asia will become a stalwart military bulwark against international communist aggression. The only bulwark against such an eventuality lies in United States power and United States readiness to use its power in defense of the area. If Moscow or Peking plot any major aggression against Southeast Asia in the future, it is clear that the United States and the members of the Southeast Asia treaty organization will have to bear the major burden of protecting the area.

Only the illusion of strength is created by military aid which serves no other purpose than to lay a crust of military force on soft political and economic foundations. Still, United States military aid should help Southeast Asian governments to establish and maintain minimum levels of internal law and order at the very least and even, in some instances, to handle internal communist disturbances and minor border clashes.

It is not reasonable to assume that United States economic and technical aid will create modern industrial societies in Southeast Asia nor that it will convert Southeast Asian governments and peoples into practitioners and advocates of the American free-enterprise system. Because Southeast Asia lacks a strong middle class to provide the initiative and capital for economic growth, its future economic institutions are certain to depend in large part on government investment and regulation in industry. The important fact is for the United States to recognize the economic and psychological limitations to Southeast Asia's full adoption of American-style capitalism and to judge Southeast Asian economic institutions by the purposes and aims which the governments of the area attempt to pursue as well as by the techniques which they are led to adopt by conditions and preference.

In the political field, it is certainly not reasonable for the United States to expect that its economic aid will ensure the last-ditch political and military allegiance of the Southeast Asian governments. Given in sufficient time and amounts and under proper circumstances, there is every reason to believe that economic aid, technical assistance, and cooperation should help Southeast Asian nations to organize and develop their economic and political resources in a manner and at a rate of speed sufficient to maintain national morale and improve the chances for economic growth and confidence. It is equally plausible that the *results* of economic and technical aid can help offset the attractions offered by communism's totalitarian techniques for economic development. Provided in a spirit of partnership and mutual interest, economic aid and technical assistance afford an excellent opportunity to improve the political and psychological conditions for mutual confidence, cooperation, and unity between the United States and the Southeast Asian states.

However, the potential accomplishments of economic and technical aid should not be overestimated. No country can be rescued from communism nor can the United States gain steadfast allies merely by the grant of economic aid and technical assistance. But the fact of such aid, buttressed by political, social, and economic efforts on the part of both the United States and recipient countries, can create conditions for desensitizing the attractions of communism and for cultivating close political and security relations.

It is unreasonable to suppose that United States policy can induce India, Burma or Indonesia and Cambodia to jettison nonalignment, which is the basic principle of the foreign policies of those countries, in favor of participation in anticommunist collective security arrangements. It is possible, however, that, in presenting and pursuing its foreign policy, the United States can accommodate the neutralist position and, avoiding antagonism, influence the neutralists to maintain an independent and responsible position which would neither fully serve communist purposes nor critically endanger American and free-world objectives.

It is unreasonable to assume that United States policy can erase quickly from Southeast Asian minds the bitterness and suspicion resulting from colonial rule. To the Southeast Asians, colonialism remains foreign domination imposed by force. No matter how free from the taint of colonialism Americans may believe themselves to be, the majority of Southeast Asians nonetheless associate the United States with Great Britain, France, and the Netherlands as bearers of Western colonialism and economic imperialism. By clearly and consistently supporting the principles of self-government and independence for subject peoples and by sympathetically considering the national aspirations of Southeast Asian peoples and governments, the United States may, in time, reduce the colonialism issue as a barrier to mutual confidence and understanding.

Even these modest potential accomplishments, however, require major United States policy effort for realization. The irony lies in the fact that although it is an arduous uphill task to improve United States relations with Southeast Asia, any disintegration of United States and Southeast Asian relations can take place rapidly and in a spectacular manner.

In the decade ahead, the test of United States policy in Southeast Asia will lie primarily in the realm of foreign economic policy and diplomacy. Although continued programs for mutual security are essential, with American military aid and assistance to the governments of the area playing a potentially critical role, United States policy can only score its decisive successes or failures on the basis of the socioeconomic progress of the Southeast Asian nations and on the ability of American diplomacy to reverse the economic, political, and psychological drift of the uncommitted Asian states toward the communist bloc.

Three dimensions exist in this challenge to United States policy: (1) the aspirations of the Southeast Asian peoples and governments; (2) Southeast Asian conditions and attitudes which must be overcome or accommodated by the United States in seeking to attain its objectives; (3) the contest for supremacy over the policies and activities of international communism.

Although previously discussed, recent communist tactics and their relevance to Southeast Asia precipitate several additional and pertinent observations on this challenge in Southeast Asia.

Beginning with the Geneva "Summit" Conference in July 1955 and gaining momentum during 1956, the Soviet Union has evolved a new approach to the noncommunist world which incorporates at least four innovations of importance to the Southeast Asian world. First, the Soviet Union has placed new emphasis on "normal" and conciliatory diplomatic attitudes and techniques, in marked contrast to its suspicious, hostile, and intransigent approach of former years. Second, the Soviet Union and the communist bloc have begun through programs of trade and aid to wield their economic power as a political weapon. Third, the Soviet Union and the communist bloc have started to export arms to certain noncommunist governments. Fourth, the Soviet Union's leaders have initiated a vigorous program to repudiate Stalin and Stalinism in a move which can be interpreted in several ways. None of these innovations, however, has been accompanied by reduction of the vast program of arms production and military build-up which the Soviet Union, the East European satellite nations, and communist China seem intent on continuing.

In the restless and revolutionary-minded Asian-African world, such communist policy changes are darkly significant and obviously present new and critical challenges to United States foreign policy. To Southeast Asia, it is evident that the new Soviet approach can bear promising fruit because it lends credence to the idea of co-existence, indeed even of close cooperation, with the communist bloc as being safe, feasible, and profitable. The Soviet offer of trade and aid appears highly attractive to neutralist governments and to other governments whose principal economic difficulties stem from the major problem of disposing of surplus production in free-world markets at competitive prices.

The repudiation of Stalin and, by implication, Stalinist methods seems to mark the Soviet régime as less menacing, more malleable, than before. In the new international communist line and in Moscow's treatment of Yugoslavia, for the moment at least, exists the slight hint of a degree of toleration of national communism relatively free of the slavish ties to Moscow which characterize the relations of East European satellites. In most of Southeast Asia, it is highly probable that these factors will soften resistance to communism and strengthen the hands of indigenous communists.

Equally important in Southeast Asia is the new Soviet effort to play down force, violence, and insurrection as the communist routes to power. The repudiation of Stalin, implying a de-emphasis of the communist methods of force and terror, was made more specific by Communist Party Secretary Khrushchev in his address to the Twentieth Congress of the Soviet Communist Party in February 1956:

> In view of the fundamental changes that have taken place in the world arena, new prospects have also opened up with regard to the transition of countries and nations to socialism.
>
> It is quite likely that the forms of the transition to socialism will become more and more variegated. Moreover, it is not obligatory for the implementation of these forms to be connected with civil war in all circumstances.
>
> The enemies are fond of depicting us, Leninists, as supporters of violence always and in all circumstances. . . .

> But there are different forms of social revolution and the allegation that we recognize force and civil war as the only way of transforming society does not correspond to reality. . . .
>
> In this connection the question arises of the possibility of employing the parliamentary form for the transition to socialism. For the Russian Bolsheviks, who were the first to accomplish the transition to socialism, this was excluded.
>
> However, since then radical changes have taken place in the historical situation that allows an approach to this question from another angle.
>
> Socialism has become a great magnetizing force for the workers, peasants and intelligentsia in all lands. The ideas of socialism are really conquering the minds of all toiling mankind. . . .
>
> In these conditions, by rallying around itself a toiling peasantry, the intelligentsia and all the patriotic forces, and by meting out a determined rebuff to opportunistic elements incapable of abandoning a policy of conciliation with the capitalists and landlords, the working class has the possibility of inflicting a defeat on the reactionary anti-popular forces and of gaining a firm majority in Parliament, and converting it from an organ of bourgeoise democracy into an instrument of genuinely popular will.[1]

In calling for a special communist effort which would rally the peasantry and intelligentsia, two invariable prime communist targets in Southeast Asia, to work for a parliamentary majority and to transform their society to Bolshevik socialism by parliamentary means rather than by force, violence, and civil war, the Khrushchev line sugarcoats what hitherto has been one of the most distasteful aspects of communism to many Southeast Asian peasants and intellectuals.

If the new Soviet line is pursued, there is menace in its alternate challenge to the present shape of United States policy in several Southeast Asian countries. In the past, the collective security alliances have been soldered together by communist-sponsored violence, threats, and obstructionism at the international and local levels. But if communism can be made to seem more palatable and less threatening to South and Southeast Asian peoples and governments, the question arises as to the validity of United States policy which is dominated by the concepts of collective security against the communist scourge, deterrence of communist aggression through massive retaliation, and military aid programs for military strength against communist threats.

In the ultimate communist objective of establishing world communism in one way or another, the Soviet leaders indicate no change of plans. Nor is any lessening of antipathy toward the United States or toward Western democratic institutions glimpsed either in recent Soviet conduct or in its statements. Only for the remainder of the noncommunist world, especially the Asian-African states, does the Soviet leadership appear to doctor the face of international communism in an effort to obscure its more sinister aspects. The morality lesson with which the Soviet leaders of the moment seem to be toying is the one about catching insects with honey and nectar rather than with vinegar. Their tentacles undoubtedly reach out for their prey with scarcely concealed satisfaction and the hope that this new approach will be effective in weakening the ties which bind NATO and SEATO and in isolating the United States politically, economically, and psychologically from the Asian-African nations.

The Soviet leaders seem to be calculating the odds in their favor for a United States policy which, immobilized by the mold of military precedence into which it was thrown by the Korean War, is unable to shift its Asian and African position in order to stop the neutralists from veering into the winds of communism and to halt the drift toward neutralism of other United States allies seeking economic development, trade, peace, and normalcy.

As it has been shaped from the onslaught of the Korean War, United States policy is scarcely prepared to meet this guileful turnabout. To this writer, the evidence would seem to point up the necessity for some important adjustments in the emphasis, attitude, and techniques of United States policy to arrest the erosion of American prestige and status in Southeast Asia and to strengthen the foundation for mutual confidence, trust, and cooperation in future United States and Southeast Asian relations.

First, and most obviously, the United States must attune its policy objectives, actions, and statements more closely to the economic, political, and psychological currents prevailing in Southeast Asia. Nothing continues to be as important for United States relations with Southeast Asia as the need for knowledge of the attitudes and thinking of Southeast Asian peoples and governments, of their aspirations, of their fears. Only within the framework of such

knowledge can United States objectives and policies take on meaning and find support in Southeast Asia.

Broadly speaking, the five principal concepts which motivate Southeast Asian nations today are:

1. All are equally determined to maintain and perfect—and, in the case of Malaya, to achieve—national sovereign independence and equality. The meaning of the phrases bites more deeply than their sound. The Southeast Asian nations, to the last one, want to participate as equals in any international decisions concerning their part of the world and their broad national interests. They want to formulate and pursue their own domestic and foreign policies in their own way. In Nehru's words, they are determined never again to "be used as pawns by others."

2. All the Southeast Asian states consider that their top priority need is economic diversification, industrialization, and development. They are anxious to end their economic impotence and the craven dependency caused by having only one or two export products on the international market. They are interested and hopeful of outside help for their economic development, but they are interested in such help only so long as their views of sovereignty and independence remain uncompromised.

3. All the Southeast Asian states, in an extension of their anticolonial struggles, continue to feel such a strong antipathy toward foreign domination in any form and anywhere in the world that they consider colonialism an incessant threat and direct their principal colonial suspicions and fears against the West. Even Thailand and the Philippines, differing from the other Southeast Asian nations on the colonial question, stand as staunch opponents of colonialism.

4. All the Southeast Asian peoples and governments remain sensitive to racial discrimination on all levels and greet manifestations of this social disease with repugnance and resentment. Mr. Nehru, in an address to the Indian Parliament, merely reflected a widespread Asian attitude when he characterized racialism as "a very important thing and at least as important as all this business of communism or anti-communism or both of them."[2]

5. All the Southeast Asian nations are ardent protagonists of peace and are in agreement over it as an essential condition for

their successful economic, political, and social progress, though each nation differs as to the best means of achieving the desirable condition.

Against this backdrop of Southeast Asian motivations, United States policies seem to focus so consistently on anticommunism, military strength, and collective security arrangements that the United States lays itself open to the Southeast Asian rejoinder that American concern for their independence seems to mean specifically Southeast Asian independence from communist influence and that American concern for their welfare seems to fluctuate with the momentary reading of the communist barometer. Although an exaggerated portrayal of American policy toward Southeast Asia, the image is flecked with spots of truth and, even more to the point, is commonly seen in that light by many Southeast Asians.

Second, the United States must adopt a more dynamic and positive central theme than anticommunism for its policies and objectives in Southeast Asia. It is only too clearly a matter of prime importance to American national security to stop the spread of communism, but this negative concept is too sterile to admit of being the heart and soul of American interest and activity or to evoke any popular enthusiasm among Southeast Asians. United States emphasis on anticommunism seems to place the Southeast Asian states in the position of pawns in the cold war and lays United States policy open to the Soviet peace offensive.

Although the United States policy defense is that American interests and activities in Southeast Asia go far beyond anticommunism, the evidence of an American concern circumscribed always by anticommunism remains only too clear to loyal Burmese, Indonesians, Thai, Cambodians, or Filipinos. Easily read on the ledger is the fact, for example, that the United States first became interested and active in Southeast Asia, except for its work in the Philippines and Thailand, following the communist victory in China and then intensified its efforts in relation to communist activities. The wide interpretation of United States support for the French effort in Indochina is that it stemmed from the idea that the Viet Minh had to be stopped whether or not the latter represented a nationalist cause because the Viet Minh leadership happened to be communist. Add to these the fact that numerous top-level Western conferences to

discuss ways and means of stopping communism in Asia have been held without Asian participation, that United States foreign aid programs have been and still are dominated by military considerations, and that the United States has placed great emphasis on the need for building an anticommunist alignment in Southeast Asia, and the Southeast Asian side becomes somewhat clearer.

Certainly, the world must be well aware by now of the fact that the United States is vehemently anticommunist and that it considers any political communist enslavement of the world the crucial issue of the present historical epoch. But the United States passes the point of diminishing returns in its investment on anticommunism when it continues to harp on the subject in its policies, public statements, and propaganda to the relative neglect of positive concepts which would have more specific meaning and importance to the peoples and governments of Southeast Asia.

For Southeast Asia, a more positive and appealing central theme could be United States interest in human progress, technical advancement, and economic growth and United States ability and willingness to help foster that growth and progress as an end in itself in the Southeast Asia area. Southeast Asia could be receptive to a policy emerging from the idea of "partnership in human progress," the United States being as silent a partner as possible; and such a policy coincidentally and fortunately could contribute to the fight against communism.

Dean Acheson felicitously phrased the thought in these words:

> People will do more damage and create more misrepresentation in the Far East by saying our interest is merely to stop the spread of Communism than in any other way. Our real interest is in those people as people. It is because Communism is hostile to that interest that we want to stop it. But it happens that the best way of doing both things is to do just exactly what the peoples of Asia want to do and what we want to help them to do, which is to develop a soundness and administration of these new governments and to develop their resources and their technical skills so that they are not subject to penetration either through ignorance, or because they believe these false promises, or because there is real distress in their areas. . . .[3]

Third, the United States, while attaining an adequate level of military preparedness against overt communist aggression, must shift the relative emphasis of its foreign aid policy to meet the

socioeconomic aspects of Southeast Asia's survival problems. Some official circles hold the theory that communism can come to power only through military means, that no nation, however bad its internal economic conditions may have been, has gone communist without external communist military pressure, and that, so long as the United States can help the Southeast Asian states build enough military power and can maintain sufficient military power of its own, communism cannot take over Southeast Asia. But such a theory is dangerously rigid, and an unimaginative interpretation of the communist potential and methods in the area. It is by no means inconceivable for the Southeast Asian peoples to be so politically paralyzed that they vote themselves into communism or to be so oppressed by economic stagnation and public despair that a communist victory is achievable by default.

Southeast Asian states face their most pressing security weakness in the uncertainty of popular mass support for the national governments, stemming from political, administrative, economic, and educational problems which do not lend themselves to military solutions.

For the Southeast Asian governments to enjoy authority and stability, certain minimum conditions which will consolidate mass loyalty to national institutions must be met. (1) The people must be provided with a sense of personal and national economic growth and progress through the achievements of their national governments. (2) The base of representative government must be expanded as rapidly as possible without serious political disruption, and an effort must be made to foster popular participation in government activities and vigorous local self-government. (3) Administrative authority in rural areas must be strengthened through efficient and noncorrupt officials. (4) The national armed forces and police must gain the respect and confidence of the people whom they must provide with security and guard against lawlessness and disorder.

Of the four conditions, American military aid can only help solve the final one, whose problem of military loyalty or discipline it still cannot guarantee. The analysis remains that Southeast Asian security requires action of a socioeconomic character. Southeast Asian leaders, perceptive enough over the threats of communist subversion and the necessity for meeting them by economic, political, and educational techniques, nonetheless have the problem of an acute shortage of funds, equipment, and trained personnel to carry through their programs of progress. Precisely these shortages are the ones which the United States can provide through economic aid and technical assistance.

The United States has not entirely neglected the factors of economic aid and technical assistance in its policy toward Southeast Asia, but it has maintained technical assistance programs on a small scale only and has conceived its economic aid programs within the context of military preparedness, frequently formulating them in terms which are politically offensive to Southeast Asian governments and peoples.

President Eisenhower's congressional message on the 1957 program for foreign aid gave little evidence of any basic change in the spirit of the program or the relative proportion of military to economic aid. His delineation of foreign aid activity in the Middle East, Africa, and Asia consists of the proposal "to help those of our allies whose economic resources cannot support their essential defense effort. This help is designed, as in former years, in part to assist projects of a nonmilitary character which further defense activities, in part to help build internal resources and economic stability, and in part to contribute to the recipient's programs of economic development." [4]

As outlined by the President, the 1957 budget-request breakdown revealed the proportionate weight attached to the program's three major purposes:

Military Aid	$2,925,000,000
Defense Support	1,130,700,000
	4,055,700,000
Development Assistance	$170,000,000
Technical Cooperation	157,000,000
	327,000,000
Special Presidential Fund	$200,000,000

For the past several years, the United States foreign aid program has amounted to approximately $5,000,000,000 annually as an investment in American national security and in free-world stability and progress. On the assumption that the United States can afford only this level of foreign aid investment or, more to the point, that American political considerations permit only this amount of foreign aid, the question arises as to whether such an investment is designed to yield America the greatest possible economic, political, and security benefits.

As far as Southeast Asia is concerned, it would seem reasonable to assume that benefits to the United States could be increased by reversing the present emphasis of United States foreign aid policy to give prime consideration to Southeast Asian requirements for economic development and progress on the following basis: (1) economic development concerns and interests the Southeast Asian governments and people far more than military development; (2) no matter how much American military equipment is supplied, the Southeast Asian states cannot be transformed into military bulwarks against determined communist military aggression; (3) communist political, economic, and ideological penetration and subversion still constitute the primary threats to Southeast Asian security and to United States interests in the area.

As a result of these factors, it seems only logical that increased emphasis on economic aid and technical assistance, even at the expense of military aid, should give the United States more security and greater political and economic returns than now obtains from the area.

In a redirected effort, the United States can take some very specific measures. It can (1) devote a larger portion of its total foreign aid investment to economic aid; (2) either shift a substantial part of defense support funds to the development assistance category or reduce eligibility conditions for defense support to those which are necessary for ensuring efficient and effective use of foreign aid, just as do the conditions attached to development assistance; (3) double, at least, the size and scope of the technical assistance program. In addition to its own binational program, the United States also can guarantee to meet 60 per cent of the United Nations technical assistance budget against any increased contributions which other United Nations members may be willing to make; (4) within reason, support any effective plan for financing economic development in underdeveloped areas through long-term loans or international development financing arrangements.

A sole Southeast Asian exception in this matter of relegating military aid to a subordinate role in American foreign aid policy is the case of South Vietnam and Laos. There, military aid is vital for the present, for those countries face the task of literally building national armies from the ground up and are threatened by considerable internal opposition from armed dissident groups and by possible armed uprisings on the part of the guerrilla units and cadres which the communists, moving northward in line with the Geneva agreements, left behind to harass and hinder the national governments.

It is also conceivable that a change in the general American attitude toward foreign aid could help produce maximum political, economic, and security returns. For one, the Southeast Asian atmosphere would be relieved of a certain amount of suspicion and resistance by the direct approach that United States foreign aid is extended in the spirit of United States interest and stake in the progress of the Asian revolution rather than as a means of buying allies. For another, the United States atmosphere could be cleared of some misapprehensions by a genuine acknowledgment that foreign aid is a firm requirement of United States national interests in the present era of global relationships. And for a third, the political and economic effectiveness of foreign aid programs would be improved through acceptance of the fact that foreign aid is likely to remain a long-term aspect of American diplomacy.

Aside from American foreign aid policy, another top aspect of United States and Southeast Asian economic and political relations calls for priority attention. That is the question of trade. If Southeast Asia's key agricultural and raw material exports, such as rice and rubber, cannot be absorbed by the free-world markets, then there is every reason to assume that Southeast Asian trade will be oriented increasingly toward the communist world. The communist bloc, apparently with a present sufficiency of capital goods for export, has indicated its willingness to accept in payment for its goods and technical assistance a wide range of Southeast Asian export products. This naturally appeals to the Southeast Asian governments, which not only are interested in increasing their trade but also must secure some ready markets for their surplus production. In fact, their preference in most instances is for financing economic development through trade rather than through foreign aid grants which are accompanied by explicit or implicit political obligations. As a result, the United States must very soon face the alternative of (1) finding free-world outlets for Southeast Asia's rice, rubber, and other export products, or (2) acquiescing as gracefully as possible to the economic fact of the Southeast Asian states increasing commercial relations with the communist world.

Fourth, United States policy must become sufficiently flexible to permit dynamic American action in Southeast Asia before, rather than after, military, economic, or political conditions are allowed to deteriorate into major crises. For example, although there was ample warning of the approaching economic crises as a result of Burma's and Thailand's increasing rice surpluses and decreasing foreign exchange, the United States did little to head off the crisis. If anything, through legislation which permitted the government to sell American surplus agricultural products abroad, the United States sharpened Thailand's and Burma's international marketing problems.[5]

Too often the United States has delayed decisive action until confronted with absolute crisis conditions when it is generally too late to provide more than emergency patchwork measures. Senator Mike Mansfield's recent report to the Senate Committee on Foreign Relations makes an interesting case in point.[6] The senator, a supporter of imaginative and effective American foreign aid, following a study mission to Southeast Asia, recommended "that the executive branch . . . review the extent of our activity in Laos and the size of the mission with a view to keeping both within the realm of the reasonable." Obviously disturbed, Senator Mansfield pointed out: "At the time of my first visit to Vientiane (Laos) in 1953 there were two American officials in the entire country. Now there are some 45."

Contrary to the senator's emphasis in his alarmed revelation, the real question which requires explanation is why there were only *two* United States officials in Laos in 1953 at a time when the situation in that strategically located country was becoming increasingly critical.

Of much greater importance is a more recent illustration of the United States policy weakness of waiting until confronted by an acute crisis before swinging into action. The new Soviet political and economic offensive in the underdeveloped areas of the world caught the United States ill prepared psychologically and politically. The Soviets began to telegraph their intentions of trying a new policy approach soon after the death of Stalin. Many American observers were so hypnotized by their own speculations regarding a major upheaval or even collapse of the communist régime in Russia that few failed to calculate that new leadership might result in new vitality, flexibility, and imagination in Soviet policy. Now, once again, the United States, having missed an opportunity to seize the initiative, is shifting the tone and emphasis of its foreign policy statements to take account of the social, psychological, and economic aspects of security. The shift, unfortunately, comes at a time and under circumstances which give the appearance of defensive maneuvers to offset the communist bloc's dramatic offers to the underdeveloped world.

If there is any one requirement essential to a successful United States foreign policy in South and Southeast Asia, it is that American actions, programs, and statements must sail ahead of the currents of economic, social, and political revolution prevailing in the area. Only once has our postwar policy dramatically and decisively leaped to the forefront of the Asian revolution and captured the imagination of Asian peoples. That was with the 1949 announcement of the Point Four idea. But the advantage was soon lost by the uncertain and feeble manner in which the idea was implemented.

It may be possible to recapture some of the spirit and dynamicism of the technical cooperation idea in Southeast Asia. The modest programs that have been carried on there provide a backlog of mutual experience and confidence and a foundation for effective, vastly expanded programs.

Fifth, the United States must determine the meaningful message in the realm of ideas which it can convey to Southeast Asians and then must decide on its most effective technique for communicating the message. To be meaningful and important to Southeast Asians, any American message must be formulated within the double context of modern Southeast Asia's revolutionary aspirations and the ancient cultural values of the Southeast Asian people. It must have direct and immediate relevance to the issues which are important to Southeast Asia—to national equality, racial equality, economic progress, self-determination, and peace.

For the exchange of ideas and for mutual understanding, both the United States information program and the exchange-of-persons program are valuable channels which, on the basis of past performance and future possibilities, merit increased government support. The constant danger of the programs, however, lies in an oversimplified course which could lose sight of long-range informational ends to interpret the United States and United States foreign policy by concentrating on a battle of words and images productive only of phantom propaganda victories in the minds of the phrase makers. But this is a course which under proper guidance and consistent appraisal need not prove meretricious but could, rather, be charted with skill.

Not yet utilized to its fullest extent is the channel of communication offered by the cultural exchange of musicians, artists, writers, theatrical groups, and entertainers.

Another channel of communication is open to Americans through such devices as the technical cooperation program which allows for extended informal contacts between Americans and Southeast Asians working in joint efforts which serve the mutual interest. Earlier limitations on the use of this channel for transmitting ideas have been the diminutive size of the technical cooperation program, the fact that a majority of administrative personnel in technical assistance missions have few personal contacts among the Southeast Asian people, that only a relatively small number of operations personnel having frequent and prolonged contact with great numbers of Southeast Asian people are included in technical assistance missions, and that many American technicians share a common lack of preparation in serving as the living "voices of America" in foreign lands.

If United States diplomacy were to accept economic aid and

technical assistance as part of its long-range aspects, then a corps of foreign service technical officers could be developed to provide the United States government with diplomat-technicians on a career basis. Development of such a corps certainly would increase the economic and psychological returns of American foreign aid programs.

Although scarcely solutions to the innumerable problems of security, economic development, and diplomacy which confront the United States in its relations with Southeast Asia today, the five enumerated adjustments in emphasis, attitudes, and techniques are delineated to provide United States policy with the broad terms of reference which would seem important in any attempt to arrest America's sliding influence in Southeast Asia.

In the final analysis, Southeast Asia's future naturally rests in the hands and the hearts and the minds of the Southeast Asian peoples and their governments. It is for Southeast Asia to show the will and determination which are vital to the maintenance of their independence and to the firmness of their security. It is for Southeast Asia to make the effort and to offer the necessary sacrifices for their economic development. To such efforts, the United States can make its contribution by adding both moral and diplomatic support, material assistance, and suggestions.

Although this reflects that the United States contribution to the nationalist and revolutionary struggles which beset Southeast Asia today can be at best only marginal and supplemental to Southeast Asia's own efforts, renewed stress must be placed on the fact that an effective American contribution can prove to be the critical margin between a choice of free democratic institutions or totalitarian communism in Southeast Asia. The degree of patience, tolerance, and understanding which American diplomacy exhibits in Southeast Asia may determine the extent of the area's future political and ideological attachment to the institutions and values of Western democracy.

Also well to remember is the choice for the United States of a Southeast Asia which raises the standard of neutralism rather than the banner of communism. It serves American interests far better to have such states as India, Burma, Indonesia, and Cambodia develop responsible, independent, and self-sufficient neutralism than to increase their economic and political fealty to the communist bloc along with militant anti-Western policies. United States diplomacy must steer a course which avoids presenting the critical international issues of the day in terms which could possibly high-light any illusion of affinity between international communism and neutralism.

For those who believe with the United States in the premise of collective security, the United States must take care that mutual defense organizations are not allowed to become sterile military clubs. Their vitality must be kept alive through political, economic, and social programs because total security is more than military security.

For the most part, Southeast Asia's political leaders are men of Western education and democratic inclination who seek to adapt the basic values of economic, political, and social democracy to the conditions which prevail in their countries. They look first to the West, especially to the United States, for understanding, sympathy, and support in their nation's struggles for economic progress, political stability, social change, and international prestige. If the West disappoints or rebuffs them, their recourse for inspiration and guidance is the communist world.

The test of United States policy in Southeast Asia is a test of humanitarian principles, of social sensitivity, of political and economic courage and imagination, as well as a test of strength.

NOTES

CHAPTER 1

[1] Halford John Mackinder. "The Geographical Pivot of History," *Geographical Journal* (April, 1904), 421–444.

CHAPTER 2

[1] J. S. Furnivall, *Colonial Policy and Practice* (Cambridge, Cambridge University Press, 1948), p. 214.

[2] Roeslan Abdulgani, "Idealogical Background of the Asian-African Conference," *United Asia* (April, 1955), p. 44.

[3] Furnivall, *op. cit.*, p. ix.

[4] George McTurnan Kahin, *Nationalism and Revolution in Indonesia* (Ithaca, Cornell University Press, 1952), pp. 2–3.

[5] Eugene Staley, *The Future of Underdeveloped Countries* (New York, Harper and Brothers, 1954), p. 279. Council on Foreign Relations.

[6] H. J. van Mook, *The Stakes of Democracy in Southeast Asia* (New York, W. W. Norton, 1950), pp. 194–195.

[7] From "Second Review of the Working of the New Order Plan," June 7, 1944, in *Burma's New Order Plan* (Rangoon, 1944), pp. 32–33. Quoted in Willard H. Elsbree, *Japan's Role in Southeast Asian Nationalist Movements, 1940 to 1945* (Cambridge, Harvard University Press, 1953), pp. 62–63. Institute of Pacific Relations.

[8] From *Burma's Fight for Freedom, Independence Commemoration,* Department of Information and Broadcasting, Government of the Union of Burma, pp. 32–33 (undated).

[9] Quoted in Elsbree, *op. cit.*, pp. 26–27.

CHAPTER 3

[1] Mohammad Hatta, "Indonesia's Foreign Policy," *Foreign Affairs* (April, 1953), p. 445.

[2] *Ibid.*, p. 444.

[3] The Five Principles are: mutual respect for territorial integrity and sovereignty; nonaggression; noninterference in internal affairs; equality and mutual benefit; and peaceful co-existence.

[4] *Indian Information,* Government of India Information Bureau, New Delhi, Oct. 15, 1946.

Chapter 4

[1] This and the following quotations of Zhdanov are from A. Zhdanov, "The International Situation," *For a Lasting Peace, For a People's Democracy!*, No. 1, Information Bureau of the Communist Parties (Belgrade, Nov. 10, 1947).

[2] The *Burman,* June 14, 1948, as quoted by Virginia Thompson and Richard Adloff in *The Left Wing in Southeast Asia* (New York, William Sloane, 1950), p. 110. Institute of Pacific Relations.

[3] Kahin, *Nationalism and Revolution in Indonesia,* pp. 257–258.

[4] Thompson and Adloff, *op. cit.,* pp. 153–155.

[5] Kahin, *op. cit.,* p. 290.

[6] *Ibid.,* p. 301.

Chapter 5

[1] Cordell Hull, *The Memoirs of Cordell Hull* (New York, The Macmillan Company, 1948), II, 1482–1483.

[2] The Act for International Development did not receive congressional approval until May of 1950. The appropriation necessary to put the Act into operation was delayed for four additional months and required the President to use his personal influence on the Senate leaders.

[3] Raymond B. Fosdick, "Asia's Challenge to Us—Ideas, Not Guns," *New York Times Magazine,* Feb. 12, 1950.

[4] An excellent analysis of this period of history is Lawrence S. Finkelstein, "United States at Impasse in Southeast Asia," *Far Eastern Survey* (Sept. 27, 1950), pp. 165–172.

Chapter 6

[1] "Evolution of Foreign Policy" address to the Council on Foreign Relations, New York, Jan. 12, 1954 (Department of State Press Release No. 8, pp. 3–4). This address was expanded and published in the April 1954 issue of *Foreign Affairs.*

[2] *New York Times,* March 14, 1954, p. 44.

[3] Chester Bowles, "A Plea for Another Great Debate," *New York Times Magazine,* Feb. 28, 1954.

[4] William F. Knowland, "The 'Instant Retaliation' Policy Defended," *New York Times Magazine,* March 21, 1954.

[5] Dean Acheson, "Instant Retaliation: The Debate Continued," *New York Times Magazine,* March 28, 1954.

[6] *Hearings Before the Committee on Foreign Relations, United States Senate,* 83rd Cong., 2nd Sess., March 19, 1954.

[7] Italics supplied.

[8] John Foster Dulles, "Policy for Peace and Security," *Foreign Affairs,* April, 1954.

[9] *Ibid.,* pp. 55–56.

[10] The four treaties received United States Senate approval on March 20, 1952.

[11] John Foster Dulles, "Security in the Pacific," January, 1952, *Foreign Affairs,* pp. 182–183.

[12] Department of State Press Release No. 549, Oct. 9, 1953.

[13] Joint communiqué, April 14, 1954.

[14] *Act for International Development, Hearings Before the Senate Committee*

on Foreign Relations, 81st Cong., 2nd Sess. (March and April, 1950), pp. 12–13.

[15] Since 1951, American foreign aid has been fragmented into five major kinds of aid. *Military assistance* primarily is in the form of military end items and training, but it also includes "facilities assistance" for equipping armaments plants, airfield construction, and financing of special-weapons development abroad. It is administered by the Department of Defense. *Direct-forces support,* another form of military assistance, provides military forces with "common-use items" such as clothing, rations, petroleum products, and medical supplies. It also finances the support of forces in Southeast Asia and the western Pacific. *Defense support* is economic aid used as indirect military assistance. It contributes to the maintenance of military forces by shoring up economies of friendly nations to increase their ability to support larger-size military establishments. This kind of aid is the same as ECA aid. The new nomenclature probably helped make the granting of ECA-type aid more palatable to Congress; however, its classification as a kind of military aid brings it under an entirely different, and more stringent, set of "conditions for eligibility" than is the case with development assistance. *Development assistance* is economic aid of the ECA type provided for economic development purposes. It is designed to promote conditions of stability and to supplement technical assistance programs with capital equipment, commodities, and funds. *Technical assistance* merely covers the exchange of knowledge, experience, techniques, and skills on a bilateral or multilateral basis, and equipment or commodities used in this connection are limited to the amounts needed for demonstration purposes.

[16] The large number of administrative reorganizations undergone by the agencies responsible for administering American economic and technical aid adds much confusion to the picture. The first special agency for the program in Southeast Asia, the Technical Cooperation Administration, was established in September 1950 within the Department of State to supervise all Point Four activity. Prior to that, however, and overlapping to some extent, between 1949 and 1951, the Economic Cooperation Administration established Special Technical and Economic Missions (STEM) in Burma, Indochina, Thailand, Indonesia, and the Philippines under authority of the Economic Assistance Act of 1950. The Mutual Security Administration, newly created in October 1951 to succeed ECA and partially absorb TCA, passed a "one country, one program" rule which it followed by certain administrative shifts in the field. In 1952, by congressional mandate, TCA took over the STEM operations in Burma and Indonesia but, while attached to and receiving policy guidance from the Department of State, received its funds and operational supervision from MSA from October 1951 to May 1953. The Foreign Operations Administration succeeded MSA in July 1953, absorbing TCA completely and unhinging TCA from the Department of State. In July 1955 the International Cooperation Administration succeeded the FOA.

[17] President Eisenhower's address to Congress, March 30, 1954.

[18] The total of American aid to Indochina increased approximately as follows: $150,000,000 in fiscal 1951, $300,000,000 in 1952, $500,000,000 in 1953, and $1,000,000,000 in 1954. The administration budget requests for 1955 called for $1,133,000,000 for Indochina.

[19] $23,000,000 for economic aid, $15,000,000 for military aid to Indochina.

[20] *New York Times,* April 13, 1950.

[21] Accounts of the events during this period are: Chalmers M. Roberts in the *Washington Post,* June 7, 1954, and the *Reporter,* Sept. 14, 1954; Joseph C.

Harsch, *Christian Science Monitor,* April 29 and May 7, 1954; James Shepley, "How Dulles Averted War," *Life,* Jan. 16, 1956.

[22] He is also reported to have favored opposing communist forces on the ground. "If Britain would join the United States, and France would stand firm, Dulles pointed out, the three Western states could combine with friendly Asian nations to oppose the communist forces on the ground in Indochina just as the United Nations stepped in against the North Korean aggression in 1950." James Shepley, "How Dulles Averted War," *Life,* Jan. 16, 1956, p. 72.

[23] *New York Times,* June 24, 1954.

Chapter 7

[1] William W. Kaufmann, *The Requirements of Deterrence* (Princeton, Center of International Studies, Nov. 19, 1954), p. 14.

[2] James Shepley, "How Dulles Averted War," *Life,* Jan. 16, 1956, p. 70.

[3] Dean Acheson, "Instant Retaliation: The Debate Continued," *New York Times Magazine,* March 28, 1954.

[4] John Foster Dulles, "Policy for Peace and Security," *Foreign Affairs,* April, 1954 (Department of State Press Release No. 139, March 16, 1954).

[5] The communists reacted quickly to the countersubversion provisions of the Manila Pact. The communist concern and line of criticism is demonstrated in the following extract from a Moscow broadcast of August 29, a week before the opening of the Manila Conference: "The inclusion in the text of the agreement of the clause regarding the struggle against subversive activities means that the colonial powers wish to make their interference in the internal affairs of Asian countries the accepted norm of international conduct. . . . The struggle against so-called subversive activities means the struggle against the right of Asian peoples to be masters in their own house" (*Soviet Home Service,* Moscow, Aug. 29, 1954).

[6] *Hearings Before the Committee on Foreign Relations, United States Senate,* 83rd Cong., 2nd Sess., Part 1, Nov. 11, 1954, p. 14.

[7] The communist use of the Pathet Lao or Free Lao name is an attempt to capitalize on the reputation of a Free Lao nationalist movement organized in 1946 to work for independence from the French.

[8] Twice during 1953, Ho Chi Minh's forces invaded Laos. On each occasion, although the Viet Minh forces retreated of their own accord, they left behind communist agents and organizers who recruited and trained Laotian and Vietnamese peasants and tribesmen as communist guerrillas.

[9] Edwin F. Stanton, "Spotlight on Thailand," *Foreign Affairs,* October 1954, p. 80.

[10] In this regard it is interesting to recall that Ho Chi Minh first built up his communist apparatus in Indochina from a headquarters in South China.

[11] During the Bandung Conference, communist China and Indonesia negotiated a treaty for ending the dual-nationality status of the overseas Chinese in Indonesia.

[12] An excellent report on the work of the Philippine Army Economic Development Corps is Alvin H. Scaff's *The Philippine Answer to Communism* (Stanford, Stanford University Press, 1955).

[13] *Time,* April 4, 1955, p. 24.

[14] *Report on Viet Nam, Cambodia and Laos to the Senate Committee on Foreign Relations* by Senator Mike Mansfield, Oct. 6, 1955.

[15] An excellent report on this problem is Joseph Alsop's, "A Man in a Mirror," *The New Yorker,* June 25, 1955.

[16] Rice accounts for three out of every four cultivated acres. Before 1941, rice sales abroad accounted for 35 per cent of Indochina's exports and totaled 25 per cent of all rice moving in the international market.

Chapter 8

[1] Norman S. Buchanan and Howard S. Ellis, *Approaches to Economic Development* (New York, Twentieth Century Fund, 1955), p. 376.

[2] *Guidelines for Point 4: Recommendations of the International Development Advisory Board* (Washington, D.C., June 5, 1952).

[3] *Report to the President on Foreign Economic Policies* (Gray Report, Washington, November, 1950).

[4] *Partners in Progress: A Report to the President by the International Development Advisory Board* (Washington, March, 1951).

[5] *Report of the Special Study Mission to Pakistan, India, Thailand and Indochina* (House Committee on Foreign Affairs, Washington, D.C., May 12, 1953), p. 60.

[6] *The Report of the Commission of Foreign Economic Policy* (Randall Report) of January 23, 1954, states: "The Commission attaches special importance to the strengthening of the technical assistance work of the United Nations. It believes, however, that no country should contribute as much as 60% of the financing of this world-wide cooperative effort" (p. 12).

[7] Clarence R. Decker, retiring as Assistant Director of the Mutual Security Agency in September, 1952, proposed that the United States draft a tentative plan of economic cooperation for a free Asia and bring together all free Asian nations in a conference similar to the one which set up OEEC. *New York Times,* Sept. 10, 1952.

[8] Article 3 of the Southeast Asia Collective Defense Treaty provides: "The Parties undertake to strengthen their free institutions and to cooperate with one another in the further development of economic measures, including technical assistance, designed both to promote economic progress and social wellbeing and to further the individual and collective efforts of governments toward these ends."

[9] *Manchester Guardian,* Dec. 23, 1954.

[10] *Report of Special Study Mission to Southeast Asia and the Pacific* (Committee on Foreign Affairs, Washington, D.C., Jan. 29, 1954).

[11] The following statement made by Senator Hickenlooper during the hearings on the Mutual Security Act of 1954 is probably representative of the view of many members of Congress: "Every year we have had the tacit understanding that except for military assistance, the program was going to end the following year. I am concerned about these various categories outside of direct defense assistance. I have no particular quarrel at this moment with items of direct defense assistance, but are these items of economic assistance justified by the fact that the economy of the country will develop and warrant the placing of the money in these development projects?" *Mutual Security Act of 1954: Hearings Before the Committee on Foreign Relations,* 83rd Cong., 2nd Sess. (Washington, D.C., 1954), p. 67.

[12] In Southeast Asia the Philippines provide the only instance in which American foreign aid as direct pressure has been successfully used to induce in-

ternal political reform. In 1950 a combination of desperate economic need and historic ties between the United States and the Philippines made it possible for the Bell Mission to lay down specific and far-reaching Philippine reforms as conditions for American aid.

[13] *Report of the Commission on Foreign Economic Policy presented to the President and to the Congress* (Washington, Jan. 13, 1954), p. 13.

[14] The United States is the third largest exporter of rice, accounting for about 13 per cent of world rice trade. Burma is first with 30 per cent and Thailand second with 26 per cent.

[15] Welles Hangen, "Moscow's Aid to Asians Is on Firm Business Basis," *New York Times,* Dec. 24, 1955.

[16] The free-world consumption of tin and rubber as projected by the Paley Commission Report is as follows:—Tin (in 1,000 long tons): in 1950 the United States consumed 71 and the rest of the free world 73; in 1975 the United States will consume 84 and the rest of the world 109. The percentage of increase for the United States will be 18 and for the rest of the free world 50. Rubber (in 1,000 long tons): in 1950 the United States consumed 1,320 and the rest of the free world 825; in 1975 the United States will consume 2,500 and the rest of the free world 2,500. The percentage of increase for the United States will be 89 and for the rest of the free world 203.

Southeast Asia has 72 per cent of the known world tin reserves divided as follows: Malaya, 30 per cent; Indonesia, 20 per cent; Thailand, 16 per cent; and Burma, 6 per cent.

Southeast Asia produces 95 per cent of the world's natural rubber.

Chapter 9

[1] Address of Secretary of State Dulles to the International Rotary Convention, Seattle, June 10, 1954. *New York Times,* June 11, 1954.

[2] *Ibid.*

[3] *Mutual Security Act of 1954: Hearings Before the Committee on Foreign Relations,* 83rd Cong., 2nd Sess. (Washington, D.C., 1954), p. 19.

[4] *Documents on American Foreign Relations, 1954,* ed. Peter V. Curl (New York, Council on Foreign Relations, 1955), pp. 370–372. Communiqué on the Bogor Conference of the Prime Ministers of South and Southeast Asia, Dec. 29, 1954.

[5] The countries represented were: Afghanistan, Burma, Cambodia, Ceylon, communist China, Egypt, Ethiopia, Gold Coast, India, Indonesia, Iran, Iraq, Japan, Jordan, Laos, Lebanon, Liberia, Libya, Nepal, Pakistan, Philippines, Saudi Arabia, Sudan, Syria, Thailand, Turkey, Vietnam, and Yemen.

[6] Tillman Durdin, "Rebuffs to Reds and Nehru Bring Bandung Discord," *New York Times,* April 19, 1955.

[7] Tillman Durdin, "Bandung Meeting Asked to Assail Red Colonialism," *New York Times,* April 22, 1955.

[8] To the Indians, the status of Goa is an emotional, not a legal question. The Portugese originally captured Goa, a port city on the west coast of India, in 1510 as one of a series of strategic outposts which would help control trade in the Indian Ocean. Since 1949 it has been a thorn in the side of independent India, which has been attempting to negotiate a settlement of the issue. Portugal's attitude that Goa and other Portuguese possessions in India, as Portuguese provinces, are integral parts of Portugal remains fixed. While exer-

cising patience and restraint, the Indian government has been vehement in its denial of Goa's absorption into Portugal as a colonial possession. The Goa issue comes up in every session of the Indian Parliament, and Nehru has announced on numerous occasions that India will never accept continuation of the present unsatisfactory conditions.

[9] Radio and television report on the Manila Pact Conference, Sept. 15, 1954.

[10] The terms "neutralism" and "neutralist," though used, for the most part, to convey the same general concept, have slightly different connotations. As a political and psychological force, neutralism is far more widespread than neutrality, the latter being an official government policy of noncommitment or nonalignment in the cold war. Neutralist foreign policies are officially pursued in such South and Southeast Asia countries as India, Indonesia, Burma, Ceylon, and Cambodia. But neutralism rates strong public attraction in many non-communist Asian and African nations, including Thailand, Pakistan, the Philippines, and Malaya. For a full discussion of the rationale and individual characteristics of neutralism and neutrality in each of the South and Southeast Asian states, see Chapter Three, "National Objectives in Southeast Asia."

[11] Mao Tse-tung, "On the People's Democratic Dictatorship," 1949. Conrad Brandt, Benjamin Schwartz and John K. Fairbank, *A Documentary History of Chinese Communism* (Cambridge, Harvard University Press, 1952), pp. 453-454.

[12] Address to the Annual Convention of Rotary International, Seattle, Wash., June 10, 1954. *New York Times,* June 11, 1954.

CHAPTER 10

[1] *New York Times,* Feb. 15, 1956.

[2] The *Hindu* (Madras), Oct. 2, 1954, reporting Mr. Nehru's speech of Sept. 30, 1954.

[3] Address to the National Press Club of Washington, D.C., Jan. 12, 1950. *Department of State Bulletin,* Jan. 23, 1950, pp. 113-114.

[4] *New York Times,* March 20, 1956.

[5] Public Law 480, the Agricultural Trade Development and Assistance Act of 1954, approved July 10, 1954, authorized the President to negotiate and carry out agreements with friendly nations for the sale of surplus agricultural commodities for foreign currencies. The foreign currencies which accrue may be used to develop new markets for United States agricultural commodities; to purchase strategic materials; to procure military equipment, materials, facilities, and services for common defense; to finance purchase of goods or services for other friendly nations; for promoting balanced economic development and trade; to pay United States obligations abroad; for loans to promote multilateral trade; and for financing international educational-exchange activities. The United States has negotiated and is negotiating such agreements with several Asian countries for sale of rice and wheat. It is difficult to convince the Burmese and the Thai that American agricultural surpluses are not being dumped on Asian markets at the expense of their necessary export trade.

[6] *Report by Senator Mike Mansfield on Vietnam, Cambodia and Laos to the Senate Committee on Foreign Relations,* Oct. 6, 1955, p. 19.

A CHRONOLOGY OF HISTORICAL EVENTS OF SPECIAL SIGNIFICANCE TO SOUTHEAST ASIA

1945

September 2 — V-J Day

1946

July 4 — Republic of the Philippines becomes independent.

November 21 — Indochina War begins as fighting breaks out at Hanoi between the French and Ho Chi Minh's Viet Minh forces.

1947

July 30 — Indonesian Case brought before United Nations.

August 15 — India and Pakistan become independent. Both elect to remain within the British Commonwealth.

1948

January 4 — Union of Burma becomes independent and rejects membership in the British Commonwealth.

1949

January 20 — President Truman's Inaugural Address calls for the United States to share its technical knowledge with the nations and peoples of the underdeveloped areas of the world.

October 1 — Mao Tse-tung formally proclaims People's Republic of China. USSR extends recognition the following day.

November 2 — Netherlands-Indonesian agreement reached at the Round Table Conference at The Hague.

December 27 — Indonesia becomes independent.

1950

February 14	The USSR and communist China sign a treaty of friendship, alliance, and mutual aid.
May 8	Agreement between France and the United States for military and economic aid to the French effort in Indochina.
June 5	President Truman signs the Foreign Economic Assistance Act providing for a Technical Cooperation Program.
June 25	Korean War begins.

1951

February 1	United Nations General Assembly brands communist China an aggressor in North Korea.
February 12	Conference of fourteen nations draws up the British Commonwealth Colombo Plan for technical assistance and cooperation.
July 18	Cease-fire talks begin at Kaesong, Korea.
August 30	United States and Philippine Mutual Defense Treaty signed. Senate ratification March 20, 1952.
September 1	United States, New Zealand, and Australia sign a Mutual Defense Treaty (ANZUS Pact). Senate ratification March 20, 1952.
September 4–8	Japanese Peace Treaty Conference at San Francisco. Senate ratification of the treaty March 20, 1952.

1953

January 20	President Eisenhower takes office.
July 27	Korean Armistice.
August 8	USSR announces United States no longer has monopoly of the hydrogen bomb.

1954

January 12	Major foreign policy address by Secretary of State Dulles explains United States security policy.
April 26	Geneva Conference on Korea and Indochina opens.
May 7	Dienbienphu falls to the Viet Minh.
July 20	Indochina armistice agreements concluded at Geneva. Armistice terms go into effect August 11.
September 6–8	Southeast Asia Defense Treaty concluded at Manila between the United States, Great Britain, France, Australia, New Zealand, Pakistan, Thailand, and the Philippines.

1955

April 18–24	Asian-African Conference at Bandung, Indonesia.

July 18–23 Geneva "Summit" Conference with President Eisenhower, Prime Minister Eden, Premier Faure, and Premier Bulganin attending.

October 10 USSR announces willingness to provide industrial and agricultural equipment and technical assistance to any underdeveloped Arab or Asian nation.

November 17 Bulganin and Khrushchev leave Moscow for month-long visit to India, Burma, and Afghanistan.

1956

February 8 Great Britain and Federation of Malaya agree that Malaya is to take over internal security, finance, commerce, and industry "immediately." Britain agrees to make every effort toward independent dominion status for Malaya by August 31, 1957.

February 14 Party Secretary Khrushchev's major address to the Twentieth Congress of the Communist Party meeting in Moscow. New party line is announced and downgrading of Stalin begun.

SELECTED READING LIST

The general literature on modern Southeast Asia and United States policy toward the area, although still scarce, has been increasing in quality and quantity during recent years. The author found the following books and periodicals especially interesting and informative. They are included here as suggested complementary reading, not as a bibliography of the subject.

Bowles, Chester. *The New Dimensions of Peace*. New York: Harper and Brothers, 1955.

Devillers, Philippe. *Histoire du Viet-Nam, 1940–1952*. Paris: Éditions du Seuil, 1952.

Emerson, Mills, and Thompson. *Government and Nationalism in Southeast Asia*. New York: Institute of Pacific Relations, 1942.

Elsbree, Willard H. *Japan's Role in Southeast Asian Nationalist Movements, 1940–1945*. Cambridge: Harvard University Press, 1953. Institute of Pacific Relations.

Farley, Miriam S. *American Relations with Southeast Asia, 1950–1954*. New York: Institute of Pacific Relations, 1954. Mimeographed.

Finkelstein, Lawrence S. *American Policy in Southeast Asia, 1945–1950*. New York: Institute of Pacific Relations, 1951. Mimeographed.

Furnivall, J. S. *Colonial Policy and Practice*. Cambridge, England: Cambridge University Press, 1948.

Hall, D. G. E. *A History of South-East Asia*. New York: St. Martin's Press, 1956.

Hammer, Ellen J. *The Struggle for Indochina*. Stanford: Stanford University Press, 1954. Institute of Pacific Relations.

Holland, William L., Editor. *Asian Nationalism and the West*. New York: The Macmillan Company, 1953. A symposium based on documents and reports of the Eleventh Conference of the Institute of Pacific Relations.

Hopkins, Harry. *New World Arising*. London: Hamish Hamilton, 1952.

Jenkins, Shirley. *American Economic Policy Toward the Philippines.* Stanford: Stanford University Press, 1954. Institute of Pacific Relations.

Kahin, George McTurnan. *Nationalism and Revolution in Indonesia.* Ithaca: Cornell University Press, 1952.

Kaufmann, William W. *The Requirements of Deterrence.* Princeton: Center of International Studies, November 15, 1954.

MacDonald, Alexander. *Bangkok Editor.* New York: The Macmillan Company, 1949.

Mende, Tibor. *South-East Asia Between Two Worlds.* New York: Library Publishers, 1955.

Mills, Lennox A., and associates. *The New World of Southeast Asia.* Minneapolis: University of Minnesota Press, 1949.

Reischauer, Edwin O. *Wanted: An Asian Policy.* New York: Alfred A. Knopf, 1955.

Rostow, W. W., in collaboration with Richard W. Hatch, Frank A. Kierman, Jr., and Alexander Eckstein. *The Prospects for Communist China.* Technology Press of Massachusetts Institute of Technology and John Wiley and Sons, New York: 1954.

Rosinger, Lawrence K., and associates. *The State of Asia.* New York: Alfred A. Knopf, 1951. Institute of Pacific Relations.

Staley, Eugene. *The Future of Underdeveloped Countries.* New York: Harper and Brothers, 1954. Council on Foreign Relations.

Stebbins, Richard P. *The United States in World Affairs.* New York: Harper and Brothers, an annual edition. Council on Foreign Relations.

Thayer, Philip W., Editor. *Southeast Asia in the Coming World.* Baltimore: The Johns Hopkins Press, 1953.

Thompson, Virginia, and Richard Adloff. *The Left Wing in Southeast Asia.* New York: William Sloane, 1950. Institute of Pacific Relations.

van Mook, H. J. *The Stakes of Democracy in Southeast Asia.* New York: W. W. Norton, 1950.

Zinkin, Maurice. *Asia and the West.* New York: Institute of Pacific Relations, 1953.

PERIODICALS

Department of State Bulletin.

Far Eastern Survey, Institute of Pacific Relations.

Foreign Affairs, Council on Foreign Relations.

Headline Series and *Foreign Policy Reports,* Foreign Policy Association.

New York Times.

The Economist, London.

INDEX